A Social History of English

Second edition

Dick Leith

London and New York

First published in 1983
by Routledge and Kegan Paul Ltd
This edition first published 1997
by Routledge
11 New Fetter Lane, London EC4P 4EE

Simultaneously published in the USA and Canada
by Routledge
29 West 35th Street, New York, NY 10001

Typeset in Times by
RefineCatch Limited, Bungay, Suffolk
Printed and bound in Great Britain by
Mackays of Chatham PLC, Chatham, Kent

Brtitish Library Cataloguing in Publication Data
A catalogue record for this book is available from the
British Library

Library of Congress Cataloguing in Publication Data
A catalogue record for this book has been requested

ISBN 0–415–16456–7 (hbk)
ISBN 0–415–09797–5 (pbk)

A Social History of English
Second edition

A Social History of English is the first history of the English language to utilise the techniques, insights and concerns of sociolinguistics. Written in a non-technical way, it takes into account standardisation, pidginisation, bi- and multi-lingualism, the issues of language maintenance and language loyalty, and linguistic variation.

This new edition has been fully revised. Additions include: up-dating of information about 'New Englishes' in different parts of the world; a new chapter entitled 'A critical linguistic history of English texts', which discusses a selection of texts from Anglo-Saxon to the present; a theoretical postscript outlining some problems in writing a history of English, and topics for further study. All terms and concepts are explained as they are introduced, and linguistic examples are chosen for their accessibility and intelligibility to the general reader.

It will be of interest to the student of Sociolinguistics, English language, Literature, History and Cultural studies.

Dick Leith has worked as a consultant in the School of Education at the Open University and is a former lecturer in linguistics. His publications include *English: History, Diversity and Change* (co-author and editor with D. Graddol and J. Swann, Routledge, 1996).

Contents

List of figures

List of tables

Author's preface to the first edition

This short introduction to the history of English is the product of teaching a subject that is often daunting to the student. It is intended to be as clear and simple as possible and therefore assumes no technical knowledge on the part of the reader.

Inevitably the debt to numerous works of scholarship is too heavy to acknowledge in copious notes and references. The book has drawn extensively on the work of historians of English like C.L. Barber, M.L. Samuels, and Barbara Strang; of linguists and language scholars like A.C. Gimson, Geoffrey Leech, Frank Palmer, Randolph Quirk, and R.A. Waldron; and of sociolinguists like Joshua Fishman, Einar Haugen, William Labov, and Peter Trudgill. And the work of Raymond Williams has proved an invaluable supplement. The more specific contributions of others have been acknowledged in the Notes and Bibliography at the end of the book.

The book is divided into three parts. Parts 1 and 2 trace the history of English within England, first by outlining a 'historical sociology' of the language and then by exploring some case studies of linguistic change. Part 3 concerns the history of English in other areas of the British Isles and in different parts of the world.

Preface to the second edition

A Social History of English has been in print for thirteen years, and a new edition is clearly overdue. But revising it has not been easy. Not only has a wealth of new material been published that relates to this vast field, but the world now seems a very different place, so that new perspectives are needed on several issues.

In English schools, successive Conservative administrations have implemented a 'National' Curriculum, with a strong focus on the teaching of 'Standard' English. Always linked conceptually, the two terms in quotation marks now require a degree of theoretical exploration which would have been desirable in the first edition, but which is now urgently necessary. One reason for this is the quite unexpected revival of nationalist ideology in many parts of the world, another the related surge of interest among English academics in the notion of 'Englishness'. In this new edition I have tried to be more discriminating and self-critical where my discussion touches on the issue of nationalism, especially in chapter six. And on the question of standardisation, I have revised chapter two in the light of recent political events and of important new work on the topic. This emphasis may seem Anglo-centric, but an Olympian view of English as a World Language is impossible, even if it were desirable.

The new edition has also been expanded to include a chapter dealing with textual extracts. Here the reader will find not only examples of English from various times and places, but also a discussion of some key issues in their analysis and interpretation. My intention here was partly to question the widely-held view that there exists a settled and agreed 'History of English' (as is suggested by such book-titles as *The History of English*). In doing this I have been guided by the work not of linguists but of historians, some of whom have in recent years made some invaluable contributions to the study of language, and who have written openly about the nature of history as a form of storytelling. As it turns out, much history has been the story of particular 'nations', often conceived as a sequence of dramatic ruptures. In revising this book I have become aware of how these story-structures also persist within *linguistic* historiography, and how easy it is to be seduced by them. I discuss these issues in the Theoretical Postscript to the book.

In the first edition of this book I tried to build a bridge between traditional histories of English and the new discipline of socio-linguistics. In this new edition I have tried to move the project beyond sociolinguistics, with its proclaimed committment to 'science', to include perspectives from history, cultural studies, literary theory and the more 'critical' kinds of linguistics now being practised.

I would like to take this opportunity to thank all of those who read parts of the manuscript of the first edition: Jen Coates, Stanley Ellis, Paul Johnston, Caroline Macafee, Derick Thomson and, in particular, John Spencer, editor of the *Language in Society* series, for his faith in the project and his dogged attention to clarity and detail. My thinking for the second edition has been clarified in conversations with Jack Aitken, Jim Milroy, Harold Rosen, Andrew Thacker and David Grad-dol, together with other former colleagues in the School of Education at the Open University. Both editions have benefited immeasurably from the support and criticism of my wife Barbara Crowther. All errors, needless to say, are my responsibility alone.

Introduction

The English language today is spoken by several hundred million people in five continents. It functions in different kinds of societies as a mother-tongue, a second language, a vehicle of officialdom, a medium of education, and as a language for science, business, and commerce. It is also used widely as a lingua franca – a language used among people who have no other tongue in common – and in some areas it has provided a base for pidgins and creoles. It is spoken by people who also use two or three or even more languages in the course of their daily lives, and it has come to symbolise many different and often sensitive issues and institutions in different areas: education, literacy, social mobility, economic advancement, Christianity, and colonial dominance.

These facts are often forgotten by people in England, most of whom tend to associate English with British nationality (the latter is sometimes even defined by it). And since they expect to spend their lives speaking only English it comes as a shock to learn that in other societies quite ordinary and unexceptional people need to be bilingual. When we look at English across the world today we find therefore that it varies enormously in accordance with its wide range of functions, and because it bears the imprints of the languages with which it has made contact. This is something that has also characterised its past – a fact that could be borne in mind when we consider the Asian, West Indian, African, and European languages and dialects that are spoken by schoolchildren in towns and cities of the United Kingdom.

So great is the variation in English that it is often difficult to say whether a certain variety in one place or another should be called English or not. But the demarcation of languages is a perennial problem in linguistics because there is no sure way of determining, on purely linguistic grounds, where one language ends and another begins. In reality there are only linguistic continua: different varieties of English shade off into each other, as English shades off into other languages. It is up to us, as social animals, to decide where to draw the lines; and the chances are that our choices will be governed by social and political considerations rather than linguistic ones. Wherever the line is drawn someone, somewhere, will be upset, since deep emotions are often aroused by issues of language – emotions widely felt, but all too easily ignored in others.

We need not look beyond England itself to find extensive variation in the ways English is used. Language varies because of the wide range of uses to which it is put, and it is a matter of common experience that we speak and write differently in different situations. But English also varies because its speakers come from different backgrounds of region and class, and variations associated with these often function as markers of group identity. Different varieties therefore acquire social values – these are often exploited, for instance, in television commercials – and these values themselves may vary according to the loyalties of different social groups. Most people in England will probably place a high value on what is called the standard variety, but recent research confirms the impression of many that regional speech shows little sign of dying out. One reason for this is that varieties of language are intimately involved with issues of power and solidarity. The so-called standard variety constitutes one dimension of the process of political centralisation, and it has recently been suggested that in much of Western Europe and North America that process has by now gone far enough to provoke a counter-reaction of 're-tribalisation', in which language has played a key role. The issue of the Welsh language is a recent example.

Many people argue that since the spread of compulsory education and the mass media there is little justification or excuse for the persistence of speech-forms that we all know lack prestige. But this is to assume that education plays only one role in contemporary society. The education system cannot compensate for a social system that despite recent claims to the contrary remains fundamentally unequal. Modification of local speech-patterns may be thought necessary to enter certain prestigious occupations, but these are few in number, and people may change their speech-habits only if they consider they have a realistic chance of securing one. Despite the best intentions of many teachers, the education system, instead of engendering a healthy interest in varieties of speech, has often functioned in a way that reproduces and reinforces the ethos of a highly competitive society. Class still plays a central part in English society, despite the erosion of manufacturing industry and, along with it, many of the traditional signs of social stratification. It seems likely that different varieties of English will continue to play a large part in the symbolism of social class.

All these considerations mean that an adequate history of English must respect no national, political, ethnic, cultural, or social boundaries. Neither need we assume that English-speaking communities in the past were any more homogeneous than they are today. Unfortunately, the study of language has been harmed by the divorce of past from present. The historical study of English has developed its own perspectives and methods, but these have been limited in part by the ways in which the subject has been institutionalised in university departments. For most students it has been associated with the translation of Old and Middle English texts, and to many it has had a rather curious preoccupation with the level of linguistic structure which in the past we can know least about – that of sounds. Above all, the emphasis has been on *linguistic* data, and by presenting linguistic history as moving in stages from Old English (a stage of infancy) through Early Modern English (robust adulthood) to the language of today (creeping senility?) the impression has sometimes been given that language changes by itself.

This book has tried to respect the actual users of English. This helps us to see language as a tool rather than as a commodity or even artefact, and prevents us from seeing its history either as a decline from a Golden Age of elegant eloquence or as progress from the unsophisticated usage of wild Anglo-Saxon tribespeople. A selection of well-known examples of linguistic change have been explored within the general framework of sociolinguistics, and some social and political factors have been suggested to help account for the changes. Much of the book is speculative: lack of evidence has always been a problem in the historical study of language. And rather than propose a general theory of linguistic change the book has been written in the conviction that the historical study of a language cannot itself be an autonomous discipline.

Note: In the interests of simplicity phonetic symbols have been kept to a minimum throughout this book, and length-marks, diacritics, etc. omitted in quotations from the Anglo-Saxon.

Part I
Emergence and consolidation

1 Languages in contact

In the Introduction we saw some of the ways in which we need to modify our conception of English as we observe its use in different kinds of communities throughout the world. The same type of adjustment must be made when we look at English across its fifteen centuries of history. In this chapter we shall outline the issues involved in the historical description of a language like English as it has been adapted to changing social functions in different periods, and as it has co-existed with other languages. The period covered is from the earliest records to the end of the Middle Ages. We shall trace the origins of English as the vernacular of certain Germanic tribes on the continent of Europe, at a time when much of that area was dominated by the institutions and language of the Roman Empire. We can use the Latin of that period, with its patterns of contact with other languages, as a model for discussing a major kind of bilingual situation, and also that particular form of standardisation known as diglossia. In describing the Anglo-Saxon settlement of what is now England, we shall see how English came into contact with the Celtic language of the Britons, and how it developed a literature under the influence of Latin. As the various kingdoms of the Anglo-Saxons created institutions and extended literacy, they came to be threatened by the Vikings, who spoke a different though closely related language. There followed two other cases of language-contact, involving different varieties of the same language: Norman French after the Norman Conquest, followed by the Central French of the Paris area after 1204. Finally, we shall see how an early form of what we can call language-loyalty surfaced in the fourteenth century, linking the English language with a patriotism based on antipathy towards France.

At no point during the period under discussion was there a standard variety of English accepted as such wherever the language was spoken. Rather we see a growing trend towards dialectal variation, as different centres of power exert their influence over local speech. We are not therefore describing English as a *taught* language; nor is it the case that the bilingual situations we shall discuss were primarily products of the schoolroom. We are dealing with language-learning, and language-contact, in contexts that are more informal, more haphazard, and unplanned: as peoples migrate, as armies occupy new territory, as settlers intermarry. What may strike the modern monoglot speaker of English is the relative ease with which new languages seem to have been acquired or old ones discarded.

Just as there was no norm of language during the first thousand years of England's history, so there was no enduring political centre. Until the late Middle Ages the concept of England itself was a fragile one. The Anglo-Saxon kingdoms were often at war with each other, and for over two centuries they suffered militarily and politically at the hands of the Vikings. The periods of centralisation under Alfred and Athelstan were short-lived; one kingdom, Northumbria, was for centuries virtually isolated. Although unity of a kind came with the Normans, it was a unity imposed by a foreign power, through a foreign language. Long after the early period of Norman setflement was over, many of the institutions of England remained saturated with French manners, ideals, and language.

Some of the changes which took place during this period in the structure of English – its sounds, its words, its grammar – will be mentioned in the following pages, and later in the book. But we shall predominantly be concerned here with changes of a different kind. The English of the Germanic tribespeople who first encountered the Celts of Britain was not the English of the Anglo-Saxon kingdoms at the time of the Viking invasions. By that time English had a written form, and was beginning to serve the functions of the developing institution of monarchy. The language had changed, that is to say, because it had been made to function in a different kind of society.

LANGUAGE AND SOCIAL FUNCTION

These considerations at once suggest the approach proposed in the Introduction: seeing language in terms of its functions, and relating language changes to changes of function. This is sometimes referred to as the *sociolinguistic profile* of a language. In the course of this chapter, we shall be attempting to sketch such profiles for the languages that came into contact with English until the end of the Middle Ages; also, of course, seeing how the profile of English itself changed, partly as a result of these contacts.

We have already referred to two of the most important factors:

standardisation and literacy. These are so central to the sociolinguistic history and description of a language that in this book they are accorded a chapter to themselves. To recognise their importance, however, is not to say that a standardised, written language is in any way better or more important than its unwritten, unstandardised counterpart. Nor would it be true to say that languages of the latter type are inferior or handicapped. It means, rather, that the demands of speakers on their language are no more than those associated with the customary, local needs of small, technologically simple societies. A larger, more centralised society will make new demands on its language or languages, as specialised institutions – administrative, legal, religious, educational – are created. As we shall see in the next chapter, the adaptation of a language to such demands is closely bound up with the cultivation of standardised varieties and the written word.

We can see, then, that the range and kinds of functions that a language serves must be borne in mind when we describe its sociolinguistic profile. In general, languages that function in the *domains* of a centralised state have been described as *developed*, while the term *oral vernacular* has been used to denote languages with the alternative characteristics we have outlined. Both developed and vernacular languages can function in societies where they are the only languages their speakers need to know; and where this is the case, we can further describe them as *autonomous*. Thus, as a standardised, literate language of a modern state, English is autonomous today within England; but no less autonomous was the oral vernacular of the Germanic tribes who first settled here.

The notion of autonomy is important, since it enables us to describe the difference between a vernacular and a dialect. The term *dialect* is used in many different ways. Our description of a vernacular language may remind us of the characteristics usually associated with dialects, in that these are not normally written; neither are they used in the 'higher' domains of the centralised state. In fact, the term dialect has been used, confusingly, to refer to languages of this type: people have written of 'the myriad dialects of Africa'. In contemporary England, however, we think of dialects as regional variants of a language which also has a standardised, and therefore non-regional form. The use of dialect in this sense is limited to certain 'everyday' domains – for instance, it is spoken among family and peer-group – but the standard variety can, in theory, be used for all purposes in all circumstances: it is fully developed, or omnifunctional. In general, then, the dialects in such a society are dominated by the existence of the more prestigious standard and are not, therefore, autonomous.

Dialects, then, can be described as undeveloped, oral varieties of a language that are *heteronomous* with respect to a standardised one. Unfortunately, different scholars at different times have used the term to denote different combinations of criteria, some social or functional, others more directly linguistic. In French usage, the term *dialecte* refers to a regional variety that has a written form, in opposition to a *patois*, which does not (we shall see the usefulness of this distinction throughout this book). Also, speech-varieties have been called dialects on the basis of purely linguistic similarities among them, such as shared words, similar sound-systems, grammatical patterns, and so on. Some scholars, therefore, have used the term to relate varieties that most of us would consider separate languages, and they have done this because they have drawn their lines on different parts of the linguistic continuum, as described in the Introduction. Thus, it has been said that the earliest speakers of English used a dialect of Germanic, similar in terms of linguistic structure to the other kinds of speech used by other, related, Germanic tribes. The term *Germanic* here denotes a kind of parent language. And in principle there is no knowing where to stop applying the term dialect, since it can be used, it seems, to relate any varieties that have some perceived linguistic feature in common. More often the line is drawn according to some notion of mutual intelligibility: when people stop understanding each other, they can be said to be speaking different languages. But this criterion is not nearly as useful as it seems. Unintelligibility can be total, or only partial; and it also depends very much on the motivation of speakers to understand each other. Indeed, some would argue that there are enough problems of intelligibility between different dialects in contemporary England to justify calling them separate languages.

Another crucial dimension in the sociolinguistic description of a language is the value placed on its different varieties by its speakers. Greater prestige tends to be attached to the notion of the standard, since it can function in higher domains, and has a written form. Developed languages, therefore, tend to be more prestigious than vernaculars. We shall see throughout this book that when developed languages come into contact with vernaculars, the latter tend to be influenced by the former. This is partly a reflection of power: developed languages tend to be used by societies that are more centralised politically, and these are usually better equipped to fight and survive in conflicts with less centralised ones. But it is also a reflection of attitudes to language. People who use a language with traditions of standardisation and literacy may develop a sense of *historicity*, a pride in their language's past, and its continuity with the present. They tend to be more keenly aware of their language's difference from other languages. They do not see their language as being under threat, and in danger of dying out: rather, they are aware of its *vitality*. These factors are extremely important in the modern world, when oppressed languages, such as the Celtic ones of Britain and France, and languages such as Pennsylvania German in the United States of America are being kept alive by their speakers. We shall bear all this in mind when we come to consider the status of Latin during the Roman Empire.

The prestige attached to standardised, written varieties of language is associated with the belief that they are the most correct forms of the language, and that they are perhaps the most 'beautiful'. Aesthetic judgments of this kind are even shared by people who may be illiterate, and who have little access to the prestige variety. This is most likely to happen where a *classical* variety, enshrining a literature either sacred or secular, develops in a language spoken over a very wide area, and where literacy is the preserve of an elite. In such conditions, the everyday spoken varieties of such a language may diverge quite sharply from the classical one. The consequences of this divergence may be seen today in the case of Arabic. This language, to put it rather simply, has two forms: one based on an ancient, classical variety, the other on the colloquial usage of the present. No contemporary speaker of Arabic uses the form deriving from the ancient literary variety as a medium of everyday conversation. In fact, the two varieties are functionally differentiated, just as they are evaluated differently by their users. The classical form, which is considered more correct and beautiful than the colloquial forms, is used in the prestigious domains like law, religion and education, and has therefore been called the *High* variety of the language. The *Low* variety – which uses many words, grammatical constructions, and sounds that are different from the High one – is subject to great regional variation (as distinct from the 'fixed' classical form codified in dictionaries and grammars) and is used in more informal contexts.

The situation just described is known as *diglossia* and it demonstrates the value of describing languages or linguistic varieties according to the ways in which they function in society. We shall return to diglossia later, in our consideration of Latin, which, like Arabic, was once the official language of a large empire.

BILINGUALISM

People will readily acquire a second language if they need one, and if they have access to its speakers. This is particularly common when speakers of different languages intermarry, and their children grow up bilingual. In some circumstances, a first, or 'native' language, may not be as useful to an individual's daily needs as a second language: this often happens when people migrate to other countries to work. And in some conditions people learn a simplified version of another language when contact with its speakers is only intermittent; and they use it for very limited purposes, such as trade. These simplified languages are known as *pidgins.*

Bilingualism can be of various kinds. Where one person commands more than one language, we can speak of individual bilingualism. But this need not mean that both languages are actually spoken: scholars, for instance, can be fluent only in the written form of another language, and translation from one language to another can introduce linguistic changes that are far-reaching. Such cultural bilingualism, as we shall call it, is of great importance in the early history of English.

Where a society regularly uses two or more languages to carry out its affairs, we can speak of societal bilingualism. The restriction of each language to certain areas is referred to as geographical bilingualism. In parts of Belgium for instance, French is spoken as a first language, whereas Flemish is natively spoken elsewhere; and both languages have official status. Some people, of course, will be bilingual; and in most bilingual societies, one language-group is more bilingual, at the individual level, than the other. This is particularly so in the very common cases where one language is the official one, used in High domains, and the other is relegated to functions that can be described as unofficial, where it is merely tolerated (as in the case of immigrant languages in English cities) or actually proscribed (see chapter six). The speakers of the Low language are much more likely to be bilingual than those whose first language is the High one. In such situations one language is clearly the dominant one, and we can adapt the term diglossia to describe them, and speak of diglossic bilingualism.

LATIN AS THE LANGUAGE OF EMPIRE

To anyone acquainted with the roles and status of English in the world today, a sociolinguistic profile of Latin at the time of the Roman Empire would make familiar reading. Latin was a developed, omnifunctional, autonomous, urbanised, highly standardised language. It had a classical variety which was codified by grammarians, and a writing system that could provide a model for other languages when it was their turn to require orthographies. This imperial language of a vast empire also became the language of an international religion, Christianity.

At first, the imposition of Roman rule over areas of ethnic, cultural, and linguistic heterogeneity would have led to the kind of bilingualism we have described as diglossic. Latin was the official language of High domains, while diverse local vernaculars served the everyday needs of many different subject populations. Thus, ordinary people would have been controlled in a language unfamiliar to them, as in so many parts of the world today. But it seems that this kind of societal bilingualism did not remain stable for long. The spread of Latin came to be not only geographical, but social as well. Subject peoples gradually, over the generations, acquired it as a second language, and subsequently as a first language. In short, the Roman Empire witnessed a process known to sociolinguists as *language shift*. The evidence for this is demonstrated by the fact that Latin formed the base of French, Spanish, Italian, Portuguese, and Romanian as they are spoken today.

There are a number of reasons why a process of language shift took place. The Romans conquered, but also administered; and their central-ised rule lasted so long – several hundred years in many places – that Latin had the chance to take root. Since it was imposed over areas of great linguistic diversity, it could also function as a lingua franca for subject peoples. And finally, there were material advantages in learning it. The characteristic instrument of Roman rule was the town (sup-ported by the agricultural economy of the villa), and to play any part in the life of the towns, it was necessary to learn Latin. Urbanisation, then, brought new influences, practices, and opportunities to people interested in exploiting them.

The successful spread of Latin over a vast area had much in common with the extension of other international languages in the ancient and early medieval worlds. The Hellenic Empire had spread Greek in the eastern Mediterranean, where Latin never displaced it. Later, over much of the Levant and parts of Africa, Islam extended the use of Arabic, religion being a powerful agency in its spread. And it has been argued that all three languages at different points in their history have exhibited the features associated with diglossia.

When today we speak of Latin we tend to think of the literary Latin used by writers like Cicero about two thousand years ago. This is because Classical Latin, as we usually call it, is the variety most often studied: it derives prestige from the great writers who used it, and it enjoys the air of regulation and fixity conferred upon it by the scholars who codified it in grammars. But we must not forget that Latin, like any language, had different varieties, just as many Classical writers them-selves could not overlook the differences that were emerging between their metropolitan written usage (described as *urbanus*, which later came to denote refinement) and the local (*rusticus*) or popular (*vulgaris*) Latin which was to provide the basis for Christian writings in the following centuries. Classical Latin is certainly of great importance in the history of English, but it is on the spoken Latin, not of Rome, but of the Imperial provinces, that we must now concentrate.

We have already mentioned the significance of towns to the imposition of Roman rule. In the major Imperial cities, a small elite of Roman citizens used the Latin of Rome as the official language, teaching it in schools to the nobility of the conquered peoples. A major function of all towns was to raise enough cash to pay for the standing armies that were so essential to the maintenance of the Empire. It is in these armies that we can see the conditions for the genesis of new, local varieties of Latin. Drawing their complements from speakers of many different languages, the armies fostered Latin as a lingua franca: and it is likely that the spoken Latin of the soldiery bore the imprints of numerous mother-tongues, as a process of pidginisation occurred. Similar conditions existed among the trading sectors of the towns. As centres of commerce, the provincial towns attracted a mercantile element almost as multilingual in character as that of the army, and this would have assisted the spread of a local variety of Latin among the neighbouring population.

The spread of Latin was not as even, however, as the above account might suggest. In at least two parts of the Empire, its position was to prove tenuous. In the provinces of the east, Latin did not displace Greek, the prestigious language of an earlier Empire, as an official language. And in the western province known as Britain, and especially among the highland population, it seems unlikely that the language was widely learned at all.

THE COLLAPSE OF THE EMPIRE IN THE NORTH

The subject populations of both Britain and Gaul were farming peoples known as Celts. Their society was a tribal one, and their language an undeveloped vernacular. The Celts were not literate (although they had an alphabet which they used for inscriptions) and it is probable that the British variety of the language could be understood in Gaul, and vice versa; hence, they could be said to have spoken different dialects of Celtic, if we use dialect in the sense of 'related language', discussed above. Under the Romans, Celtic would have been the Low language, though the pattern of individual bilingualism may have varied widely. Thus, in the remoter, less urbanised areas, monoglot speakers of Celtic may have predominated, while in the towns Latin may have been the only language used. In the areas influenced by the towns bilingualism was probably quite common.

It is impossible to gauge the extent to which Latin displaced Celtic in either Gaul or Britain. But as one of its most enduring and valued possessions, Gaul is more likely to have been the more thoroughly Romanised. In Britain, however, bilingualism may have had a strongly geographical character. Throughout the more inaccessible northern and western regions, including much of what is now called England, Celtic customs, organisation, and language remained to threaten Roman rule; whereas it is at least conceivable that in certain areas Latin had displaced Celtic. Unfortunately, we can do little more than speculate on these matters; and, as we shall see, the oblique and even contradictory nature of what evidence exists is very much bound up with the subsequent fortunes of these two outposts of Roman rule. By the fifth century AD, both had fallen to invading Germanic tribespeople; among them, the Angles and Saxons, the speakers of a language that was later to be called English.

Of these Germanic tribes little is known. Like the Celts, they had developed none of the social, political, and economic institutions which demand the cultivation of a standardised language. They were farming peoples, locally organised on the principle of personal loyalty to a chieftain; tribal kings were only elected in times of crisis. Unlike the Celts, however, they had managed to keep the Romans out of their homelands north of the Rhine and Danube. But in their sustained defence of these areas, many of the tribes came into contact with the Romans, siding with them in campaigns against other tribes, and enlisting in the Roman legions. Such contact had its linguistic consequences: the word *cheese* was probably adapted from Latin *caseus* at this time, its pronunciation changing to fit the sound-patterns of the Angles and Saxons.

During the period of the Roman Empire, it seems that the inclination of the Germanic tribes was to expand, generally towards the south and west; but the organisational superiority of Rome kept them bottled up. As Roman rule faltered, however, it came to depend on some of the more Romanised tribes for its survival, and these often had imperial ambitions of their own. The Visigoths of the lower Danube area, for instance, were originally employed to regain what is now Spain from other Germanic adventurers; but as the collapse of Roman rule became imminent, they created their own Empire there. But Roman ways lived on. The Visigoths were rapidly Christianised. Above all, they adopted Latin; at first for writing, later in speech. It is their version of spoken Latin that forms the basis of the Spanish language.

Even those tribes who had not been caught in the Imperial net seem to have been impressed by the apparatus of the Empire when they encountered it in their invasions of the fifth century. At least, this is true of mainland Europe. The spectacularly successful Franks, who overran Gaul from their homelands by the lower Rhine in less than half a century, seemed content to respect the institutions of Roman rule and leave them intact. Quickly united under one leader, the Franks had been baptised before the end of the fifth century. With Christianity came Latinisation. Latin remained the language of administration and religion, and soon became the language of law. In the end the Franks, like the Visigoths, discarded their Germanic speech and adopted the spoken Latin of Gaul, the language that was to become French. It is probable that these two cases of language shift were led from above, by each ruling group.

THE GERMANIC INVASION OF BRITAIN

The rapidity with which the Franks settled Gaul and embraced the trappings of Latin civilisation contrasts markedly with the slow, less co-ordinated progress of the Germanic invaders of Britain. The groups of Angles, Saxons, Frisians, and Jutes who left their north German homelands for Britain in the course of the fifth century were not united under one leader; neither did they so swiftly secure military success. While the Franks seemed content to allow the town-and-villa economy of Gaul to continue untouched, the Angles and Saxons found resistance from Celtic chieftains, to whom authority had now passed after the withdrawal of the standing army had left Roman institutions undefended. The Germanic invaders of Britain might well have been content to co-exist peaceably with the Celts, as appears to have happened in Gaul; but naturally enough, British resistance was met with force. This resistance is likely, however, to have been relatively uncentralised and sporadic, so the pattern of Anglo-Saxon invasion would have varied in different places. Some Celts would have been killed in battle; others fled west, and some perhaps into what is now Brittany; some may have been enslaved; many would probably have carried on much as before. But without the possibility of a military response, those Celts who remained would have been gradually absorbed through intermarriage into the Anglo-Saxon hegemony.

We know very little about the early relations between Anglo-Saxons and Celts. Although the Germanic tribes possessed a runic alphabet for purposes of inscription, they had no use for written history, and have bequeathed us no contemporary account of their invasion. But we are left with one striking fact. The Anglo-Saxons did not abandon their language. The Celtic language was displaced, and English developed not from a local variety of spoken Latin, but from the Germanic language of the invaders. Unfortunately, much of the speculation about Anglo-Celtic relations at this time is based on linguistic evidence, which, as we shall see, is of uncertain value when other crucial information is missing.

One problem concerns the extent to which Latin was spoken in the south and east of Britain. Since the Anglo-Saxons landed on the eastern shores, they would first have encountered Latin-speaking Celts, if that language had taken root. The fact that the Germanic invaders did not then learn Latin may have two possible explanations. First, the Celtic resistance may have been long and bloody enough to have embittered relations with the invaders. Alternatively, it may have been the case that the Anglo-Saxons were simply unimpressed by what remained of Latin civilisation in Britain. Either the economy of town and villa was less flourishing than in Gaul, or the Anglo-Saxons had no desire to ape or adopt the institutions and language of Imperial Rome. As we shall see, Christianity, which was a potent force for Latinisation, came only slowly and gradually, like the process of settlement itself.

It is more commonly assumed that the Anglo-Saxons encountered a Celtic-speaking population rather than one speaking Latin. If this is the case, it is difficult to know how to interpret the linguistic evidence that exists. When we examine the origins of place-names, we find that Celtic elements are not uncommon in the west of what we now call England, suggesting that Celtic communities co-existed alongside sparser Anglo-Saxon ones. River-names (such as Axe and Avon) are often of Celtic origin, but this evidence conflicts with the extremely low incidence of Celtic loan-words into Anglo-Saxon. The place-name evidence has been taken to show that Celts and Anglo-Saxons co-existed peaceably, at least in some areas, while the dearth of loan-words might suggest wholesale slaughter, expulsion, or enslavement of a dominated people. The only conclusion we may be justified in drawing here is that we do not know how to evaluate these different kinds of linguistic evidence in the absence of other kinds of data.

There are in any case great difficulties involved in making predictions or projections about the language-habits of a particular community on the basis of comparisons with situations elsewhere. It would be wrong, for instance, to argue that because the Anglo-Saxons did not learn Latin, as the Franks did in Gaul, the British Celts *must* have remained Celtic-speaking. In trying to specify the vital factors which influence the adoption of new languages by conquering peoples and subjugated populations, we need to bear in mind the numerical strength of the invaders, the degree of centralisation of their political organisation, their intentions (the establishment of a ruling caste, for instance, or the settlement of land for farming), the extent to which intermarriage occurs, and so on. We might also need to know something about the degree of resistance put up by the defending inhabitants, and their own degree of centralisation and military strength, as well as the extent to which they, and the invaders, share an international written culture or religion. Even if we were to have detailed knowledge of this kind, it would still be impossible to *predict* which language would prevail in any given case. On the available evidence, it seems likely that any comparison between the linguistic histories of Britain and Gaul would need to bear in mind the differing degrees of Romanisation, and the different aims of the Germanic invaders. We shall see the relevance of this discussion again, later in this chapter.

Whatever languages the British Celts spoke, the Anglo-Saxons successfully imposed their own undeveloped, oral vernacular. But this case of language imposition is very different from that of Latin as the language of an empire. While Anglo-Saxon was almost certainly the dominant language, its relationship with either Celtic or Latin could not be described as diglossic: each Anglo-Saxon kingdom took generations to establish. At first, too, bilingualism would have been societal, in that language use was determined by ethnic background, and was to a large extent geographical, since Celtic would have been stronger in the west. This pattern is likely to have been replaced by individual bilingualism on the part of Celts and in some areas Celtic survived, perhaps for several centuries. It has been claimed that a vestige of it may even have survived into the nineteenth century, particularly in the area of the northern Pennines, in the numeral systems associated with counting sheep, stitches in knitting, and perhaps children's games: a Cumbrian version has *pedera* (four) and *pump* (five); the equivalent numerals in modern Welsh are *pedwar* and *pump.* But while the Celtic language was preserved in Wales and Cornwall – only to experience a further attack from English in later centuries – it was eventually displaced from most of England altogether.

THE ANGLO-SAXON SETTLEMENT

The fact that the Angles and Saxons had to cross the sea before reaching their chosen territory greatly influenced the process and pattern of their settlement. It is likely that their tribal organisation was disrupted by the voyages: a charismatic leader might attract a boatload of adventurers drawn from different tribal units. The boats would sail up the major rivers like the Thames and the Humber and establish the first settlements – probably strongly fortified – at places on the banks, and then wait for the next boatloads before advancing further. It seems likely that the invaders largely took over existing agricultural practices. Archaeological and place-name evidence suggests that the settlers used Roman roads and sites when it suited them: but it seems that the Anglo-Saxons preferred to take over the kind of site called in Latin a *vicus*, where civilians had settled outside the walls of military centres (giving place-names ending in *-wich*, *-wicham*, etc.). This contrasts markedly with the pattern in Gaul, where Roman villa sites became villages, and where towns remained intact and flourishing.

It sems to have been the Anglo-Saxon settlers who largely established the structure of villages in the territory we now call England. An overwhelming proportion of these villages have Anglo-Saxon names, many incorporating the names of local leaders, others the vocabulary of wood management, drainage, and cultivation (see chapter three). In many places, the relatively undisturbed character of village life, and a largely immobile population, created over the centuries the conditions for sharp divergences in local speech. But in parts of the more strongly Celtic west, Anglo-Saxon settlement was often later, and less dense. The settlers did not venture into Wales or Cornwall (although a heavy 'buffer' settlement occurred in parts of Devon, where Anglo-Saxon boundaries are still a dominant feature in the landscape), and it seems they found the Cumbrian hills uninviting. Here, pockets of Celts remained, and in other parts of the northwest their presence may be attested by the Celtic place-name *Eccles*, an adoption from Latin *ecclesia*, which denotes a place of worship. In these areas the Celtic language may have influenced the local Germanic speech in ways that are no longer recoverable, accounting, perhaps, for characteristic pronunciations of words like *boot* and *soon* in the local accent of both Devon and Lancashire; the vowel has a fronted quality, rather like that in French *tu*, which is unusual elsewhere in England.

The small communities of Angles and Saxons, with their oral culture, were gradually organised into larger political units under petty kings. At one point there seem to have been at least seven kings in different parts of England, often warring amongst themselves. The most important were those of Northumbria (the land north of the River Humber), Mercia (the land with a *march* or border with Wales), Wessex (the land of the West Saxons, who lived to the south of the western part of the Thames), and Kent; but there were also kingdoms of East Anglia, Essex, and Sussex. We shall see the importance of these separate kingdoms in establishing regional varieties of English in the following paragraphs.

With the institution of kingship came the gradual introduction of Christianity. And with Christianity came literacy. But for the Anglo-Saxon kings, unlike their Germanic counterparts on the European mainland, Christianity was not synonymous with the use of Latin in both speech and writing. Conversion in early English society was often the work of Irish missionaries, and Ireland, never part of the Roman Empire although influenced by it, developed as well as its own style of Christianity a tradition of writing in its own language. Rather than use Latin, they adapted its alphabet in Ireland for their own purposes, and this knowledge they shared with the Anglo-Saxons. Each Anglo-Saxon kingdom eventually developed its own traditions of writing, using the local variety of English. Perhaps the finest examples of Germanic poetry, like the epic *Beowulf* and the elegiac *Seafarer*, are recorded in Anglo-Saxon. But it is significant that much early writing in English was prose, used for laws, charters, chronicles, and also for sermons.

The development of any literary tradition at this time could not, however, escape the influence of Latin. Christianity and Latin were virtually inseparable over much of Europe, just as the Church was the stablest and most highly structured political institution. The traditions of philosophical, theological, legal, and administrative writing in Latin were so long, pervasive, and prestigious that for Anglo-Saxon scholars like Bede in the eighth century and Aelfric in the tenth, it would almost have been the instinctive choice. Thus, while Latin was a spoken medium at this time in the monasteries, its use is most directly associated with writing, and it is on this level that the language comes into contact with English. Anglo-Saxon scholars would have been bilingual in English and Latin, but it was a bilingualism that was cultural in character, the preserve of an educated elite. And contact with Latin meant exposure to ideas, practices, and concepts that were Christian. The pagan tradition in poetry, as it was written down, was re-interpreted in Christian terms, and loan-words from Latin in the period of early Anglo-Saxon literacy were often associated with religion (*abbot, apostle, choir, mass*).

The fact that Latin was a model and an inspiration for the first writers in Anglo-Saxon England does not mean that it was in any way superior to the language of the English. Any language, or dialect for that matter, has the potential for use in any domain, and for any purpose. But if the speakers of a vernacular come into contact with a developed language, they will often interpret traditions of use within certain domains as evidence of linguistic superiority. The Anglo-Saxon scholars may well have thought that Latin was the natural and most suitable vehicle for, say, philosophical writing (just as many people think, or used to think, that French is particularly suited to theoretical argument). What was happening in Anglo-Saxon England was a process of language development, under the influence of another language. Latin may have continued as a High language, but English ceased to be an oral vernacular, as it came to be cultivated in the other's shadow. As English was made to serve some of the functions of the developing monarchies, and as it came to be written down, we can describe its profile as that of a partially developed, literate language. As yet, however, it was unstandardised. What scanty records remain show that distinctive regional varieties of English were emerging in the different kingdoms. And in time these varieties were to diverge to a point where we should need to describe them as different languages if the criterion of mutual intelligibility were to be the only one applied. It is more usual, however, to refer to these varieties as dialects. If this term is to be used, it should be remembered that each dialect of English at this time was, from a sociolinguistic point of view, a partially developed *language*.

In that they established centres of influence in different parts of England, the Anglo-Saxon kingdoms have often been seen as highly significant in the history of English. Recent research into English dialects shows that these ancient divisions continue to underpin the traditional regional varieties of English, nine centuries or more after the demise of the monarchies themselves. More recently, however, it has been suggested that the Church, with its superior administration and regional diocese structure, may have been more influential. Unfortunately, we do not know very much about the Anglo-Saxon dialects, since very few texts have survived from the period, and we do not know anything about the relationship of written Anglo-Saxon to the spoken usage of the ordinary families as they toiled in the fields. A great deal of writing has been lost over the last thousand years. But the indifference, or vandalism, of subsequent centuries is not the only reason for the dearth of records. More Germanic settlers, this time from Scandinavia, very nearly overturned the few institutions of centralised monarchy that existed in the different kingdoms. Hostile to the developing Christian culture of monasteries and books, at least if contemporary accounts are to be believed, it was the Vikings who, ironically enough, succeeded in pushing the Anglo-Saxons into taking the first steps towards centralisation under *one* monarch.

THE VIKINGS

The pattern of Germanic expansion which we have described above was continued into the eighth and following centuries by the Scandinavian tribes of the north. For nearly two centuries and a half, Anglo-Saxons and Vikings came into contact of one kind or another. A period of piracy was followed by military campaigns. One after another the Anglo-Saxon kingdoms were overturned, until Wessex was the only source of English resistance. Extensive settlement in much of northern and eastern England was followed by a further round of armed incursions, culminating in the accession to the English throne of the kings of Denmark themselves.

It is the period of settlement that chiefly concerns us here. As great traders, the Scandinavians were interested in securing footholds in the urban centres of Europe; and as farmers, they wanted new land, like the Anglo-Saxons before them. While Norwegians colonised Ireland, the Scottish Islands, the Isle of Man, and parts of England's north-west, Danes settled thickly in the north and east. The place-name evidence for Yorkshire, Lincolnshire, and Leicestershire suggests that Danes here outnumbered the earlier settlers: the Danish form *Ingleby*, 'settlement of the English', in north Yorkshire, suggests that Anglo-Saxons were scattered enough to have a settlement named after them. Wherever they settled, the Scandinavians brought with them their leaders, laws, and their own language.

Very little is known about the relations between the English and the newcomers. While at times these must have been bitter, it appears from recent research into place-names and settlement sites that on many occasions the Scandinavians did not displace the Anglo-Saxons from their own settlements, but grouped themselves near them, often in less fertile places. And although a third of England was occupied by speakers of Danish and Norse, the newcomers did not, and could not, impose an alien set of customs and institutions; nor could they impose their language even if, for a time, it may have been socially dominant. The independence of the area of Danish settlement, known as Danelaw, was undermined by the baptising of the Danish leaders, who knew that Christianity was a useful form of control over their subjects. And it was further undermined by the resurgent dynasty of Wessex. Alfred checked the Danes militarily and defined the limits of the Danelaw, while his progeny, Edward and Athelstan, carried the authority of Wessex throughout England during the tenth century. Finally, the period of Danish kingship under Svein and Cnut in the early eleventh century was short-lived. Danish could not, therefore, become the official language of England – unlike Norn, which persisted in Orkney and Shetland for nearly a thousand years, during a period of unbroken Norwegian hegemony.

The language that the Scandinavians spoke was an undeveloped, oral vernacular. Similar in sociolinguistic profile to the language of the Anglo-Saxons four centuries earlier, it was also similar in its linguistic structure. It is not improbable that the Anglo-Saxon small-holders were able to follow the speech of their Scandinavian neighbours. The records suggest that differences between the languages might have been akin to those characterising, say, the dialect of Devon compared to that of Aberdeenshire today. There would have been some predictable variations: the word for 'bone' in Anglo-Saxon might have sounded like *ban*, but with a longer vowel sound; in Scandinavian, like *bane*. But there may have been as many differences among the dialects of English as there were between English and Scandinavian (as in the relationship between British English and American English today). At any rate, similarity in language, as in custom and social organisation, facilitated the absorption of the new-comers in many parts of England, although some distinctive Scandinavian practices, such as land-measurement, survived in what was formerly the Danelaw.

Contact between the languages occurred at the oral level, in those areas where ordinary English people encountered, in face-to-face inter-action, their Danish counterparts. In situations such as this, where the communication of basic information is at a premium, we are likely to find a process similar to pidginisation. Language is reduced to bare essentials, as it is when we send a telegram; and one of the clearest means of achieving this is to delete, or simplify, some of the patterns in our grammar. It is probable that grammatical re-structuring, a process described more fully in chapter four, took place wherever contacts were made, and the new forms gradually spread, at the spoken level, beyond the area of Scandinavian influence. As in the case of Anglo-Celtic contact, such innovations will have taken place in conditions where exact evidence is almost entirely lacking.

More obvious evidence of linguistic contact is the massive borrowing into English of loan-words. Not only have numerous words like *angry*, *awkward*, *get*, and *take* been borrowed into the core of our everyday usage, but indispensable pronoun forms such as *they* and *she* derive either directly or indirectly from Scandinavian. These words are now no longer regional; but in much of northern England, local dialect is still heavily 'Scandinavianised'. Forms such as *kirk* (church), *steg* (gander), *laik* (play), as well as pronunciations and grammatical forms (see chapters four and five) are still part of traditional usage, or were until very recently.

We do not know how long an 'unmixed' Scandinavian language survived in England. But the presence in Cumbria of Norse runic inscriptions from the eleventh century confirms the impression given by recent dialect research, that it was the area associated with part of the ancient kingdom of Northumbria that best preserved the Scandinavian culture. With York an important centre of Viking trade, Northumbria stood aloof from the rest of England. The strongly regional character of Scandinavian influence means that if we are to speak of Anglo/Scandinavian bilingualism, we should describe it as geographical in nature. The Anglo-Saxons could not dominate the newcomers as they dominated the Celts. Perhaps the linguistic relations between the two languages can best be described as a continuum, ranging from a relatively unmixed Scandinavian at one end of the scale to a relatively uninfluenced English speech at the other. In between, the languages co-existed, and then merged, with English forms and structures competing at first with the Scandinavian ones, then gradually spreading northwards.

At the other end of the country from Northumbria, a concept of 'Englishness' was kept alive by the kings of Wessex. Alfred doggedly maintained the tradition of writing in Anglo-Saxon, particularly in prose; and his desire to translate works from Latin into English makes him one of the first vernacularisers in education (see chapters six and seven). Winchester became the important centre for English writing, and the West Saxon dialect became a kind of literary standard. Works written in different dialects at earlier times were copied into it, giving us a somewhat indirect insight into the output of the other Anglo-Saxon kingdoms. As we shall see in the next chapter, the influence of the Winchester scriptoria long outlived the period of West Saxon power.

Later kings of Wessex introduced political changes that also had far-reaching linguistic consequences. Athelstan instituted the system of shires, political boundaries that by establishing new centres of power could influence the usage of surrounding areas. But the West Saxon dynasty itself was fragile. After further Scandinavian invasions and depredations had brought a Danish king, Cnut, to the English throne, another foreign dynasty was to be imposed on England; Scandinavian in origin, but speaking another language.

Figure 1.1 Linguistic map of the British Isles *c.* AD 1000

THE NORMANS

The Viking adventurers who settled in Normandy in northern France during the early tenth century were also baptised and ceded territory like their counterparts in England. Again, they did not impose their oral vernacular, but were gradually assimilated to the customs and language of the more centralised lands they colonised. In France, however, they had to learn a language that was structurally very different from their own. That they did this, within about four or five generations, is evidenced by the fact that it was a variety of French that they imposed on England when, as Normans, they added this territory to their possessions by the military Conquest of 1066. For the next three centuries or so, French was to be a living force in England, and its influence continued to be felt, though less directly, for centuries after that.

The Norman invaders were few in number, but well-organised. Their intentions were not those of their colonising ancestors, nor of the Anglo-Saxons before them. The Normans were interested in territorial annexation, and they overcame the English by means of efficient military campaigns. The superstructure of political and economic power – based on the ownership of land – was then almost exclusively wrested from English hands and given to Norman friends of William the Conqueror. The positions of power, in respect to both king and Church, were thus in the hands of French speakers, who spent the next 150 years 'commuting' between their possessions on both sides of the Channel. It was only when this ruling class lost its possessions in Normandy at the beginning of the thirteenth century that it could begin to think of itself as English. By that time, French had become firmly established in England as the High language of law, government, administration, and also, to some extent, courtly literature and religion. It was not until the fourteenth century that English was re-developed within these domains.

We need to distinguish, therefore, two phases of contact with French. The first involves the Scandinavianised French of the Norman elite. This language would not have been more developed or more prestigious than that of the English; neither was Norman culture more international or more literate in character: probably the only technical advantages it enjoyed were military organisation and the wider use of stone as a building material. Norman French was imposed by a ruling caste; but since Latin continued in its spoken form in the Church, and as the written language of scholarship, the linguistic situation after 1066 may be described as *triglossic*.

There has been some controversy about the extent to which this state of societal bilingualism was realised at the individual level. Some have argued that French was very widely learned throughout English society; others, that its use was very limited. One thing that we can be sure about is that French did not displace English. Unlike Latin in the age of Empire, Norman French did not offer linguistic unity or a prestigious, literate language to linguistically diverse, uncentralised tribespeople. Neither is it apparent that the Normans took much trouble to encourage English people to learn their language, still less to offer them material advantages. Norman French was exclusive, the property of the major, and often absent, landowner.

While no wholesale language shift took place, it is probable that individual bilingualism came to exist among certain social groups. The motivation for learning a second language, however, may have been different in each case. Some groups would need to be bilingual, whereas for others opportunities for contact with the other language would have been minimal. Certain domains of usage would make different demands on people's linguistic repertoire. Moreover, we should not assume that language-learning was always in one direction.

About the social extremes there is some agreement. We know that the *first* language of the English monarchs was French until the end of the fourteenth century – long after the Norman dynasty. It is also probable that the upper aristocracy were monolingual French-speakers for a considerable time after the Conquest. It seems too that the upper aristocracy continued to use French for a considerable time after 1066, although there is also evidence that some of them began to learn English quite soon after that date. At the other end of the social scale, there is no reason to believe that the ordinary people who worked the land spoke any language other than their local variety of English. In a society overwhelmingly agrarian, this class would constitute the vast majority of the population. During the period of French dominance, then, the regional variation of the Anglo-Saxon era was intensified.

Not all the Normans were aristocrats, however. They brought with them people who could administer their feudal estates; and these would have needed to be bilingual in their role as mediators between overlord and land-labourers. There were also adventurers who became lesser landowners: these were thinly spread in the countryside, and it is likely they would have adapted to local ways and language, just as many of those who went on to settle in Ireland eventually learned Gaelic (see chapter six). Norman craftsmen, merchants, and artisans settled in English towns in greater numbers, but they were never more than a small minority of the urban population. It is questionable whether they ever dominated trade, or even particular crafts, and it is not certain whether French was ever institutionalised as the language of commerce.

The garrisons of Norman soldiers may have retained their language, as a marker of the male peer-group (so that bread-and-butter transactions with local people took place in a kind of Anglo-French pidgin), but in general it may well have been the Normans in the towns who learned a second language, rather than the English. If at this time bilingualism was at all common, it was perhaps quite unremarkable, as it is in so many parts of the world today. We do know that many Normans married English women, so it is likely that children in the towns grew up as bilinguals.

French was also less strongly institutionalised in the domain of religion. Writings in English emanated from the monasteries throughout the period of French dominance: the Anglo-Saxon Chronicle was continued for nearly a century after the Conquest, and in following centuries didactic religious texts circulated from mainly west midland sources. Sermons continued to be delivered in English, although there is some evidence for French. It has been argued that most of the lesser clergy were monoglot speakers of English, and that even in the monasteries newly founded by the Normans, bilingualism, rather than French, was expected. As an institution of learning, then, the Church tended to promote fluency in more than one language, as it had done in Anglo-Saxon times.

At the top of the social pyramid, however, Norman French was secure, with Latin, as the language of official transactions and decrees, and of diversions for the powerful: a great deal of Norman French literature was produced in England. About one hundred years after the Conquest, the first loan-words into English show how the language was associated with the instruments and offices of power: *prison* and *castle*, *cardinal* and *prior*. But the full weight of loan-words comes later, during the second phase of contact with French, this time with another variety of the language.

CULTURAL CONTACT WITH THE FRENCH OF PARIS

In 1204, the dukedom of Normandy was won by the king of France. While the kings of England still retained possessions in more southerly parts of France, the descendants of the Norman conquerors lost the sense of their ancestry. The ruling class of England became increasingly Anglicised, but it maintained its contacts with the French of the kings of France, a monarchy which by the end of the thirteenth century had become the strongest and most centralised in Europe.

From a sociolinguistic point of view, this second phase of contact with French is probably more interesting than the first. We see language come to be regarded as a social symbol, as it is identified with social groups of declared interests. The old Norman French is seen as provincial and unfashionable, while the language of the French court is seen as the emblem of the most sophisticated and prestigious culture in the contemporary world. To use this French, then, is to impress. In the eyes of many, English had perhaps the aura of a peasant language, much like that of Gaelic in nineteenth-century Ireland. But among others, it became a marker of what today we might call ethnicity.

Individual bilingualism would have been extensive during this phase. While the court retained its devotion to French language and culture, the ruling class gradually acquired English. By the fourteenth century, we begin to see the linguistic consequence of this process. English is saturated with French loan-words, some of which have become such common currency that we tend to forget their ancestry – words like *pass, join, butcher, large*. Some, like *chase* and *guarantee*, had even been borrowed earlier, in the forms *catch* and *warranty*, from Norman French. The taste of the Francophile court was reflected in much of the English poetry of this phase, which borrows French themes, techniques, and language; and in so far as the English poet was brought up in this atmosphere, we can best describe this period of contact as one of cultural bilingualism.

It is also the case that many English people learned French. The prestige of French as a marker of high social status meant that some people learned it for its snob value. Since the Conquest, French had been the medium of education, and schools were a means of acquiring the language. A fourteenth-century writer, Higden, records that even people from the country busied themselves 'to speke Freynsh', so they could sound like 'gentil men'. If there was a demand for the language, people who could teach it had a vested interest in its continuance. Thus, we see in the same century edicts enforcing French in the domains of education and religion. That a similar entrenchment existed in the domain of law can be seen by the fact that 'Law French' was still in use, for some purposes, in the seventeenth century. For a lawyer, the possession of a special language is a powerful weapon, as can be seen in many multilingual societies today. The 'professionalisation' of law in the course of the twelfth and thirteenth centuries meant that its practitioners could exploit the advantages of knowing a special language: they could become parasitic on the people they were meant to serve.

If for some the French language meant social advancement, for others it aroused antagonisms. Cultural contacts with France were an increasing source of tension in English life. The monarchy of France came to be seen as a foreign power, whose interests often clashed with those of the people of England. Moreover, while some kings of England waged long, costly, and fruitless wars against France, others lavished the wealth of England on French favourites. Either was likely to upset baron, lesser landowner, and merchant alike. Frenchmen, and the French language, were increasingly disparaged. From its position as a tolerated language under the Normans, English became what sociolinguists might call a *promoted* language, a mark of 'Englishness'.

The promotion of English was associated with gradual changes that had been taking place in English society. The old feudal structure so successfully sustained by the Norman kings, the system of obligations between king and aristocracy, was giving way to an economy based, not on land, but on money. We see the emergence of new bases of power, new feelings of group loyalty. Alliances were made between lesser landowners, who were making money out of raising sheep for wool, and the rising merchant class in the towns, a pact institutionalised in the thirteenth century by the assembly that came to be called Parliament. The founding of universities stimulated mobility, both geographical and social, among certain sections of the population; and by the fourteenth century mobility had even spread to the land-labourers, who could bargain for wages now that labour was scarce. By that time, the balance of forces was beginning to favour an increasingly articulate, English-speaking merchant class. It was this class, with London as its base, that spoke the basis of what came to be called standard English.

2 Standardisation and writing

In the last chapter we outlined the conditions for the emergence of a standard variety. The last 600 years has seen the attempt to establish one as a superordinate variety, and today, at least within Britain, the process is probably as complete as it will ever be. In this chapter we shall trace this long and complex process, by first examining one of its key components, the writing system. We shall need to know about the nature of English spelling, and the sort of writing system inherited by the first printers, who played such a vital role in standardisation. We shall then assess how far the process can be understood from a narrowly sociolinguistic point of view, by seeing it in terms of four inter-linked and often overlapping stages. First, we see the *selection* of the East Midland dialect as the dominant variety; then we discuss the conditions of its *acceptance* by the powerful and educated classes, and the implications this has for speakers of other dialects. Third, we chart the *elaboration* of its functions, as this variety was developed in the domains previously associated with French and Latin. Fourth, we describe the stage of *codification*, the attempts to 'fix' a standard variety in dictionaries and grammars, a process most clearly associated with the eighteenth century. Finally, we shall see how codification can be regarded as the expression of class attitudes to language.

The stages we have outlined above are in some sense applicable to the process of standardisation everywhere. Throughout the world, moreover, the process can be characterised by an important feature: it involves somewhere along the line an element of engineering, a conscious attempt to cultivate a variety that can be used for all purposes. A standard variety is therefore seen to be a fully developed one, to use the terminology of the last chapter. Coupled with this trend is the desire to have it recorded and regularised, to eliminate variations and, if possible, change. While the latter may be unattainable, the aims of standardisation remain inviolate. They have been described as maximal variation in function, and minimal variation in form.

The consequences of this process are far-reaching, but also controversial. To some commentators, including many educators and politicians, the 'standard' is seen as a product of centuries of careful cultivation. It is seen as a 'national' norm, a lingua franca for all speakers of English within Britain (and even a supranational one across the Anglophone world). It is both the 'native' spoken language of educated people, and the variety we expect to find in print. And it is also what we are all taught to write in school (and in many instances encouraged also to speak).

Given the weight of these different meanings, it is not surprising that discussion of the term 'standard' often gets bogged down by misunderstanding and polemic. As we shall see, any references to the 'nation' or to the 'educated' beg the question as to how those concepts are to be defined. This problem is exacerbated by the habit of many influential commentators to talk about the 'standard' as an ideal of usage, restricted to the written medium and inseparably linked to the notion of literary greatness. This pulls the meaning away from any idea of a norm and invests the notion of the standard with the aura of transcendence, so that like the nation, the law and the market it supposedly operates at a level above the merely human.

It would be a mistake to dismiss these meanings as 'unscientific', as many of them have been present ever since the term 'standard' was first applied to the discussion of language in the early eighteenth century. Indeed, the earliest recorded meanings of the term have to do with literary excellence. The term 'Standard English' is not used until over a century later. So, one conclusion we can draw from this is that in writing a history of English we have to be aware of the changing meanings of the very words we use in writing that history. The danger if we do not is to apply the term standard retrospectively across a range of historical contexts where nineteenth- or twentieth-century meanings are not really appropriate. We shall see the relevance of this point throughout the present chapter.

Sociolinguists have tended to see the standard in less idealised terms, as a linguistic variety, describable as such, much like any other dialect. But there are immense problems involved in drawing a boundary between such a 'standard' and whatever is felt to be 'not-standard' usage. Applied too loosely, the 'standard' includes virtually the whole of English, with dialect, slang and perhaps jargon constituting only an exotic fringe. Applied too restrictively, the standard is associated with only a very limited range of supposedly correct forms. On this latter view, which is not the one adopted by sociolinguists, the standard is an ideal that has to be constantly fought for (despite the claim that it is simultaneously a 'national' norm).

In this chapter we shall not deal with the idea of the standard as an entity or product; rather we shall see standardisation as a project, which took different forms at different times. It is only with hindsight, after all, that we can interpret the process at all: things may have felt very different in the past. One thing we can be clear about is that the process of standardisation cannot be seen as merely a matter of communal choice, an innocent attempt on the part of society as a whole to choose a variety that can be used for official purposes and, in addition, as a lingua franca among speakers of divergent dialects. It involves from the first the cultivation, by an elite, of a variety that can be regarded as exclusive. The embryonic standard is not seen as the most useful, or the most widely-used variety, but as the best. Moreover, all sorts of arbitrary and at times spurious arguments are found to justify its forms and structures. In short, the process means the creation of a class dialect, that is imposed on an often resentful, and sometimes bewildered, populace.

The notion of 'Standard English' has gathered so many different political, social and even moral meanings that teaching it in the classroom has always been fraught with difficulty. Although standardisation, as we saw in chapter one, gives speakers a sense of historicity in relation to their language, many have been led to believe that the so-called standard variety is the language itself. From this comes the unfortunate belief (still aired in newspaper columns) that most people do not speak their own language, or at least do not speak it 'properly'. Many people are quite unsure whether or not they speak 'Standard English', although, as a result of codification, they are quite sure what they are not supposed to say. One of the most widespread assumptions about 'Standard English' is that it is restricted only to formal kinds of utterance. This idea has gained acceptance, presumably, from its association in people's minds with contexts where power is exercised – the classroom, the courtroom, the institutions of government.

The concept of Standard English makes most sense when we limit discussion to the written word. It is not only that speech, by its very nature, is less amenable than writing to being fixed. Writing can be seen to be an indispensable component of standardisation. Indeed, it is difficult to imagine the process without the existence of a written form. At the same time, the existence of a writing system does not presuppose the existence of a standard, as we saw in the last chapter. But once a particular variety has become dominant, writing is a powerful agent for its dissemination especially as literacy spreads and printing makes written materials more readily available. As the written forms acquire prestige, and are considered 'correct', they increasingly exert a pressure on speech. Written forms (despite their immense variability across different genres and levels of formality) act as a norm, a yardstick, and a guide.

In view of what has just been said, it may seem ironical that for many people still 'Standard English' has less to do with writing than speaking in a particular accent, which linguists today call Received Pronunciation. Since this accent is used only by a tiny minority it cannot be described as a norm, but only as an ideal for people to emulate. This is despite the insistence on the part of linguists that there is no 'standard' accent, and that pronunciation, moreover, is the least fixable level of linguistic structure. Historically, however, the process of standardisation has often been caught up with the idea of correct pronunciation, as we shall see. And the association between 'Standard English' and Received Pronunciation is not altogether surprising. Socially, pronunciation is the most pervasive aspect of speech, and carries with it a host of associations. In the case of RP, these include power and influence – the very qualities also projected onto the notion of standard English.

It is instructive to consider how far the meaning of the term standard has often been taken from the terms to which it is opposed. Although it is often contrasted with the creatively informal vocabulary usually called slang, the term to which it is most often opposed is dialect. One dimension of this contrast concerns writing: dialect is not usually associated with writing, still less with print. Another dimension has to do with functional elaboration: the dialects have not been developed in the same range of formal functions. A third is that dialects have often been seen as barriers to communication, thereby 'holding back' their speakers. Finally, dialect is seen as regional, whereas the standard is seen as national, even mainstream. It is questionable, however, whether most speakers of English see it as anything other than a dominant variety, one associated, moreover, with its historical base in the South-East, especially London. As such the notion of the standard is also partly regional, but, in a special sense, associated with the status of London as a metropolis.

In the discussion that follows, and throughout the rest of this book, the terms dominant variety, metropolitan variety and 'Standard English' (referring to the English taught in schools since the nineteenth century) are used, where appropriate, to try to distinguish the various strands in the process of standardisation.

THE NATURE OF THE WRITING SYSTEM

The spellings we use today were largely fixed in the eighteenth century. Such was the prestige of Johnson's *Dictionary* of 1755 that it was Dr Johnson's decisions about the spelling of words that have influenced modern practice. Since that time, the idea that words should have only one spelling has become so deeply rooted that it takes considerable effort to accept the fact that until quite recently in the history of English, invariant spelling was not even regarded as a desideratum.

A degree of fixity was conferred before the eighteenth century, however, by the introduction of printing in the 1470s. It is too expensive for compositors to keep changing spellings, either through personal whim or social custom, so that since the fifteenth century certain spellings owe their continued existence to the convenience of the printers. But in personal correspondence, and hand-written documents of many kinds, spelling continued to vary enormously long after the time of Caxton. While it is essential to bear in mind this distinction between printed and hand-written traditions – the relevance of which we shall see again below – we should note the crucial fact that the use of print is nearly as old as the process of standardisation. Very loosely, then, the period of printing corresponds with the period of standardisation.

Although spelling may be fixed, pronunciation continues to vary and change, so that the relationship between sounds and spelling is likely to be somewhat indirect, to say the least. If we remember that the spellings of many words represent their pronunciation, in a particular region, of centuries ago, it is not surprising that we find what seem to be disparities between how we pronounce and what we write. But there are a number of misunderstandings about the nature of this relationship. It is not uncommon to find many people, including some historians of English, describe our spelling as arbitrary, illogical, and even chaotic. Yet it can only be described thus if we perversely expect it to do what it no longer can. In order to understand this we must look more closely at the nature of writing systems in general.

Different languages have developed writing systems which represent different levels of linguistic structure. In simplified terms, some languages, such as Chinese, symbolise whole words, or syllabic components, by using a very large set of characters. This kind of *logographic* system represents language at its most expansible level, since in principle there is no limit to the number of new words or concepts a language can acquire. Other languages, such as those of Europe, make use of an alphabet, a series of letters which encode the most restricted and limited level of linguistic structure, that of sounds. In so far as users of the first kind of system must master an enormous number of symbols when learning to read, they may be considered to be at a disadvantage in comparison with those who have access to alphabetic writing.

The potential for mass literacy, therefore, is greater when the second kind of system is available, and the reason for this is that alphabets encode the sounds of language in a very specific way. While in the course of speech we make a vast number of different sounds, all of those sounds are related, and relateable, to a finite number of sound-units, called *phonemes*. It is ultimately to these units that the letters of the alphabet relate. For no alphabet can represent the wealth of phonetic variation that exists in any variety of speech. For instance, we pronounce the initial sound of *pit* in a slightly different way from the same sound in *spit*: the *p* is aspirated in the first example only. But while that distinction might be important in some languages, such as Urdu, it is not so in any variety of English, so there is no reason why it should be signalled in spelling. At best, then, a spelling system might be *phonemic*, in that there is one spelling for each phoneme – about 44 in most varieties of our language. But as any modern reader knows, the writing system we have inherited is decidedly not of this kind. There are at least seven ways of representing what is for most people the same vowel sound, for instance, in *tree, these, leaf, field, seize, key*, and *machine*.

The reasons for this lack of fit are very complex. But before we try to discuss them, it is essential to point out that there are insuperable problems involved in establishing a standard, consistent spelling system. Quite simply, this is because sounds vary enormously, as we have already said. We pronounce differently according to whether we are speaking formally or casually (as we shall see in chapter five). And sometimes the same word has different phonemes associated with the amount of stress placed upon it. *Must* and *from*, for instance, are differentiated when stressed, but in unstressed positions they have the same 'neutral' vowel /ə/. Finally there is the problem associated with regional pronunciation, or accent. Our sounds relate us to different localities and social backgrounds, and to some extent accents have different sound-systems, with varying numbers of phonemes. A phonemic spelling system can only hope to represent one accent, but the problem is, whose? The selection of one discriminates, in principle, against speakers with other accents.

By encoding the sounds of speech in an inconsistent and often arbitrary way, our spelling system at least manages to favour nobody. Contrary to what some people think, it is not a representation of the accent spoken by a small minority of the wealthy and privileged. We are all equally disadvantaged by it, and that is one of its strengths. Moreover there is often more pattern in it than is at first apparent, particularly if we abandon the expectation that at all points spellings must represent different sounds. The plural ending in *cats*, *dogs*, and *horses* is pronounced in three different ways, but little would be gained by replacing a useful grammatical marker with an unnecessary amount of phonemic information. Secondly, our spelling signals lexical relationships: connections among related words, such as *nation* (the first syllable of which has the vowel of *name*) and *national* – with the sound of *nag*. Finally, our spelling often usefully separates homophones, different words which, in some accents at least, sound alike, like *meat* and *meet*. This example shows us the value of knowing about other kinds of writing systems than our own, for here we see something of the logographic principle: we have learned to read *meat* and *meet* not as sequences of sound, but as individual words with different *meanings*.

THE SCRIBAL TRADITION

The devising of a phonemic writing system has posed problems since the earliest times. The first scribes in Anglo-Saxon England did not invent their own letters, which could unambiguously represent the sounds they needed to symbolise. As we have seen, they were taught to write by monks from Ireland, who had themselves adapted the alphabet of Latin. The Romans, in their turn, had borrowed their letters from the Greeks, to whom the principle of alphabetic writing had spread from the Middle East. Largely the same stock of letters, therefore, came to be used to represent the myriad sounds of many languages. The Anglo-Saxons had to try and match up the symbols to the sounds of English, in so far as the Latin sound-values of those symbols were reminiscent of English sounds. Where there was no symbol available for particular sounds, as in the *th* sound, the scribes had to use their ingenuity. Sometimes they adapted signs from the runic alphabet: the sound just mentioned was represented by þ. In sum, alphabetic writing has always been characterised by a process of adaptation.

The spelling traditions of the Anglo-Saxon scribes were further complicated by the superposition of French spelling habits after the Norman Conquest. Words of French origin were spelt in the French way, so that the /s/ in *grace* is written *ce*, while the Anglo-Saxon *grass* retains the native *s* graph; but French spellings were also used to 'reform' the representation of Anglo-Saxon words. *Cwic* has adopted the French *qu* spelling, and become *quick*. Thus we have at least two different traditions in our spelling – a Germanic one, and a Romance one – and there was, as can be appreciated, an arbitrariness as to which tradition was resorted to in different cases.

Other features of scribal practice led to further heterogeneity in the writing system. Before the printing press, spelling habits were characterised by spectacular diversity. When we look up a word in the *Oxford English Dictionary*, we are immediately confronted by a bewildering range of spellings. There are two main reasons for this. First, scribes wrote in their own dialects, so there were different spelling systems in different parts of the country. Second, scribes were more often guided by their own speech-habits than by written precedent, which meant that changes in pronunciation were often mirrored in spelling. 'Bone' in Anglo-Saxon was spelt *ban*, but by the fourteenth century it was *boon*. It is impossible to know the extent of this sensitivity to sound-change, but we can gauge some of the sociolinguistic implications of these practices. In particular, scribes would not have developed a responsiveness to the individual word. We know, for instance, that when they copied manuscripts written in dialects other than their own, they showed little concern for the original spellings, but changed them to accord with their own traditions and preferences. Moreover, if they failed to understand a word in the passage they were copying, they would change it to one they did know. We shall explore this matter further in the next chapter.

We may summarise the scribal writing system by saying that in general, spellings were less consistent, more individual, more subject to variation in space and time, then they were to become in the subsequent period of print and standardisation. But before we go on to discuss the latter, we need to mention two developments in the scribal era which tended towards fixity rather than diversity. The first of these was the establishing of a written norm based on the West Saxon dialect of the tenth and eleventh centuries. Spellings associated with the Winchester 'house style' persisted well into the early days of printing, as we shall see. The second concerns the growth, by the end of the fourteenth century, of a class of scribes who were professional. Up to that time, the copying of texts had been undertaken in ecclesiastical institutions; but from then on a young man could be trained in the writing conventions of a particular secular scriptorium, and get paid for it. And by then, of course, it was the written dialect of the East Midlands that could be disseminated from these institutions.

STANDARDISATION: THE SELECTION OF A DOMINANT VARIETY

The origins of a dominant variety of English – on which notions of the standard were subsequently built – lie with the merchant class based in London. The dialect they spoke was the East Midland one – associated at first with Norfolk, later with Northamptonshire, Leicestershire, Bedfordshire – and already by the fourteenth century this was a class dialect within London. The lower class spoke another dialect, a south-eastern one, the antecedent of Cockney. The dialects were similar in many respects but there were some regular differences; for instance, the merchant would say *mill*, with the short *i* of *pin*, but the tradesman said *mell*, with the *e* of *pen*. Vestiges of this pattern have been found in Cockney speech today. It is important to stress this linguistic stratification in London, since the subsequent history of standardisation has much to do with its relationship to the speech of the Londoner in the street.

By the end of the fourteenth century, East Midland can be seen as an embryonic written standard. Within the dialect, however, there were variations, often associated with the birthplaces of bourgeois immigrants into London; so at first we see in use a number of different written standards. After about 1430, however, one of these variants became increasingly dominant, its use in government and official documents aided by the newly-established secular scriptoria mentioned above. By the end of that century, the fixing of the selected variety was greatly strengthened, and accelerated, by the printing press.

We cannot yet assume the existence of any standard of spoken usage. It is one thing for a minority of literate people to adopt a different written form; quite another for them to change their speech-habits overnight. As we shall see, it took some time for the East Midland speech of the London merchants to acquire prestige. But there is another reason why East Midland, or variants of it, may have been quite widely adopted during the later Middle Ages. Students from all over England mixed in the two universities of Oxford and Cambridge, both only about sixty miles from London. In the triangle formed by these three centres, a great deal of East Midland speech would have been heard, and possibly used as a kind of lingua franca among a mobile social group.

If such a norm of popular communication existed, it would have helped to spread East Midland, not because of its prestige value, or because it was imposed by the most powerful group, but because of its usefulness in communicating with people who spoke another dialect. It has long been recognised that in new situations contact among speakers of different dialects often results in a process of levelling, and recent sociolinguistic research shows that this is by no means always in the direction of the dominant variety. The use of *them* as a demonstrative, for instance, as in *them books*, has now become generalised across many dialects. If such a new norm is to be called a standard, then it is so in a very different sense from those usually associated with the term. For such developments to have taken place during the fourteenth century a measure of popular mobility was necessary: the conditions for this have already been described in the previous chapter.

There is some evidence to suggest that a popular East Midland norm existed as a medium for folk-song. From the printed broadsheets of the sixteenth century to the song-collections of contemporary singers, the linguistic medium for folk-song is one that does not, on the whole, reflect regional differences. We do not know whether this is to be attributed to the people themselves, or to the commercial presses: but it seems clear that while ordinary people spoke in their local dialect, they were less likely to sing in it.

So far, we have identified both regional and socio-economic factors in the selection process. There is a political dimension as well. A dominant variety tends to emerge when ideas about political autonomy are gaining currency: and we find that in other European kingdoms where a degree of centralisation had occurred early, dominant varieties were emerging at this time. But they were not always associated with the same power base in society. In both France and Spain, it was the usage of Court and monasteries in the areas of political power – the regions of Paris and Castile respectively – that determined its selection. In countries where political autonomy was achieved relatively recently, standardisation took a different course. Thus, while Tuscan developed as a literary norm during the later Middle Ages in Italy, it did not have a political dimension until the unification of the country in the 1860s. By that time, the municipal varieties of Italian in the old, independent city-states had become regional norms; and not only do these persist today, but they are tolerated to an extent unknown in France and England. Norway today is said to have two competing standards: one a Danish-influenced legacy of Danish rule, the other consciously engineered after independence from Denmark in 1814, and based on the Norwegian dialects of the west. These examples show the inextricability of language standardisation and social, political, and economic processes; and we shall be seeing this again in Part 3.

STANDARDISATION: ACCEPTANCE OF THE DOMINANT VARIETY

By about the middle of the fifteenth century, the East Midland dialect had been accepted as a written norm by those who wrote official documents. But its acceptance was tacit rather than explicit, a matter of convention rather than *diktat*. For when Caxton – who had spent much of his life on the continent – came to set up his press, he did not realise that the variety he was printing was already a written norm. Instead, he complained about the difficulty of choosing a dialect that all could understand, and also – like a good many people since – about how English had changed since he was young.

By the sixteenth century, this variety was well-established in the domain of literature. If we contrast the literary output of the Elizabethans with the great flowering of literature in the fourteenth century, we find a striking difference in language. For the dialect of Chaucer was not the dialect of Langland, who wrote *Piers Plowman*; and different again was the dialect of the unknown poet who wrote *Sir Gawain and the Green Knight*. The student of fourteenth-century English literature must come to terms with a range of regional vocabularies, grammars, and spelling-systems that seem bewildering in their diversity. Thus, while Chaucer wrote in the East Midland dialect as it was spoken in London, he was not yet writing in a *national* literary standard, since his contemporaries had their own, local norms. By Shakespeare's time this regional variation in the language of printed literature had all but disappeared, although there have been isolated examples since and a re-emergence in the industrial north of England in the nineteenth century.

The establishment of a national literary norm had crucial repercussions for imaginative literature. In medieval England, there could be no sense of a norm for English usage, for reasons already explained above. Once a norm has been established, at least in the written language, it becomes possible to break it for stylistic purposes – in particular, for representing the speech of people from regions far away or belonging to social groups whose language is supposed to have certain clearly identifiable characteristics. In the later Middle Ages, regional differences in speech were as familiar to some people as they were to Caxton in the fifteenth century – and, in the writing of the Cornishman Trevisa, subject for some caustic descriptions – but it was hardly possible for a medieval writer to try to represent dialects other than his own, if the scribes copying the manuscript in other parts of the country were going to change it into their own dialect. A famous example of this in fourteenth-century literature is Chaucer's depiction of northern speech in *The Reeve's Tale.* When the manuscript was copied in the north midlands, the language was changed to such an extent that the linguistic differences between the speech of the north country students and the rest of the poem were ironed out. Chaucer's norm was not the norm elsewhere, so his copyists could not appreciate his attempt at deviation.

In the course of the sixteenth century, the growing sense of a literary norm can be seen by the numerous attempts to represent the speech of foreigners, the linguistic characteristics of Welsh, Scottish, and Irish people, and the speakers of other dialects of English. It is now that we begin to see the social stereotyping of such speakers. Increasingly, they play the role of buffoon or boor. Non-standard speech is equated with simplicity or roughness; and in order to depict those qualities in literature, some form of *marking* for non-standard features is adopted. A tradition is established which has lasted until the present day, and which has been translated into cinema and television soap-opera: deviation from the norm implies social comment in the minds of author and audience alike.

Acceptance of such a norm, therefore, occasions a rejection of kinds of English that are felt to be outside it. While in the fourteenth century Chaucer could depict the speech of people whose dialect was not his own, and Trevisa could rail at the 'scharp, slyttyng and unschape' speech of the York area – the words are so expressive of the writer's attitude that they barely need a modern translation – differences in dialect were only differences, even if regrettable: dialects spoken in areas outside London were not automatically the emblems of stupid, quaint, or base-born people. But in the earliest years of the sixteenth century, one dialect had already been singled out by playwrights and others as the butt for a cheap laugh. That dialect was Kentish. A county that had long been densely populated, and often visited, Kent was close enough to London for its dialect to be well-known. At this time, Kentish shared features with dialects to the west – those which had developed from the old dialect of Wessex – and these features were sufficiently different from the dominant East Midland forms to be easily exploited as a marker of comedy, boorishness, or rusticity. The latter quality is exemplified in *King Lear.* The high-born Edgar, forced to disguise himself throughout the play as various lowly-born characters, switches to the dialect when defending his blind father from their enemy, Oswald. Responding to Oswald's challenge of 'base peasant', Edgar is shown, in a striking piece of textual deviation, to pronounce *sir* and *so* as *zir* and *zo*, *folk* and *fortnight* as *volk* and *vortnight* (along with other dialectalisms). What is interesting here is that by Shakespeare's time the dialect seems to have been conventionalised, in that the selection of dialect features is rather a random one. This stage Kentish, moreover, was known and appreciated by the playwright's London audience, who must have seen the point of the stereotype.

Such literary practices reflect the growing awareness of a dominant variety in the course of the sixteenth century. By then, attempts were being made to *define* it. But these attempts were supplemented by a more general interest in what could be classed as the 'best' English, and not only the best literary English. So while it might be appropriate here to suggest a stage of explicit acceptance, we must not forget that it was only a small minority of educated, courtly people who were in the business of defining it. We do not really know how far their comments are descriptions of current usage, or merely desiderata; how far they were reflecting opinion, or leading it. On balance, the latter seems more likely. As we shall see, the 'market' for scholarly ideas about usage does not really open up until the latter half of the eighteenth century.

For the first time, significantly, it was the issue of speech that was raised. Most important, much of the discussion addressed the notion of an *ideal* variety of speech rather than a norm. And while the comments of the sixteenth-century scholars are sometimes difficult to interpret – we often do not know, for instance, whether they are talking about sounds, grammar, vocabulary, or even style – it is clear that many of these writers were concerned about matters of pronunciation as much as anything else. In the course of the century a number of references are made to a 'natural' and 'true' pronunciation. As we shall see, early phoneticians were already noticing discrepancies between sound and spellings, which were prompting them to comment; but the interest in pronunciation may reflect uncertainties about usage, itself suggestive of extensive variation.

In the absence of other guides or models, an ideal or norm of spoken usage has to be anchored to a particular social group. It was a phonetician, Hart, who did this most clearly. In three works (1551, 1569, 1570) he mentions the 'learned' and 'literate' elements, and this theme is renewed during the following century by Price (1665) and Coles (1674). What these people were ultimately doing was describing their own usage – a tendency not uncommon among linguists of the twentieth century. Other observers are more specific about locale. A famous observer, Puttenham, writing in 1589, may be referring to the London-Oxford-Cambridge triangle mentioned earlier when he states that the best speech can be heard within a radius of sixty miles round London. The educated speech of the Court in London was now prestigious, and people like Hart and Puttenham were concerned with the speech-habits of aristocratic and wealthy people living in other regions. For now that urban speech in London was also *urbane*, speech in the countryside was 'barbarous', as Edmund Coote described it in 1597. It was incumbent on the provincial gentry to adapt to the standards cultivated in the capital.

A crucial question to be asked about this stage of the standardisation process is, acceptance by whom? Acceptance by government functionaries and small groups of literati is not the same as acceptance by the aristocracy of the shires; still less is it acceptance by the vast majority of ordinary people who worked in the fields. But by the end of the sixteenth century, we have an accepted printed standard, and some prestigious speech forms, that were being promoted consciously and unconsciously by a tiny elite. We do not know, however, how widespread that pronunciation was among the aristocracy in general. What we can be sure of is that the prestige of one dialect triggers the disparagement of the others. Kentish is only the first to be stigmatised. In the course of the following centuries, the dialects of other parts of England are labelled variously as 'offensive', 'disgusting', 'barbarous', and 'cant'. And by the beginning of the twentieth century, the mudslinging has come back to its source. Disparagement is directed this time towards an urban dialect, that of London itself; but it is the working class dialect, Cockney, that is singled out in a School Board report as speech unworthy of citizens living in the capital city of an Empire. By then, of course, 'Standard English' is a subject taught in schools: and 'acceptance' is backed up with the teacher's rod.

ELABORATION OF FUNCTION

The dialects lost status for another reason. As we have seen, their writing systems came to be used only rarely for literary purposes, and no longer for devotional ones. In short, their range of functions was restricted as those of the dominant metropolitan variety were elaborated. They became *patois*, unwritten vehicles for informal, everyday conversation among equals. The process of standardisation may be said, therefore, to have involved an accompanying process of patoisation.

The new metropolitan variety had to function in those domains previously associated, either fully or in part, with the use of Latin and French: law, government, literature, religion, scholarship, and education. Progress for English against the incumbent languages in these domains was often rather uneven, slow, and at times controversial, and the circumstances of its adoption were often different in each case. Inertia, the jealous guarding of ancient privileges, or feelings about the inadequacy of English delayed its advance. Occasionally even Acts of Parliament were required to support its implementation.

The stage we are describing points towards one of the two major goals of standardisation: maximal variation in function. And since a standardised language, according to our model, has to be omnifunctional, it will develop new structures and new meanings, appropriate to its use in different domains. Each group of specialists – lawyers, the writers of religious texts, administrators, and later, journalists and advertisers – cultivate their own varieties and these have to be learned by each new recruit to these professions. Thus the metropolitan variety cannot be as monolithic as people like to imagine: it has to develop variations to suit its wide range of functions.

The linguistic consequences of this process were profound. The major source of variation was no longer regional, as different styles (some linguists call them *fields of discourse*) developed their own particularities. Often these were influenced by Latin and French usage, as though the early practitioners were trying to match the dignity of those languages by distancing their use of English from the everyday. Extreme cases of this are the English of religion and the English of law, whose special qualities today derive in part from the fact that they were in process of formulation during the sixteenth and seventeenth centuries. In all styles, words developed additional technical meanings as they came to be used in certain contexts, and these technical meanings often influenced casual spoken usage, as we shall see in chapter three. In sum, English vocabulary became differentiated to an extent previously unknown, in that words can be identified as 'literary', or 'legal', or 'technical' in one sphere or another.

We have already seen the importance of the fourteenth century in the process of standardisation. In 1362, for example, English was used for the first time in the domains of both government and law. But in the first of these, the use of French in written documents persisted for about a century after this date; and in law, it was used in some circumstances until the eighteenth century. An Act was passed in 1731 to limit its use in this domain once and for all, along with Latin (which was also occasionally used for keeping records). Today, legal English still employs Law French and Law Latin phraseology, such as *fee simple* and *habeas corpus*.

By the end of the sixteenth century some observers felt that English could function as a medium for serious literature; but any acceptance of its potential in this respect was won only after a great deal of controversy. For many writers and scholars had a crisis of confidence about the suitability of English for this purpose; they felt it could never match the heights achieved by the writers of ancient Rome and Greece. What is important here is not that English was in any way actually impoverished as a language, but that some people apparently felt that it was. At one extreme, English was described as so 'dull', 'cankered', and 'barbarous' that it was irredeemable. At the other, some thought that there was nothing worth saying that could not be said in English. A compromise view held that English could attain the *eloquence* of the classical languages if two courses of action were taken. The first was to produce handbooks of composition, based on the classical manuals of rhetoric, to guide writers of English. The second was to inject thousands of Latin loan-words into the language. Some advocates of this second course – contemptuously known as *inkhorns* – went overboard in larding their speech with Latinisms, and became figures of fun in Elizabethan drama. In *Love's Labour's Lost*, the pedantic Holofernes spends a great deal of time exercising his ability to translate backwards and forwards between Latin and English.

By about the 1580s, some authors were declaring English to have achieved a state of eloquence. On this view, a balance had been achieved between native usage and foreign importation, and the patterns of rhetoric had been successfully applied to literature in English. Moreover, some poets like Spenser and Sydney had written works that many felt were a match for any literature. And with this new-found self-confidence came a self-*conscious* delight in the flamboyant manipulation of stylistic levels. We can see this in the way Shakespeare sets off the native English idiom against the polysyllabic Latin one, by associating them with different kinds of character, or different moods. Also, he dramatises such differences of vocabulary, either by juxtaposing them within the same speech, or by intensifying a dramatic moment with the most simple language. In *Measure for Measure*, the returning Duke pretends to honour his self-righteous but corrupt deputy, Angelo, by saying his record in office deserves 'A forted residence 'gainst the tooth of time/And razure of oblivion' (V. i. 12–13). 'Tooth of time' is native; 'razure of oblivion', latinate. But when it is Mariana's turn to plead for Angelo's life, a key moment in the play, every word is from the Anglo-Saxon: 'O my dear lord, /I crave no other, nor no better man' (V. i. 428–9).

The power of the Anglo-Saxon tradition can also be felt in another domain, that of religion. Protestantism gave the English monarchy a further chance to assert political autonomy by appropriating the Church, which was re-constructed as a specifically 'English' institution with English, appropriately enough, its language. The sixteenth century witnessed a flurry of Biblical translation, and the preparation of prayer books and other Christian texts. While people had been used to hearing sermons spoken in English, these printed texts seemed to the most devout to bring to them the word of God itself, in their own language. This process of vernacularisation culminated in the publication of the Authorised Version of the Bible in 1611, a text often regarded as a landmark in the history of English. It furnished English with a dignified and elevated language of worship, what might even be called a classical variety of its own to match the Latin of Catholicism. In addition, it gave many households the possibility of owning a text that greatly enhanced the status of their language: increasingly, it came to be seen as a monument, a reference-point, and a stimulus towards a sense of historicity. These sentiments were very important when English people came to settle overseas, as we shall see; and they can also be a vital focus in the maintenance of minority or suppressed languages. For the possession of a Bible in a vernacular language has been seen as one way of generating feelings of language-loyalty, a matter to be discussed in Part 3.

The air of dignity associated with the language of the Bible derives from the fact that it is distanced from ordinary spoken usage. This distancing is achieved, however, not by the use of either French or Latin models of prose, nor by the adoption of a polysyllabic vocabulary derived from those languages. Rather is it achieved by archaism, by setting the text in the tradition of native religious discourse, particularly the sermons of the Middle Ages. It is noteworthy that already in the early seventeenth century the Authorised Version reflected the usage of a couple of generations before. We shall see in chapter four how it is the Anglo-Saxon mode of clause- and sentence-linking that is exploited in this text, rather than the mode associated with Latin.

It has been suggested that the crucial stage in functional elaboration is the development of a medium for serious, expository prose. Inspired by the example of the Authorised Version, writers began to cultivate prose to such an extent that the seventeenth century has been called the century of prose: and a significant aspect of that trend was the increased use of English in writing of a scientific and scholarly nature. Although, as we have seen, the tradition of prose in English stretches back as far as King Alfred, and persisted during the Middle Ages for religious texts of a didactic or devotional nature – written, it has been suggested, for women, who were not allowed to learn Latin – that tradition had been weakened in contact with French and Latin. This was particularly so where scholarship is concerned. The tradition of scholarly writing in Latin was so long, its audience so wide, that as late as

1687 Newton chose to write his *Principia* in that language. But this choice of Newton's stands at the end of a tradition. Fed by a developing interest in science and philosophy, people wrote political pamphlets, journals, essays, and the first newspapers, in English. By the end of the seventeenth century, the range of possibilities for expression in prose had expanded to cover imaginative, fictional writing. Such a wide functional range engendered further self-consciousness among writers of English, and enhanced the status of the language.

The displacement of Latin as the automatic language of scholarship was part of a wider process, the extension of English in education. In considering the roles of language in education, we need to distinguish between languages that are taught, and those that function as media of learning. In the Middle Ages, Latin had been both a taught language and the medium of instruction in the universities. But in schools the latter role had been filled by French. Both languages were being challenged in the education system by English as far back as the fourteenth century. A contemporary observer, Trevisa, records that in grammar schools throughout England French was being abandoned as the medium of instruction; and in the University of Oxford an edict of 1340 forbidding the use of English among students suggests that the latter had made their preferences clear. Two trends underlie these changes: the general reaction against French, and the gradual loosening of the Church's hold on institutions of learning and literacy.

Formal education was extended throughout the fifteenth and sixteenth centuries. Grammar schools were founded, often for the children of merchants; and some of these deliberately excluded clergy from teaching positions. The growth of secular education increased the demand for learning in English: and this was met after the introduction of printing. Books in English sold more widely than those in Latin. And when the Protestant Reformation had promoted the English language as a medium for religious instruction, the identification of Latin with learning was undermined still further.

A major goal of education still remained: the learning of Latin, and the cultivation of a good written style in that language. During the literary and cultural Renaissance of the sixteenth century, Greek was added to the syllabus; and Latin, ironically enough, was the object of renewed interest and enthusiasm. But it was the classical Latin of writers like Cicero, rather than the medieval variety of the Church, that was studied and analysed. Latin had received a fresh boost, but as a taught language rather than as a medium of learning. Paradoxically, enthusiasm for Latin ultimately furthered the cause of English. It promoted the debate about the suitability of English discussed earlier, and it led to massive translation into English, which in turn directed people's minds to the forms and structures of the vernacular. One outcome of this was the beginnings of interest in the history of English itself.

During the Renaissance, education seems to have lost some of its exclusiveness. We must remember, moreover, that in this period, like any other, education was not synonymous with schooling. There is evidence of extensive elementary literacy during the Tudor and early Stuart periods: in Shakespeare's London, perhaps half the population could read. The broadside presses printed ballads in their hundreds of thousands; and by familiarising people with written English, the Authorised Version provided the basis for the teaching of reading and writing in the many different kinds of schools that were established for ordinary people until education was made compulsory after 1870. Latin remained important to the education of elites: it was still a requirement for certain university courses, and hence for certain occupations until well into the present century. But education for most people, if, when, and where it was available, had been vernacularised; the medium of teaching had become a variety increasingly *codified* for this purpose, as is explained below. In time, however, it was also to become the form of English taught not only to foreign and second-language learners, but to the English themselves.

CODIFICATION

Some degree of standardisation is usually involved if a language is to be formally taught, if only because a highly centralised nation-state will tend to select one linguistic variety for this purpose. A taught language inevitably becomes increasingly subject to attention and scrutiny, aimed at describing its forms and structures. But as we have seen, one of the two goals of standardisation is the attainment of minimal variation of form. In practice, this means two things. First, eliminating variation within the standardised variety, a process at odds in many respects with the other goal functional elaboration. Second, it means trying to stop linguistic change. Both these interrelated aims – which run counter to the natural development of language – constitute the stage in the standardisation process that has been called codification.

Codification is undertaken by a small elite of scholars. Its method has less to do with description of linguistic forms, however, than with *prescription:* the evaluation of variants as 'correct', and the stigmatisation of variants which, for one reason or another, are felt to be undesirable. As we shall see, the arguments for justifying one variant in preference to another are often arbitrary, irrational, and inconsistent. This is because variants are associated, inevitably, with particular social groups; and certain social groups are felt to be more worthy of emulation than others. Unfortunately for the codifiers, the usage of London in the early years of standardisation was extremely mixed. There was still considerable variation in pronunciation, for instance, amongst the upper class; what is more, such usage was constantly being pulled hither and thither by aristocratic fashion, educated pedantry, and the unmonitored speech of ordinary Londoners. But by the early nineteenth century, the recommendations of the codifiers could be embraced by those social classes who felt the need to mark their speech off from that of the class below.

In the codification of English, the example set by other languages is of paramount importance. The codifiers looked back at Classical Latin, and envied the illusion of fixity and order lent by the Latin grammarians, and the matching usage of the great writers like Cicero. But they also had other models to go on. Both Italy (in 1582) and France (in 1635) had developed Academies – bodies of learned men, who could make pronouncements on particular variants and changes. For a time, the idea of an English Academy was mooted. But by the middle of the eighteenth century, support for such an institution had fallen away. The Académie Française, it seemed, had failed to fix the unfixable, just as it is failing today. Perhaps also, the English codifiers wanted to retain the freedom to make, and break, the rules as they chose. Thus codification in France has always been a more centralised and formalised affair than in England, where it has tended to be more *ad hoc.* Either way, the effects are much the same. It seems the higher the premium on codification is set, the less tolerant and the more rigid is the attitude to linguistic variation and change.

Recommended usage in England, therefore, is identified not with the decisions of a committee, but with particular books, written or compiled by established scholars and literary men. The most famous of these is undoubtedly the *Dictionary* of Dr Samuel Johnson. We have already mentioned this in connection with spelling; but it is even more important for the codification of words and meanings. When we think of dictionaries today, we probably have in mind what Johnson achieved – an alphabetical list of all those words which are neither dialectal or slang, together with their meanings. Before Johnson, what dictionaries were available were not of this type. They were either dictionaries of hard words, or bilingual ones. The first was a list of those words which were felt to be difficult to understand because they were largely unassimilated into the mainstream of usage: they were often polysyllabic, Latinate words. The time for such dictionaries, not surprisingly, was the early seventeenth century; the 'inkhorn controversy' might have been resolved, but people needed to know about those foreign loan-words which made English 'eloquent' (see page 46 above). The second type of dictionary corresponded largely with our idea of a 'French–English' one – an aid to translation. What Johnson did was altogether different. He listed the *range* of meanings for each word, including the commonest; and he illustrated each strand of meaning with quotations from writers. But in addition to this, Johnson saw lexicography as a contribution to the study of a language. Not only does he catalogue words and meanings, but he also has something to say about the nature of language, its history, and also its grammar.

The prestige enjoyed by the *Dictionary* during the late eighteenth and early nineteenth centuries was enormous. This was partly because it answered a need frequently felt by educated and literary people, and voiced as early as two centuries before by the scholar Mulcaster. But it was also because Johnson was regarded as a great man, with an established literary reputation. A dominant element in our cultural tradition has been the cultivation of the idea of the great mind, whether literary, philosophical, or whatever; and just as Classical scholars needed their Cicero, so the English literati of the late eighteenth century saw Johnson as the source of knowledge and wisdom about the English language. His *Dictionary* could even be viewed as constituting the language itself.

Partly because of this, Johnson for all his erudition occasionally strikes the modern reader as frivolous, prejudiced or even wrong, in some of his definitions. But we are also often reminded of his personality. Since Johnson, unfortunately, we have tended to forget the fact that dictionaries are compiled by people. Instead, we tend to revere them as the products of some mysterious, superhuman omniscience. The effects of this legacy, especially regarding our perception of words and meanings, will be discussed in the next chapter.

The second half of the eighteenth century was also the high water mark for the codification of grammar. It is with regard to this aspect of linguistic structure that the prescriptive nature of codification can be seen most clearly. Certain grammatical forms and structures were judged as 'correct', while others were stigmatised as 'vulgar'. The legacy of these pronouncements is still strong today: many people are extremely nervous about being incorrect in speaking and writing. And certain of the stigmatised usages have become embedded in our present-day consciousness, as pitfalls to avoid. In general, people have a much clearer idea about what they are supposed to *avoid* saying, than what the codifiers recommend for them.

The grammarians sought to justify one usage at the expense of another by applying certain principles. The most important of these is probably the example of Latin. Grammars of Latin had been available for centuries, and all scholars knew and used them; hence, the grammatical categories established by the Latin scholars were applied, ready-made, to the grammar of English. The fact that by the eighteenth century Latin was usually encountered only in its written form gave rise to the idea that it was a fixed, regulated, and invariant language. English, by comparison, seemed untidy: it was therefore felt to be appropriate to promote grammatical variants which corresponded, in one way or another, to equivalents in Latin. Thus, the English pattern *it's me*, which had been common for centuries and still is, was deemed incorrect since the Latin construction *ego sum* made use of the subject form of the pronoun, *ego*, rather than the object form *me*: English people should therefore say *it's I*. The pervasiveness of such reasoning can be judged by the fact that people still write about this shibboleth in letters to the press.

Knowledge of Latin presupposed a knowledge of etymology, the origins of words. As well as disliking variation, the grammarians also hated change: hence, correctness was associated with what used to be the case, and the further back you could go, the better. Such arguments were very common where the meanings of words are concerned, but the 'etymological fallacy' was also applied to justify certain constructions. *Different from* was preferable to *different to*, or *different than*, because the *di* part of the word originally indicated 'division' or 'separateness'; and therefore *from* suits the etymological argument better. Similarly, the constructions *averse to* and *under the circumstances* were considered incorrect, since the meanings of the *a* in *averse* and the *circum* in *circumstance* are respectively 'from' and 'around', and these meanings were not felt to be congruent with those of *to* and *under*. The grammarians failed to see that the use of such prepositions as *to* and *from* is in any language highly idiomatic.

A final principle involved the application of a kind of algebraic logic to stigmatise some constructions and promote others. Perhaps the most notorious example concerns the pattern of negation in English. In common with many languages today, English had since Anglo-Saxon times signalled negation by the cumulative use of negative particles. Hence, *I don't know nothing* was a traditional English pattern. By the end of the eighteenth century this had been condemned as illogical, by applying the principle that 'two negatives make a positive'. That great writers like Shakespeare used the traditional construction was a source of some embarrassment to the grammarians.

As in the case of dictionaries, we tend to forget today that grammars are written by people, who are not only individuals, but who also may reflect the interests of certain social groups. Grammar also has its great mind, to some extent, in that many people today look to Fowler and his *Modern English Usage* as an arbiter of usage. In Fowler, too, we find a personality, who is able moreover to temper the tradition of prescriptivism with a liberalism that acknowledges linguistic variation and change. But the strength of that tradition should not be underestimated today, and we shall see how our perceptions of grammar are dominated by it in the course of chapter four.

Pronunciation is the most difficult aspect of language to codify. As we have seen, our spelling is a most imperfect and inappropriate model for the sounds we make; yet people have felt bound by it for more than 400 years. Already in the sixteenth century some scholars interested in the codification of pronunciation had begun to consider the relationship between sounds and spellings: their arguments in effect are a rehearsal of those discussed above. Hart, a phonetician, argued that spelling should be reformed so as to draw it into line with pronunciation. Mulcaster, a headmaster, rejected this plea for a phonemic model, arguing that people pronounced differently. But others were already proposing the inversion of this priority. Sir Thomas Elyot, author of the immensely influential *Governor* of 1531, wrote that noblemen's sons should omit no letter in their pronunciation, a view echoed by the pronouncing dictionaries of 300 years later, and heard ever since.

Attempts to base pronunciation on spelling were not helped by developments in the writing system in the early phase of standardisation. The early printers introduced spellings that had nothing to do with sounds, like the *ue* of *tongue*. Other spellings were remodelled by scholars themselves, to show their origins: the nativised spelling *dette* had a *b* inserted to show that it came from Latin *debitum*. In cases like *debt* and *island* (where the scholars got the etymology wrong: they put an *s* into *iland*, thinking it to be from Latin *insula*) pronunciation has remained unaffected, and we are left with a spelling difficulty; but in other cases, as in *perfect*, the etymological spelling gives us the basis for modern pronunciation, displacing *parfit*. Such pedantry was not the only complicating factor. As we said before, the metropolitan variety was at first a very mixed one, mingling not only the pronunciations of different areas, but also to some extent their traditional spelling systems. The spelling of *busy*, for instance, may reflect the old Winchester standard, whereas its pronunciation is an East Midland one. Some pronunciations themselves appear to have a south-western origin. The glide consonant /w/ in *one* can be heard at the onset of other words, such as *oak* (*wuk*), in that area today. (Other dialects, for example those in Northumberland, have a different glide, the initial sound of *yet*; hence, *one* is *yan*.) Finally, some pronunciations seem to have had an East Anglian source. The famous example of spelling irregularity in *bough, though, rough, cough*, and *tough* shows how spelling can create the illusion of relationship among words that are either of different origin (the vowels of some of these words are historically unrelated) or whose pronunciations have diverged. We find that in the first two words, the final consonant, represented by *gh*, is no longer sounded, but the last three have the eastern /f/.

We do not know the circumstances governing the adoption of some pronunciations rather than others. It has been suggested that in some cases choice was motivated by a desire to maintain or even establish distinctions among pronunciations that were either not made in other dialects, or were being lost in them. Thus, the adoption of a south-western pronunciation of *one* could create a useful distinction between that word and *own*. Though this may be true in some instances, it is wrong in any event to conclude that either a prestigious or a taught pronunciation (or grammar and vocabulary for that matter) is richer in distinctions than other dialects or varieties, as we shall see in the next three chapters. Traditional distinctions may be preserved by teaching them as correct, but adherence to tradition may deprive us of a variety of useful innovations.

In the early years of standardisation, the precepts of the codifiers had to compete with the push and pull of fashion. Some pronunciations were undoubtedly adopted because, for one reason or another, they were considered prestigious. But by the end of the eighteenth century, codification of the other levels of structure led to the production of the pronouncing dictionary, a book in which the pronunciation of words in the prestige variety could be looked up. In these works, there is both an appeal to spelling as a guide, but also an appeal to tradition.

Johnson's *Dictionary* had codified not only words but their spellings also; and now that spelling was virtually fixed, it was a good deal easier to recommend pronunciations based on them. Moreover, Johnson himself had written that the best pronunciations were those that accorded with the spelling. This precept was put into effect by John Walker, the writer of *A Critical Pronouncing Dictionary* (1791). If there was an *h* in the spelling, then *h* should be sounded. The verbal ending *-ing*, as in *going*, should not be pronounced *-in'*, for the same reason. The pronunciation of whole words, like *forehead, often*, and *waistcoat*, should moreover be reformed in accordance with spelling, to replace *forrid*, *offen*, and *weskit*. Certain pronunciations, however, were too firmly entrenched in upper-class society to be changed. Admitting that the new pronunciation of *cucumber* suited the spelling better than the old *cowcumber*, Walker felt reluctant to recommend it. But the spelling-pronunciation won out in the metropolitan variety, and *cowcumber* is now only heard in dialect.

There is another crucial dimension to Walker's approach. Notions of correct pronunciation are formulated against a background of what to avoid; and it becomes increasingly clear that it is lower-class pronunciations that must be avoided. And the most barbarous kind of pronunciation was that associated with the Cockney speech of London. Cockneys, said Walker, should know better, since they did not have the excuse of living miles away from the centre of power, culture, and fashion. Thus, the differences that existed between their speech and that of so-called polite society were 'a thousand times more offensive and disgusting' than differences which occurred elsewhere.

By the early nineteenth century, then, correct pronunciation was an issue of class. And the identification of the 'best' pronunciation with a particular social class is given institutional expression by the development of the fee-paying public school system. In these schools, a pronunciation that may be described as codified grew up, or was cultivated and taught. The desiderata of the scholars could at last be put into practice in controlled conditions. But the recipients of this privilege have always been only a tiny minority, a minority drawn primarily from the wealthy and powerful groups in English society. In no other country in the world are pronunciation and social class so closely and clearly linked.

In the public schools, the predominantly East Midland basis of the upper-class London pronunciation gradually lost its regional colour. It became a purely class accent, and was accordingly evaluated in ways which reflect the attitudes of the most powerful social group. Known today to linguists as Received Pronunciation – a term in which the adjective 'received' has the now obsolete sense of 'socially acceptable in the best circles' – this accent is still widely claimed to be the best form of pronunciation (although linguists themselves usually attest their neutrality on this matter). Received Pronunciation (RP) is often described, not in terms of the class that uses it, but as the most beautiful and euphonious of accents. Most strikingly, its status as an accent has even been denied: if you speak RP, you speak English 'without an accent'.

It need hardly be said that this view was often accepted and even fostered by ordinary people wherever English was spoken. Persuaded that their own regional accents were ugly or slovenly, people have often accepted the view that RP offers a prestigious norm. Many of our popular designations of RP – 'Queen's English', 'Oxford English', 'BBC English' – reflect its association with power, learning, and influence. And as we shall see in chapter five, RP has been a powerful agent in the re-structuring of regional pronunciations which originally had quite different sound-systems. Yet while RP exerts prestige at the overt level, there has been no widespread, wholesale adoption of the accent. For the vast majority of the population, RP may be all the things we have listed above, but it is also the speech of a social class that they have no ambition to emulate.

CODIFICATION AND SOCIAL CLASS

We have seen that from the first the process of standardisation is associated with power in society. Throughout the period of standardisation, an increasingly dominant source of power has been the ownership of capital. By the nineteenth century, the factory system was producing enough wealth for its owners to acquire positions in society. But ownership of a fortune does not guarantee refined behaviour or courtly manners. The new entrepreneurs needed to be 'socially acceptable in the best circles'. What more accessible way of doing this than to embrace the standards of correctness in speech, now that these had been codified and made widely available?

Recent research in both England and the USA suggests that the class most anxious about linguistic usage is the lower middle class. Insecurity about social status is reflected in nervousness about being incorrect in linguistic behaviour. In the early nineteenth century, it was the industrialists who felt insecure about status, and who therefore provided the need for a 'superior' kind of English. The adoption of the codified standard would mean that your speech could be sharply different from that of the working class, who, as a consequence of the process of industrialisation, were flooding into the cities in their hundreds of thousands. It was in *their* speech, appropriately enough, that the stigmatised pronunciations and grammatical items could be found.

Codification could be said to have become a weapon of class. What the codifiers had done, ultimately, was to propose and cultivate a code of linguistic forms which were in some degree different from those in use among the vast majority of the population. By analysing 'correct' usage in terms that only a tiny minority of educated people could command, the codifiers ensured that correctness remained the preserve of an elite. The usage of most people was wrong, precisely because it was the usage of the majority. The worst aspects of the codification process were institutionalised in the compulsory state education system introduced after 1870. The doctrine of correctness was preached with mechanical inflexibility: attention to linguistic form overrode all considerations of linguistic function. Not surprisingly, millions of people left school convinced that not only were they ignorant of their own language, but they were stupid as well.

It would, however, be mistaken to suggest that the codifiers were a tightly-knit group of conspirators extending across several generations, intent on laying traps for the unwary. In fact, they did not by any means represent a homogeneous body of opinion; they often argued amongst themselves, and some laid the foundations for the serious study of language and of linguistic history. But the codifiers did pave the way, however unwittingly, for the mystification that has often characterised discussion about language. Many people today, when they examine the work of the eighteenth-century grammarians, are struck by the triviality of the examples cited, and by the tortuousness of the arguments. And if the judgments are arbitrary, and the result of special pleading, it may well be because the codifiers themselves were not unaffected by allegiances of class and background.

Codification was not based on an informed and systematic analysis of language. It is not surprising, therefore, that there is little consensus today about what items upset us or gladden our hearts. A recent survey among employers, examiners, and teachers shows that while some people make a fuss about *it's me*, others like to wax haughty on *different to/than/from*. We all have a linguistic *bête noir*. But one of the most depressing results of codification is that as well as encouraging this prescriptive stance, it has tended to elevate personal taste into a norm, a characteristic particularly apparent in the pages of Johnson, Walker, and Fowler. In view of the social history of the past two centuries, this was perhaps unavoidable: but we should remember today that individual preference and informed understanding are not necessarily the same thing.

Part II
Changing patterns of usage

3   Words and meanings

Contact with other languages, as we saw in chapter one, has greatly influenced the word-stock of English. New words are more easily added to a language than grammatical forms or structures, or sounds, and so the word-stock of a language, or its lexicon, can be considered to be more open-ended than its grammar or sound-system. Social and cultural changes are accordingly clearly reflected in changes in vocabulary: and this is one aspect of the history of English about which it is possible to make some simple, clear, and fairly safe observations. We know, for instance, that the vocabulary of English has vastly increased in size during the last 1500 years, as an accompaniment to the process of functional elaboration discussed in chapter two. In the present chapter we shall examine the process of word-borrowing, and some socio-linguistic issues raised by it, such as how it might reflect social needs; and this in turn will lead us to further issues, such as the ways in which our notion of the word as an isolable unit has been shaped by literacy and the dictionary. We shall need to look at the complexity involved in the study of meaning (and again, the way in which our perceptions are influenced by the dictionary), and consider how many traditional accounts of semantic change tend to underplay the importance of different groups of users in changing meanings, or in adding new meanings to particular words. We shall try to illustrate the role of these factors by considering in detail three recent examples of semantic change. Finally, we shall explore parts of our vocabulary which can be shown to have been socially sensitive, by discussing the notion of 'key-words', the vocabulary of power and status, terms of address, and words which refer to women.

From a social point of view, more interesting than the mere addition of new words to our vocabulary is the change in the character of our word-stock, from one which can be called Germanic to one that is also partly Romance. Exposure to Latin, and its offspring French, has been sustained throughout much of the recorded history of English, and it is this that helps give the language its European flavour, in that many of our words are quickly recognisable to speakers of French, Italian, and Spanish. This exposure has been pervasive enough to give rise to some popular notions and stereotypes about parts of the English lexicon. Speaking 'in words of one syllable' appeals to the Anglo-Saxon element (the reason for this monosyllabic quality, the loss of inflexions, is discussed in the next chapter); 'talking like a book', to the more learned, polysyllabic lexical material derived from the Romance languages. Like most popular ideas about language, these associations are only partly justified: 'four-letter words', for instance, are not generally recorded in Anglo-Saxon texts, and there are plenty of words from French that have entered dialectal English and have rarely been used in writing. But these associations do square with an important *stylistic* trait in the language. Romance loan-words are common in domains associated with power and prestige, and it is a matter of everyday experience that formal business letters tend to favour the French *request* rather than the Anglo-Saxon *ask*, and that military medals are awarded for *gallantry* or *courage*, rather than for *guts* (deriving from an Anglo-Saxon word denoting bowels and entrails).

There have also been fundamental developments in the principles of word *formation*. In Anglo-Saxon times, new words could be coined from established ones, a process generally known as compounding. There were some productive prefixes, such as *for-, under-, mis-*, and suffixes like *-some, -craft, -dom*, and *-ness*, and these could be combined in various ways with other words: thus, poetry was *wordcraeft*, medicine *laececraeft*. The technique is similar to that often found in modern German, which might have *Ausgang* ('way out') where we are likely to use the Latinate *Exit*. While we have not abandoned this technique altogether, it has often been said that English has been particularly receptive to the possibility of absorbing foreign words; as well as making up new words, we borrow them; and not only, of course, from the languages mentioned. On this view, the borrowing process has been so dynamic that we have taken up prefixes and suffixes as well as words: the French *-able*, for instance, can be tacked on to words of Anglo-Saxon origin, for instance, as in *likeable*.

The tendency to borrow rather than create has its social consequences. It has been argued that the Anglo-Saxon habit of word-formation kept the meaning of a word transparent and was therefore democratic: you can work out what a new word means, because you know the meanings of the parts. It is certainly true that foreign vocabulary has often been used, and is still used, to dominate or mystify; and it is easy to laugh at people who, unfamiliar with the sound- and syllable-patterns of the Latinate vocabulary of, say, medicine, mispronounce words or use them inappropriately. On the other hand, can words in themselves exemplify either a democratic or an undemocratic trend in a language's development? The desire to be either of these things must be in reality a matter for the users of a language. Indeed, when it comes to demagogy, it is just as possible to manipulate people by using words drawn from a less heterogeneous vocabulary. The meanings of Anglo-Saxon words like *hearth, home, kith, kin, child, father, mother*, can easily be exploited in persuasive language, since they are words to which strong emotions are often attached; often learned early in life, some resonate with associations of familiarity and intimacy.

THE MOTIVATION FOR BORROWING

A number of sociolinguistic issues are raised by the question of why words are borrowed in the first place. It is a common misconception that some languages are inferior, or more handicapped than others, because they lack not only words but concepts that can be seen to find expression in other languages. These misconceptions falsely assume that certain topics, and some modes of discourse, depend on particular vocabulary ranges. Therefore, the argument goes, English borrowed words because it needed them. There are several objections that can be made to these notions. First, as we have seen, words are often borrowed into particular varieties of a language, and become part of the technical or specialised usage of certain groups of users only. Writers used to reading, say, philosophy, in another language, will grow accustomed to a certain range of vocabulary and a particular kind of expression; and they may well conclude that their own language is deficient by comparison. But the association of a vocabulary with such subjects is largely traditional. Though we might expect to hear in a discussion of economics words like *profit, demand*, and *recession*, there is no reason why these terms could not be glossed by others, or that notions akin to them should not be expressed differently. Second, as we have already noted, words borrowed from other languages often develop a particular resonance that is stylistic: we expect to encounter them in certain contexts, either written or spoken, formal or informal, official or literary. Thus, they can be said to parallel already existing usages rather than fill in the gaps of an impoverished language. Third, borrowed vocabulary is very often used as a means of marking social distance. Since ordinary people might be impressed by a high-sounding utterance, there is a demand among elites for foreign vocabulary: thus, the motivation for borrowing may be as much to do with social snobbery or social differentiation as anything else. Finally, it can be shown that thousands of borrowed words introduced nothing that was conceptually new; English was already adequately served. One consequence of this, as we shall see, is that the meanings of older words tend to be changed by the admission of the new.

Linguists usually argue against the notion of handicapped languages by asserting that all languages develop vocabularies that fully serve the needs of their users. In general, vocabulary is more finely differentiated in fields or subject areas which are culturally valued and significant; so that if a language has more words than another in relation to, say, rice, it will reflect the interests of its speakers. The fact that English has borrowed so many words in its history is not, however, so much a reflection of need as of the enduring cultural dominance of languages like French and Latin. Unfortunately, global statements about the needs of different speech-communities mask an important fact about language and its relation to society. Different groups of speakers may have different needs. Within one language like English, for instance, it will be necessary for a group such as farmers to classify cows and bulls with a more specific vocabulary – more sensitive to age – than most of us have need of. Similarly, I have a richer vocabulary of address to a loved one – ranging from Christian name, nickname, pet-name, terms of jocular abuse – than to a colleague of only slight acquaintance. In culturally diverse, literate, technologically complex societies such as our own it is more difficult to identify areas of general social need than in more homogeneous societies (a famous if now contested example is that of Eskimos and their many words for different kinds of snow). At the same time, it is fair to assume that the more homogeneous Anglo-Saxon tribes had a clearer need for a vocabulary denoting natural topo-graphical features than we do today. For the Anglo-Saxons, the process of settlement was of crucial importance, and it is reflected in a great many English place-names whose meaning is obscured for us. Unless we are foresters, we no longer need single words to refer to such features as 'wood on a slope' (*hangra*, preserved in Oakhanger, Hants), 'sacred grove' (*hearg*, as in Harrow, Middx), 'land covered with brush or small trees' (*hese*, as in Hayes, Herts), or 'wet land liable to be overgrown with alders' (*sceage*, as in Shaugh, Devon).

Despite what has been said in the paragraph above, it is still possible to point to certain areas of human life in which all the groups of users of English have a common interest. There is a general sensitivity about subjects like sex, defecation, drunkenness, and death, and there are clear social norms about ways of referring to them. Vocabulary tends to proliferate around such taboos, as we might expect of subjects that are culturally salient. When we examine the relevant vocabulary, however, two clearly different modes of reference can be distinguished. One, associated with the more 'polite' social groups is towards euphemism. New words are selected, or coined, to replace existing ones which are thought to have picked up the unpleasant or undesirable associations characteristic of the referent. Thus, in some contexts *die* is felt to be abrupt, and phrases such as *passed away*, *departed this life* are used to soften the fact of death. Other social contexts, however, permit a more jocular periphrasis, such as *snuffed it*, *kicked the bucket*, etc. What both tendencies have in common is the need for novelty: with euphemism, the need to find new ways of avoiding unpleasantness, and with slang, new ways of sensationalising, humourising, or actually cultivating offensiveness. The desire for newness, then, provides another motivation for borrowing.

Unfortunately for the historian of English, detailed information about words and meanings in these socially sensitive spheres is often lacking for past centuries. This is partly because ways of referring to them are covert, and partly because many such terms were until very recently rarely written down. If they ever reached print, they may have changed their meaning, and so do not provide evidence of ways of verbalising taboo subjects. The further back in history we go, the narrower the range of texts available. On the basis of the texts we possess, it is very difficult to know what subjects, if any, were taboo for the Anglo-Saxons. It might be argued, however, that the Anglo-Saxons had already devised euphemisms for death and dying. Our word *die* is not firmly evidenced in Anglo-Saxon (although related forms *deaþ* and *dead* exist) and it is possible that the concept was referred to by means of words which were historically euphemisms: *sweltan* (compare modern *swelter*), which originally meant 'burn slowly'; and *steorfan* (cf. modern *starve*), originally meaning 'become stiff'. The modern form *die* is probably a borrowing from Scandinavian *deyja*, and the reason for its borrowing may well have been that the other words had become too closely identified with their sensitive referent. The other words develop modified meanings: *swelt* does not become part of the metropolitan variety, but it survives in dialect to mean 'faint with heat'; in *starve* the meaning is specialised, with the cause of death specified: cold in dialect, hunger more generally.

A further meaning of *starve* in contemporary English brings us to one more 'universal' in our discussion of users' needs – this time of a more abstract nature. It is quite common to hear people say *I'm starving* when they are only more than a little hungry. In other words, they achieve emphasis by choosing a word whose dictionary meaning, as it were, is too strong for the context. The desire for emphasis has weakened the meanings of a great many words, such as *awfully*, *terribly*, *frightfully*, *marvellous*, *glorious*, *stupendous*, because they have been used where what is of paramount importance are the attitudes of the speaker. In such *affective* uses of language, the desire for emphasis creates the need for new terms, in that the affective content of words rapidly becomes diluted: we therefore find a motivation for borrowing similar to that discussed in the last paragraph. Furthermore, an important dimension of attitude is the desire to register approval or disapproval of certain objects, practices, ideas, and so on. A great part of our everyday vocabulary tells other people about our likes and dislikes: we often want to place things on a scale of evaluation, and our vocabulary is often correspondingly vague, as in the ubiquitous *nice*. At the extreme ends of the favourable/unfavourable continuum, new words are constantly being introduced – like *fabulous*, and more recently *magic*, with its handy antonym, *tragic*.

CODIFICATION OF WORDS AND MEANINGS

Having discussed some of the general changes in our vocabulary, and some of our ways with words, it is now time to consider how the process of codification, outlined in the last chapter, has influenced our perception of words and meanings. We need to do this not only because a number of intrinsically interesting issues are involved, but because we cannot begin to understand the process of semantic change unless we try to free ourselves from the notions of fixity and correctness associated with standardisation. We can do this if we remember that codified varieties of language are by no means universal, that many of them are relatively new, and that their influence is not uniformly felt throughout society. Since these observations can also be made about literacy, we shall also need to bear in mind the importance of the written word in our cultural experience.

A significant effect of the codification process is that we tend to think that the primary unit of linguistic structure is the word. This is partly because the most accessible handbook of English is the dictionary, a list of words; and our perception of words as isolable, fixed forms is reinforced by our writing tradition, which accustoms us to the spaces between words on the page. Above all, we perceive the word as something that is spelt, in an invariant form. When we consider the importance of the word in the school system, as a means of assessing linguistic competence (by estimating vocabulary size), or in such things as spelling tests, it is not surprising that it is this component of linguistic structure that tends to be uppermost in our minds when we think or talk about language.

In unmonitored, informal conversation, however, our perception of words is quite different. We treat them almost as abstractions: changing their pronunciation in different environments, altering their function in different kinds of sentences and making them mean many different – and sometimes apparently contradictory – things. No one, moreover, keeps words separated when they are talking off-the-cuff. Despite what many of us think, it is not only speakers of 'non-standard' English who run words into each other. In our everyday use of language, words are not treated as isolable entities, but as parts of bigger units, the utterances of speech; these, in turn, form part of larger units, which may be called discourses or texts. It is in this way that we first encounter words as children; and such pre-literate perceptions underlie our unselfconscious speech, however much we may prefer to think that it accords with the precepts of a fixed, codified, literate norm. It is only when we learn to read and write that our natural tendency to think of words as parts of larger units is broken down, and the history of the form *alright* shows how the failure to analyse a familiar phrase into its constituent parts brings into being a new, single word. In similar fashion, schoolchildren often write *a lot* as one word.

A great deal of what we have said about our informal treatment of words is relevant when we consider how words are perceived in nonliterate societies. We need to remember that if words are only encountered in face-to-face, oral interaction, their *meanings* will be more immediately tied to specific contexts. Literacy, by contrast, diversifies culture, introducing new traditions; hence words come to be experienced in a wider range of contexts, and consequently a more generalised, less concrete, and less immediate perception of their meanings may arise. And as the functions of language are elaborated, words take on meanings associated with particular domains of usage. So we can begin here to see a process of contact between specialised usage and the language of the everyday: just as languages can borrow words from each other, so borrowing can occur among varieties of the same language. A word consequently accrues layers of meanings as it is used in a widening range of contexts, the more so if it is used in many different kinds of writing. Thus, consciousness of the individual word may be reflected much more strongly in the poetry of a literate culture than in an oral one. While the former may cultivate ambiguity and word-play, oral poetry makes use of the formula, usually a string of words, habitually co-occurring, to express common ideas, actions, and processes; it chooses words for their overall sound-effect rather than for their subtleties of meaning. Even within a literate culture oral poetry can survive, as in the case of the sung ballad; and we can find some of its characteristics in the literature of the Anglo-Saxons, and to a lesser extent in the poetry of the Middle Ages. The absence of a standardised codified variety, and of a universal spelling system, meant that the medieval poets could not expect their works to remain unchanged if they were written down by scribes in other parts of the country. Not only words, but even whole phrases might be changed in the course of transmission.

The way in which literacy affects our perception of words is subtler than the more dramatic and overt influence of the dictionary. Unfortunately, many people tend to treat dictionaries with reverence: rather than being seen as a record of usage, they are often regarded as the arbiter of it, a source of enlightenment for the ignorant non-specialist. In fact, the traditional arrangement of words in dictionaries gives people a strange idea about language. The alphabetic arrangement disassociates a word from the company it keeps, presenting it as a unit isolated from context and words of similar meaning. More important, many dictionaries give the impression that words have only one meaning, to be found on the right-hand side of the page. Even the fullest dictionary, the *Oxford English Dictionary* (*OED*), which shows the whole range of meanings by citing examples of a word *in use* at different periods of its history, puts the meanings first, then lists the examples, thereby obscuring the process involved in deriving the meanings; for we learn the meanings of new words most efficiently by hearing them in a wide range of contexts. Most dictionaries, for economic reasons, cannot run to several volumes like the *OED*, so tend even more to give the idea that meaning is clear-cut and straightforward. It is not surprising, therefore, that people often misunderstand them.

The dictionary is the one reference book about language that is widely used. People writing to newspapers, for example, often preface their comments with something like 'I see from my dictionary...'. Unfortunately, a great deal of public debate about words and their meanings is conducted in an atmosphere of prescriptivism. It is assumed that the meaning listed in the dictionary is the true or real one, to which usage should conform. Identifying 'true meanings' is a favourite game in media discussions about language, and newspaper letter columns regularly print letters which highlight alleged errors or imprecisions in the use of *infer* or *sophisticated*, and so on. An assumption that underlies correspondence of this kind is that the etymology, or origin, of a word is a guide to its true meaning; in other words, the first recorded meaning is the correct one. The consequence of applying this logic through the entire English lexicon would produce strange results indeed. *Deer* would then mean any kind of animal (like the German *Tier*) and a *glamour* contest would be a test of brains, not beauty. But many people have a sincere desire to preserve distinctions that they feel are valuable, such as that existing between *infer* and *imply*. A careless use of the two words blurs a useful line between different processes; the original meanings therefore need defending. Though the concern for precision is laudable, it is rather an apocalyptic view of language that focuses its attention solely on 'lost distinctions'. The same so-called careless usage which is blurring *disinterested* and *uninterested* also failed to distinguish between *r* and *l* in *grammar*: we now have two words, with separate meanings, for the price of one – the other is *glamour*. A contrast lost, a contrast gained; such is linguistic change. The temperature needs to be lowered when meanings and changes in meaning are being discussed.

A final point to be made about dictionaries reminds us that it is not only the non-specialist who adopts a reverent attitude to dictionary authority. Many linguists and other scholars tend to regard the *OED* as definitive, even oracular, as if it had not been compiled by a group of people with certain presuppositions and even prejudices. Certain social and political values lie behind its apparent impersonality. The aura of objectivity associated with the *OED* is dangerous, since it expresses such values in a covert and anonymous way, unlike say, the dictionary of Dr Johnson. In any case, the particular tradition of scholarship which gave rise to the *OED* was more concerned with the origins of words and their variations of form and meaning, than with the ways in which words of similar or related meaning have influenced each other. An inquiry into certain parts of our vocabulary, such as the words associated with political discourse, shows the problems involved in establishing definitive meanings. Different groups in society use words like *class*, *democracy*, or *radical* to mean very different things, and the editors of the *OED* may have displayed, however unconsciously, the 'consensus' values of university academics whose work began in the 1870s and was largely completed in the 1920s. (Subsequent changes recorded in the Supplements to the *Dictionary* have involved additions rather than revisions.) We cannot write a social history of English without exploring the social position of those who study, or comment on, the language.

THE COMPLEXITY OF MEANING

The dictionary is of limited usefulness in the study of meaning and semantic change because the notion of meaning itself is so complex. We shall confine our discussion here to that part of our vocabulary that comprises so-called lexical words: nouns, like *horse*, *kettle*, *army*; verbs, like *walk*, *start*, *ride*; adjectives like *hard*, *brave*, *refreshed*; adverbs like *slowly*, *fast*, *noisily*. Lexical words such as these can be discussed in terms of their 'meaning content', in contrast to grammatical words, such as articles, prepositions, conjunctions, and pronouns.

We shall distinguish six types of meaning. The first, and most important kind, we shall call *conceptual* meaning. The meaning of many lexical words may be discussed in terms of what they denote; or, to put it another way, what their reference is. This type of meaning is sometimes called denotative or referential meaning. Many words 'stand for' objects, events, or processes that exist, or are felt to exist, in the real world; and such objects, and so on, are called referents. If we take the two words *woman* and *lady*, we can see that despite differences in meaning between them (which we shall discuss below) both words refer to an entity that is human, adult and female. Thus the conceptual meaning of both words may be related to this irreducible core of meaning.

This notion of reference is often misunderstood. It should be emphasised that the relationship between the form *woman*, and the thing it refers to, is a purely conventional one: there is nothing inherently feminine about the word itself, and in principle any other word would do to signify a woman, as long as we all agreed on the matter! But many arguments about the real meanings of words are based on an assumption of identity between word and referent. Such 'magical thinking' has a part to play in all cultures, but it will not get us far in trying to understand, in a linguistic sense, the problem of meaning and semantic change.

The relationship between words and referents, then, is a fluid one; and this comes about because as human beings we must *conceptualise* the objects, events, and processes that we find around us. These conceptualisations, being products of the human mind, are themselves inclined to change. There are of course different kinds of conceptualisation, according to the criteria used for relating words to referents. We use the word *mountain* to apply to a range of objects which conform to certain criteria, such as height, size, shape, substance, and so on; in sum, we apply the word to referents whose form satisfies the criteria listed. *Formal* criteria of this kind are less important, however, in applying the term *boat* to a range of objects. If we want to cross water, we need something that will carry our weight and stay afloat; size, shape, substance are of less concern, and a raft might do as well as an ocean liner. The word *boat* can refer to all shapes and sizes of things, as long as they *function* in a particular way (thus, we need to exclude model boats from this discussion). So far, then, we can distinguish very broadly between formal and functional criteria in our exploration of conceptual meaning, and we can test their validity by assessing the role of formal criteria in the applications of *boat*, and functional ones in the case of *mountain*. While we may think of a certain range of shapes when we use the term *boat*, it would not be true to say that the word is applicable to anything that happens to be boat-shaped, unless we are speaking metaphorically. Similarly, a mountain is something that can be climbed; but this aspect is not criterial, since we are not justified in applying the word *mountain* to, say, a ladder, simply because we can climb it. A third kind of conceptualisation involves criteria that are *evaluative*. When we use the term *hovel*, we specify a residence that seems to us to be dirty, tumbledown, or squalid. What is uppermost in our minds is our attitude to the referent: we have placed it on a scale of evaluation, of approval or disapproval. The importance of this dimension of meaning cannot be over-emphasised: the impetus towards evaluation, as we saw earlier, is very strong, and we shall see this again as we examine the history of some English words.

So far, we have discussed what is perhaps the most important dimension of meaning, but we have yet to account for other, incidental perceptions, that may not form part of the central core of meaning, but that are highly relevant when we consider how language functions in society. They are also instrumental in the process of semantic change. Another type of meaning, for instance, can be termed *connotative*. We saw above that *woman* and *lady* have roughly the same conceptual meaning, but a moment's reflection will remind us that we use the two words very differently. *Woman*, for instance, might connote a relatively open-ended set of properties, including the ability to bear children, the tendency to be warm and sensitive, the ability to satisfy men's sexual needs, and so on. The connotations of *lady*, on the other hand, tend to be associated with social status and graces. It is important to remember that though a word's connotations may vary from one individual to another, they are not purely personal or subjective; they often reflect the values and ideology of a particular social group at a particular time, and in the case of *woman*, the word will probably connote different things to men than to women.

The next type of meaning can be called *stylistic* meaning. Certain words advertise themselves as belonging to particular contexts of use.

Thus, while we may agree that, say, *horse* and *steed* have the same conceptual meaning, we are unlikely to take a steed for a Saturday morning's ride (neither would we take our *gee-gee*, unless we were talking to very young children). We recognise *steed* as a word appropriate to certain contexts of use, such as poetry, or prose romance: it belongs to a particular 'style'. From a historical point of view, stylistic meanings develop as the language is functionally elaborated, and certain words are specialised in particular fields of usage. Thus, *steed*, from an Anglo-Saxon word meaning stallion, has been associated with poetic language since the sixteenth century.

Our fourth type is *affective* meaning. We have already noted the importance of attitude and evaluation in shaping our use of language. The words we use to address, or refer to, other people are often highly partisan, particularly where differences of social class, race, sex, region of origin, or political persuasion are concerned. Certain words become so emblematic of a point of view that their conceptual content is pushed into the background. *Nigger*, originally a word denoting a racial type, has virtually become a term of abuse; and a similar development has occurred with parts of the political vocabulary, such as *fascist*.

The fifth and sixth types of meaning are respectively *reflected* and *collocative* meaning. Certain words over the centuries have developed more than one conceptual meaning, and sometimes more than one meaning is perceived by the user. The Anglo-Saxon word *deore* originally denoted things of great value, and was later applied to people in the sense of 'esteemed', from which the sense 'dear' subsequently arose. It is possible for poets to exploit both meanings, 'costly' and 'beloved', so that such words in certain contexts may be said to *reflect* both. Finally, collocative meaning concerns the somewhat idiosyncratic properties of certain words like *pretty* and *handsome*. While both words share a similar conceptual meaning, they habitually co-occur with different sets of nouns, from which they contract associations. Thus, *pretty* collocates with *girl* rather than *boy*, *village* rather than *typewriter*. While both *pretty* and *handsome* mean much the same thing, they are not normally interchangeable, for part of their associative meaning is derived from the collocational company they keep.

Collocational meaning reminds us of a vital point about words made earlier in this chapter. We are accustomed to hearing them strung together with other words: and the rules which specify which words can collocate with a particular word constitute an important part of that word's meaning. Thus, we can extend the notion of collocational meaning, and speak of collocational *range*. Some words, like *big*, can qualify almost any noun, referring to a wide range of referents, human and non-human, animate and inanimate, abstract and concrete, and so on; whereas *rancid* can collocate with very few, and *flaxen* with only one. As we shall see, extension or contraction in the collocational range often promotes a change in meaning; and a change in meaning of one word usually brings about a change in another. For words enter also into another series of relationships with other words, forming little systems of meaning: *big* patterns with *large* on one scale, with *gigantic* on another, with *small* on yet another, and so on. Thus, it is unwise to pluck a single word from its network, and discuss it in isolation, as is so often done; we should keep an eye on the fortunes of its peers.

TYPES OF SEMANTIC CHANGE

We have already encountered the difficulty of explaining the notion of meaning without referring to the past. For the rest of this chapter, we shall be seeing the relevance of our six types of meaning in discussing the processes of semantic change. This again is an issue of great complexity, and many histories of English present it in rather a forbidding way. For example, they often present us with instances of spectacular change, isolated from contexts of users and use, and with no attempt to show how these instances pattern with words of related meaning. Thus, to read that *treacle* once meant 'pertaining to wild animals' may afford a shock of pleasure or puzzlement, but if we are denied discussion of the intermediate links in the chain we can easily get the impression that words change their meanings by themselves, while the user stands helpless on the sidelines.

To give some idea of the *process* of semantic change, let us look at three words which have developed new meanings within living memory. All three are borrowings from either French or Latin. Each has a meaning that is not accepted by everybody in contemporary English society; though this need not surprise us, since speech-communities are never truly homogeneous, and there is no reason to believe they ever were. What is more, each has been cause for overt comment from people who object to certain meanings; and this shows that changes of meaning are in general more consciously felt than changes in grammar or pronunciation.

Our first example is the well-known case of *sophisticated*. A borrowing from Latin, the word is first recorded in English in the form of the verb *sophisticate* during the fifteenth century. Letters to the press, especially in the 1960s, often complained that the word had come to be used to describe technologically advanced weapons or other devices, with the sense 'elaborate' or 'highly refined'. This use of the word, associated sometimes with certain groups, such as broadcasters, or scientific and military commentators, was at variance with the so-called definitions of the word's meaning in the *OED*, which lists 'adulterated', 'artificial', or 'falsified'. Such complaints show how misleading a dictionary can be: the meanings it lists do not seem to square with the ways in which the word is most commonly used. (The most recent meanings are now recorded in the Second Edition of the *OED*.) When we inspect the kinds of words with which *sophisticated* collocates, and the kinds of people who use the new meanings, we can begin to see how changes in meaning are brought about. We shall find above all that these depend on whether *sophisticated* collocates with words having inanimate referents (where the meanings already discussed are appropriate) or human ones (where it has the contemporary meanings 'urbane', 'worldly-wise', or 'refined'). In this respect, it is rather like *dear*, as we saw from our discussion of reflected meaning. In its earliest usage, *sophisticated* clearly had an evaluative meaning, implying disapproval, and its use seems to have been limited to the description of inanimate things: if you sophisticated wine, you adulterated it, and if Art, or pleasures, were sophisticated, all primitive simplicity and naturalness were taken out of them. In all probability it was a word more appropriate to written than spoken discourse. Gradually, the connotations of the word changed, as it was used in a widening range of contexts by different groups of users. What is natural and pure to some, is to others naive and ingenuous, and such new connotations affected the word's conceptual meaning by the time it was applied, at the end of the nineteenth century, to people. The word has now lost its disapproving sense, and is used in popular speech to mean 'refined'; and when the word is re-applied to objects, it denotes those things that appeal to people of taste and experience. It is thus only a short step to the sense of 'technically advanced' in the usage of certain groups of specialists. And today, taking our cue from this latest application of the word, we speak of sophisticated cameras, tape recorders, stereo equipment, and so on.

In many histories of English, *sophisticated* is cited as an example of the process of *amelioration*, a type of semantic change in which a word originally denoting disapproval is given either a neutral or even a favourable meaning by its users. The use of terms such as this, though they may highlight dramatic shifts in meaning, not only obscures the complex and subtle pattern of interaction among varieties of the language, written versus spoken, technical versus everyday, but also the variations in connotation at a given time. For today, many educated speakers of English may try to monitor their use of *sophisticated* by restricting its use to descriptions of people; and even then many groups of people may acknowledge the meaning 'urbane' without necessarily upholding the values associated with this meaning. In other words, this meaning is 'quoted', as it were, by the speaker.

One word with which *sophisticated* patterned, in its early sense, was *vulgar*. Here, the relationship was one of contrast: *sophisticated* meant 'artificial', *vulgar* 'ordinary', 'everyday'. Deriving from the Latin *vulgus* (the common people: hence Vulgar Latin), *vulgar*, like *sophisticated*, originally collocated with words denoting inanimate referents; but by the sixteenth century it was being applied to people. By the mid-seventeenth century, it had developed its modern meaning, 'coarse', by a process known as *pejoration*, in which a word acquires a negative evaluation – the reverse of amelioration. If what was ordinary had become coarse, then what was adulterated could be refined; so that the development of new meanings in both words could have been mutually influential. We shall see later how words similar in meaning to *vulgar* have followed a similar semantic development.

Educated speakers today may also balk at using our second example, *chronic* in its recent sense of 'bad' or 'awful'. The word was borrowed in the course of the seventeenth century from Latin *chronicus* (reinforced by the French form of the same word) in the sense 'relating to time'; but the most usual meaning was that associated with the field of medicine in late Latin, where the word meant 'persistent', in contrast to 'acute'. By the nineteenth century this technical application of the word had loosened, and we find wars and doubts defined as chronic. The shift to its present meaning, however, probably comes from popular use. People were most likely to hear the word in medical contexts, as in 'he's got chronic bronchitis', and gradually the word acquired evaluative connotations: persistent bronchitis is unpleasant. What starts as a connotation becomes, in time, criterial; and now, in the sense of 'bad', it can collocate with a wide range of words – teachers, holidays, cars, can be chronic. In this meaning, it is used affectively: it conveys first and foremost information about the speaker's attitude, and has thus become a handy word to fill the evaluative slots discussed above. Also, an important part of the word's meaning is, as we have said, stylistic; this now belongs to informal spoken usage. The Second Edition of the *OED* records the new meaning from the very end of the last century, describing it as 'vulgar', not, it should be added, in the sense of 'coarse', but in the older meaning – though it is difficult for the modern reader not to feel the disapproving sense *reflected* in this use of the word!

Our third example is a word whose recent semantic development is of a less organic, and more consciously manipulative kind than those of the two cases already discussed. With *gay*, in the recent sense of 'homosexual', we are dealing with a word where a specific group-consciousness is involved, and where a very deliberate concern with language is manifested. A fourteenth-century borrowing from French, the word has retained the meaning 'merry', 'jolly', 'light-hearted' from that time, but by the seventeenth century an additional meaning had developed. Light-heartedness could also be interpreted as frivolity, lack of seriousness, or even hedonism. The meaning 'addicted to social pleasures' developed, and the word came to be used euphemistically, of people who lived immoral and dissipated lives. Its downward path continued into the nineteenth century: in slang usage, a gay woman was a whore. And by the first third of the present century, a gay man, in slang, was 'homosexual'. The last few decades have seen the attempt by homosexuals to get the word accepted as a standard term of reference, now that the earlier associations with immorality and prostitution have been forgotten.

Groups who occupy a subordinate or oppressed position in society invariably suffer from linguistic disparagement. Homosexuality is regarded as deviant behaviour, and is often referred to in abusive terms (like *bent* and *queer*), just as women and Black people find themselves at the receiving end of a rich vocabulary range, at best patronising, at worst offensive. Sometimes these words are wielded innocently, in that some people are genuinely unaware of their pejorative meaning; but more often than not they are used as conscious symbols of an attitude. And, just as politically-conscious Black people have struggled to promote words like *Black* at the expense of *nigger* or *coon*, so *gay* has become instrumental in the cause of homosexual equality; moreover, people who support such causes are expected to use these terms, since the use of the traditional terms is an index of a social stance. Thus, on a range of sensitive social and political issues we have to choose our vocabulary with care, and cultivate a conscious, highly self-critical attitude to the issue of words and meanings.

The heightened awareness of language exhibited by such groups as gays and feminists is the intelligent response of the exploited or the powerless. It stems above all from the recognition that language has a vital part to play in the exercise and consolidation of power. Not unnaturally, the powerful in society have long recognised this. It is a matter of everyday experience that in political discourse meanings are manipulated and words chosen to load the dice in favour of one point of view. Evaluative connotations of words like *democratic* are cultivated at the expense of their conceptual meaning, so that a word denoting particular kinds of political organisation becomes what we might call a 'purr' word, used merely to win approval for a particular position.

Formerly, however, *democratic* was a 'snarl' word when used by the ruling class in England, for whom it was linked with the ideas of the French Revolution. The word *moderate*, connotatively favourable but referentially vague when applied to politics, has been widely used to enlist support for people whose political views are often fundamentally conservative.

Since the early 1980s a new vocabulary has developed in Britain to reflect the re-emergence of de-regulated, 'market' capitalism with its aggressive form of management and commitment to 'enterprise'. Many terms shared by both government and managers can be seen as euphemistic: mass redundancy is re-labelled *downsizing*, working on short-term contracts *flexible working*. The words clearly reflect the point of view of the powerful. The relatively powerless, on the other hand, have been re-cast as *consumers*; the metaphor of consumption has even been applied to formal education, in which students are now called *customers*. The term *citizen* has been revived in the context of consumer or customer rights, rather than in the context of legal and democratic rights and responsibilities as on the Continent and in the USA.

KEY-WORDS

If certain words are emblematic of particular social stances, other words act as keys to whole systems of belief. Students of medieval English literature need to learn that the thirteenth-century French borrowing *cortaysye* cannot be translated by its modern form *courtesy*; more than just politeness and respect are involved, since for poets and audience the word was a central element in the conceptual edifice of chivalry. Similarly, we need to recognise the theological assumptions underlying the use of *grace*, *mercy*, and *nature* – again, all medieval borrowings from French – in the plays of Shakespeare. These words reflect critical social, political, and ethical concerns, but we must beware of assuming that particular systems of belief were always accepted by all groups in society. There can be little question that at all times a *dominant* set of beliefs existed; but at times certain groups articulate different values, and evolve their own vocabulary, or their set of meanings for common words, to express them. The meaning of *nature*, for instance, has been adapted in the course of over 500 years to suit various ideologies. Its fourteenth-century meaning, 'inherent force directing the world, or the human race, or both' was fluid enough to permit significant variations of focus. By the early eighteenth century, the word referred to the material world, and part of that included the world of people: their way of doing things. Thus, a set of social relations could be legitimised by appealing to the notion that it was 'natural'. By the late eighteenth century, however, nature had become the state of original innocence before human beings had created imperfection. These essentially static conceptions of nature were challenged in the nineteenth century by the post-Darwinian focus on the competitive and destructive aspects of nature as an inherent force; and again, certain types of human behaviour and organisation could be justified by citing what happens 'in nature'. As contemporary arguments about 'human nature' show, you can almost make the word mean whatever you like.

It is clear that in the past words were manipulated by their users just as they are today. And in so far as words emblematic of certain values are handed down through the generations, it is arguable that the vocabulary we learn conditions or even determines our thoughts on various subjects. Earlier in this chapter we noted how some languages, or some varieties within a language, had richer vocabularies with respect to certain fields of thought or activity, and it is often claimed that differences of this kind lead to differences of perception: where the gardener sees weeds, the botanist, or Native American, sees a variety of interesting or potentially useful plants. A bolder articulation of this idea was that advanced by the American anthropological-linguist Benjamin Lee Whorf, who, influenced by his teacher Edward Sapir, suggested that different languages structured the perceptions and thoughts of their users in very different ways. By comparing languages like English with some of those spoken by Native Americans, Whorf concluded that there existed very different notions of time in the different speech-communities, notions based on differences of grammatical structure. English, for instance, could 'objectify' time by permitting such constructions as *they stayed ten days*, in which a day is treated as a discrete entity, like a man or a chair; whereas Hopi, a Native American language, handled time as a continuum. Language, then, as viewed by Whorf is a kind of perceptual strait-jacket: we are at the mercy of the inherited vocabulary and grammar of our mother tongue.

The Sapir–Whorf Hypothesis seems to ignore the fact that languages are not homogeneous, and that they are subject to change. It seems more fruitful, therefore, to concentrate on how our thoughts and responses are shaped by particular users of our language, since we know that various kinds of propaganda will not work unless they can exploit the fact that much of our thinking is habitual and unreflecting. In this way, we may be able to see more clearly how some words change their meanings.

THE VOCABULARY OF POWER, RANK, AND STATUS

The proposition that different social groups may use words differently extends to the words used for the social groups themselves. As we have said, such words are particularly sensitive to the development of pejorative or affective meanings. It is therefore instructive to explore some aspects of the vocabulary of rank and status: how reference is made to the social hierarchy, and how people of different status address each other. We shall suggest three major trends in the history of the words chosen. First, terms originally denotative of rank often become evaluative; second, those denoting the more powerful groups are most likely to retain their status as rank-terms; and third, there are interesting changes in the possibilities of using these words in direct address.

While the relationships among these status and rank terms, being based on a hierarchy of power in society, are clear, they are more fluid than those of more highly structured hierarchies, such as the army. The army has evolved a *set* of mutually exclusive terms, the individual meaning of which depends entirely on an understanding of the meaning of the others: thus, we can only know what *captain* means if we understand its relation to *major*, *lieutenant*, and *corporal*, and so on. Social relations are in general, however, less static, so the meanings of their terminology are more susceptible to change; but we must beware of assuming that any change in meaning automatically accompanies, or signals, a change in social structure. The relationships between the words and the things they signify are more complex than that, as we shall see.

The Anglo-Saxon system of rank-terms was largely re-structured after the Norman Conquest. *Cyning* and *cwen* (king and queen), *hlafweard* and *hlaefdige* (lord and lady – the former being a warden of loaves, the latter a kneader of them) survive, in senses known to the Anglo-Saxons; but other terms were pushed into new meanings by the introduction from French of *duke*, *prince*, *squire*, *villain*, etc. The Anglo-Saxons used *aldormann* to denote a man responsible to the king for administrating a large territory, *þegn* (modern 'thane' or 'thegn'), a lesser landowner, and *ceorl* (churl) to denote the lowest rank of freeman. Another word was *eorl*, which denoted high status in general, and which, like *þegn*, was used in poetic texts in the sense of 'warrior'. In the period of Viking power, the meaning of *eorl* was influenced by the related Scandinavian word *jarl*, which had a similar meaning to *aldormann;* and the word has survived the Norman Conquest in this later sense. *Aldormann* has become specialised, in terms of municipal power and status, while *þegn* has been superseded by the French *baron*, and interestingly enough by the Anglo-Saxon term *cniht*. Originally *cniht* was not a rank term, but denoted a boy or lad; inferiority in age gave way to inferiority of status, and the word came to mean a servant. But there are different kinds of servant: a king's servant or knight, had to be of noble blood, and the word was specialised to the kinds of meaning hitherto represented by *þegn*.

The meanings of words denoting low social status seem to have been affected by further borrowings from French. One of these, *gentle*, had already acquired an evaluation of approval by the time it was borrowed into English in the thirteenth century. Originally it had meant 'high-born', but its meaning widened to include those characteristics felt by the high-born to be appropriate to their social position. If *gentle* – something of a key-word in the history of English – denoted good breeding and gracious behaviour, then words like *churl* could be associated with coarseness. By about 1300, *churl* had lost its technical sense as a term of rank, and indicated low breeding in general; from that point, connotations of 'rudeness' gradually became criterial. Interestingly enough, the French borrowing *villein* dropped even further. By 1300 again, its primary meaning was 'base'; from there it is only a short step to the present wholly pejorative meaning of 'villain'. While both these words have become pejorised, a later borrowing, *peasant*, has retained its early meaning, 'one who works the land', as well as a later pejorative one. By the end of the sixteenth century we find it used affectively – almost as a 'snarl' word – in Elizabethan drama, notably in Marlowe's *Edward II*.

In the examples cited, the criteria relating word to referent have shifted from the functional to the evaluative. It is difficult not to interpret this development as the projection of attitudes that are upper-class on to the words. To put it another way, the connotations that become criterial originate with the socially powerful: the dominant class imposes the dominant connotations. We see this process at work among words that were not associated with rank, like *vulgar, common, illiterate*, and *lewd*. The last two examples show the high social value that has come to be placed on literacy and learning. *Illiterate* is now a rough synonym for 'stupid', and the meaning of *lewd* has changed dramatically over the last thousand years. Originally meaning 'lay' at a time when learning and the Church were virtually synonymous, it could also mean 'unlearned'. By the seventeenth century it was applied to those of low social status, implying that by that time learning was associated with class. By about 1700 it meant 'worthless' of objects, 'unprincipled' of people; and from the latter meaning, a special kind of unprincipled-ness became criterial, that relating to sexual conduct. Hence the meaning 'lecherous'.

A more complex pattern of class attitudes has affected the history of *bourgeois*. As a word that has not been thoroughly assimilated into English from French, *bourgeois* is an excellent example of a word whose meaning depends on the loyalties of its users. This is partly because, like *exploitation*, and so on, it forms part of the technical vocabulary of Marxist thought, and has therefore acquired a certain stylistic meaning. For this reason many people avoid using it. On the other hand, it has been more recently used in a more affective sense, by groups such as students, who see it as a term exemplifying certain tastes and types of behaviour which are 'respectable'. The fortunes of the word have depended on the attitudes of the classes in the social hierarchy above and below the bourgeoisie. Its thirteenth-century Anglicised form *burgess* (town-dweller, enjoying full municipal rights) points to its association with the mercantile town, and this meaning remains in the background, as it were, of the re-borrowed form *bourgeois*, which retains more of the phonetic characteristics of its source. Originally *bourgeois* in French was rather like a rank term: it denoted, for instance, residence of long standing. Associated by the eighteenth century with the commercial class, especially those able to live off invested income, the term came to be used contemptuously by the class above, the landed aristocracy. The evaluative meaning arose because the characteristics of the mercantile class – solidity, stability, sobriety – were perceived as being small-minded, narrow, and complacent by the upper class. The same attitude came to be shared by artists, writers, and some intellectuals who derided the 'respectability' and 'safe' views of the bourgeoisie. But the *technical* sense of the word, as used by Marx, arose from a recognition of the dominance of the bourgeoisie in society: they were the employing class, the group who controlled capital, in whose factories things were manufactured. These roles and functions gave them definite ideas about society and their place within it, and, according to Marx, it is they who have been able to present their own values and ideology as given, universal, immutable, and necessary.

ELIZABETHAN TERMS OF ADDRESS

If we follow the fortunes of *gentle* into the sixteenth century, we find that it acquires, in the compound *gentleman*, a considerable social significance. It has been considered the most important rank term in use at this time, since it differentiated the privileged and unprivileged. By the sixteenth century, however, the sources of privilege were changing. Power and status could increasingly be achieved through education or entrepreneurialism: hence *gentle* could in principle be extended to people whose status no longer derived from its traditional source, the ownership of land. By the 1580s a *gentleman* could be someone who was able to live comfortably without having to 'engage in trade'. (And since then, of course, it has lost its function as a term of rank and become a polite word for any kind of man.) In many respects *gentleman* was filling the social vacuum left by the obsolescence of the knight. In medieval times a knight was one of three 'estates' ordained by God. His duty was to fight, whereas that of the clerk was to pray, while it was the lot of the labourer to toil. By the sixteenth century not only had the role of warrior declined but the Reformation had turned that of the clergy into a profession like any other. The older medieval triad of 'estates' was giving way to a new system in which the social imperative was differentiating yourself from 'the common sorte'.

It seems that the Elizabethans were particularly sensitive to the issue of rank and status. If a social hierarchy is *felt* to be changing, people will become uncertain about who is entitled to be called a *gentleman*. The same can be said for the word *master*, another class-defining term, which was widening its range of application at the same time. It may be this uncertainty that underlay the Elizabethan fondness for using terms of address. It has been concluded from a survey of such usage in Shakespeare's Falstaff plays that in about 1600 people liked to 'place' each other in the social hierarchy when they were conversing in the more formal contexts. Thus, titles, occupational terms like *parson* or *cook*, generic terms like *man, woman*, and *gentleman*, even terms of relationship like *husband* and *wife* (used freely between spouses on good terms) were frequently used in direct address; and if none of these was appropriate or available, a vague word like *neighbour* was even used. Condescension, even open insult, could be indicated by the deliberate use of terms inappropriate to the status of an addressee. The Germanic word *fellow* used to mean, literally, one who lays down money (*fee*), thus a partner in business; by the fourteenth century, as a term of address it implied polite condescension; and in Shakespearean address its use is an insult to anyone not greatly inferior in social status. Similarly, *goodman* denoted in its early sense the master of an establishment: as *gentleman* expanded down the social scale, it pushed *goodman* with it, so that by the seventeenth century it could be a term of abuse. In *Measure for Measure*, Lucio addresses the Duke, in his disguise as a Friar, as 'goodman baldpate'. So that we can see that new meanings may develop as words are used, in face-to-face interaction, as terms of address.

This aspect of Elizabethan speech-behaviour contrasts in certain ways with usage today. Many people now limit their terms of address to the Title + Last Name pattern (indicating a respectful, neutral distance), and reserve *sir* or *madam* to mark greater politeness, Christian names or terms of endearment like *darling* or *sweetheart* to mark intimacy, nicknames or generic terms like *mate* to mark solidarity. While our usage depends to a certain extent on social class and group loyalties, it is possible to make some generalisations: for the Elizabethans, greater intimacy was required before 'first-naming' was possible. There was greater fluctuation between the use of first names and surnames, and men could be freely addressed with both.

There is another way in which our language of address contrasts with that of four centuries ago. The Elizabethan habit of referring to social status in their mode of address is similar to that of some modern Europeans. Power relationships in the sixteenth century could be marked by a choice in the grammar, involving the pronouns *thou* and *you*: you could say *thou* to a subordinate, and expect a polite *you* in return, a choice still found in many European languages which have retained the two second person pronouns. As we shall see in the next chapter, this system has given way to one based on mutual respect where one pronoun, *you*, is used reciprocally. What is interesting is that it is the pronoun of neutral distance that becomes generalised, like the Title + Last Name pattern among the terms of address. More interesting, however, is the fact that at the same time as the Elizabethans were showing such concern about naming in direct address they were beginning to discard the traditional use of second person pronouns. We shall explore this matter in the next chapter.

THE SEMANTIC DISPARAGEMENT OF WOMEN

Power relationships do not of course necessarily involve social stratification. Adults have generally exercised power over minors, and women have been controlled by men, in ways that cut across class boundaries. Male power, and male attitudes, therefore, are reflected in the ways in which women are talked about. Men have developed a rich vocabulary of affective words which denigrate women who do not conform to a male ideal; and there has been a constant tendency to develop new meanings denoting the availability of women as sex objects. It has been estimated that there are over 1000 words which in their history have denoted women and have also meant 'whore'.

Words which classify women by age tend to reflect the male predilection for the younger, sexually attractive female. Unfortunately, many of these words are not recorded in early varieties of English, so that it is often difficult to trace their history. *Crone* may derive from a Norman

French word for a cantankerous woman (from the fourteenth century it has meant 'withered old woman', and suchlike), but it could also come from a Germanic word for an old ewe – a sense in which it is used between the sixteenth and nineteenth centuries. Either way, women are hardly flattered. If old age is unforgivable in a woman, ugliness or slovenliness invites further ridicule. *Drab*, a possible loan from Irish Gaelic, is recorded in the sense 'ugly woman' in 1515, and *slut*, deriving perhaps from Scandinavian, means a dirty one from the fifteenth century. Some words denoting young women had at first no sexual connotations, but they were not slow to develop them. *Doll*, originally a pet name for Dorothy, was used in the sixteenth century as a generic pet name for a mistress; and *mynx*, deriving perhaps from *minickin*, a word for a pet, came to mean a young girl, and later a wanton one.

A great many of these words developed the meaning of 'whore' at some stage in their history. The same is true of many other endearment terms, such as *sweetmeat* and *Kitty*, occupational terms like *nun*, *spinster*, even *laundress*; and kinship terms, such as *aunt* and *cousin*. But this process of semantic 'disparagement' does not necessarily mean that men have always regarded women of all kinds as little more than objects to be bought for self-gratification. Sexual relations among men and women have often depended on the brothel. Although even the most powerful in the land might indulge in it, whoring was socially taboo; and like all taboo subjects it generated a proliferation of terms, many of them euphemistic. In the covert patronage of prostitutes, it was necessary to keep the flow of terms going; hence even words like *nun* and *laundress* found themselves used in this sense.

We shall end this chapter by considering a word which may show the influence of male attitudes in a more complex and subtle way. The meanings of *buxom* have changed dramatically over the last 800 years. Today its meaning unites two separate properties; one associated with physical appearance, of 'plump comeliness', even voluptuousness; the other involving mental attributes, 'jolliness', 'openness', perhaps 'sexual uninhibitedness'. Today, the word is used only to refer to women, and even then it collocates with a very restricted range of words – like *barmaid*, *wench*, *lass* – which lend it a stylistic flavour that is mock-poetic or even archaic. When we look back at how the word has been used in the past, however, we find that there were far fewer restrictions on the kinds of word it could modify: men, and also inanimate objects like air, can be buxom. Like *sophisticated*, then, the change in meaning is closely linked to changes in the kinds of words with which it could co-occur. In its earliest recorded uses the word meant obedient, in the moral sense, and this meaning remained fairly constant from the twelfth century until the nineteenth. (Originally it may have meant something like 'ready to bow', as its elements were *bow* + *some*, as in *handsome*, *winsome*, etc.) Out of this core meaning other related senses developed: 'submissive' by about 1300, then in the course of the fourteenth century 'gracious' or 'kindly'. Until about the middle of the sixteenth century, then, to be buxom meant to be generally well disposed and tractable; and we find by the end of that century a new set of connotations developing, related to the old, but gradually replacing them. Throughout the seventeenth century the word could be used in the sense of 'physically obedient', or 'pliant', and we begin to see the origins of the modern sense of the word as it is used in relation to women. At the same time as 'physically pliant', the old sense of 'kindly' was extended, so that from the sixteenth to the nineteenth centuries it also meant 'blithe', 'lively'; and this gives us the second dimension in the meaning of the word at present. The sense 'blithe' was re-applied, as it were, in the physical dimension: the physical counterpart of 'jolliness' was 'comeliness', 'healthy well-favouredness', and we find the word used in this sense from the end of the sixteenth century until the present day, with the use of *buxom* gradually limiting itself only to women from the nineteenth century (influenced, perhaps, by *bust*). It is difficult not to see the projection of masculine attitudes towards women embodied in this example of semantic change. An important aspect of male desire, it seems, is to want not only women who are sexually submissive, but if possible comely and well-favoured too.

4 Grammar

There are probably more misconceptions about the term 'grammar' than any other term in the popular vocabulary of linguistics. Disseminated in classrooms, and therefore widely believed throughout society, these misconceptions tend to identify grammar with a certain kind of book which has been written about a language; more specifically, about the *codified* variety of a language, in its written manifestation. In this chapter, we shall examine the nature and the source of some of these notions, and show how inadequate they are to describe either the variation in a language at any given time, or the process of grammatical change. We shall need to look at some basic categories of grammatical description, and subject to scrutiny some common misunderstandings about the nature of rules in grammar. Aspects of the grammar of the Anglo-Saxons will be discussed, in particular its reliance on a system of endings known as inflexions; and we shall see how these inflexions can be said to have been simplified in the course of centuries. This process of grammatical simplification will be examined in the light of sociolinguistic variables, such as pidginisation. The agency of social factors will be clearly seen as we describe changes in the system of pronouns, and we shall see the importance of linguistic variation for describing the trend towards syntactic elaboration. Finally, we shall ask how the grammar of written English has acquired not only great prestige, but also a reputation for cognitive superiority.

Grammatical change is often less consciously felt than the adoption of new words or the creation of new meanings. Thus, it is difficult to isolate and describe changes that have been recently introduced into English. Yet when we stand back and view the changes that have occurred during the last 1500 years, we see developments of a particularly striking kind. The grammar that the Anglo-Saxons used seems to have been a radically different kind of grammar from the one we use today (subject to the qualifications we shall note below). It has been suggested that this difference entitles us to classify Anglo-Saxon English and the English of today as languages of quite distinct types. In making sweeping comparisons of this kind, however, it is as well to remember that Anglo-Saxon English was no more monolithic than the language we use today. Though the dimensions of variability may have been fewer, Anglo-Saxon grammar had its own variations, associated with region, the difference between speech and writing, emphatic and unemphatic language, and formal and informal usage. We shall see the importance of these variations in the course of this chapter, and in particular, the process by which new variants come to be associated with certain social groups, and hence acquire either prestige or stigma.

The emphasis in linguistics until very recently has been less on the social aspects of grammar and more on its psychological implications. Grammar has been seen as the crucial level of linguistic structure. Many linguists have been absorbed by the process of language acquisition, the apparently effortless and highly efficient way in which people learn their first language from a very early age. While we cannot do justice here to this recent and important tradition of inquiry, we can abstract one of its most important precepts. By about the age of five, we have mentally internalised an immensely complex system of grammatical rules. The essential feature of these rules is that they are creative: they enable us to make up new sentences. From a social point of view, our attitude to these rules is revealing. We do not regard them as rules, since we have been educated to think that grammatical rules are something formulated by people who know better than we do, who incorporate them in grammar books, rather than part of our birthright. Thus, our treatment of our grammatical knowledge is much like our attitude to words discussed in the last chapter. We apply our internalised system of grammatical rules unreflectingly and unconsciously; and just as words change shape and meaning in new environments and contexts, so we constantly adapt and extend our grammatical patterns as similarities with other patterns and forms are perceived.

SOME MISCONCEPTIONS ABOUT GRAMMAR

We can find at least five ways in which the word *grammar* is used to give a misleading idea of the nature of this part of language structure. One of these is the notion mentioned above, that some people are supposed to 'know' the grammar of the language, while others do not. A second is that grammar is something which belongs to the written language, but not to the spoken. Third, there is the somewhat archaic use of the term to refer to a book, a written account of a language's grammar; so that someone might say 'lend me your grammar'. Fourth, grammar is something that can be either 'good' or 'bad'. And finally, grammar is something which some languages have more of than others; people say that language *x* has more grammar than language *y*.

These misconceptions stem from the view of language held by the people who began to codify English grammar during the eighteenth century. To a large extent, our whole perception of grammar has been distorted by their work. Many people have been left with the impression that the grammar of the language they speak is the preserve, even the invention, of a small group of scholars. From this, the whole idea of what constitutes a grammatical rule has been perverted: for many people, such rules consist of do's and don't's, such as the prescription that 'whom did you see' is more correct than 'who did you see'. In other words, the notion of a grammatical rule has been taken in its prescriptive sense – it tells you what you should or should not say. But as we have already seen in chapter two, such prescriptive rules were formulated, unsystematically and often arbitrarily, with respect to the structure of Latin, to the written mode, in its formal tenor. The rules, then, apply to only a small part of our linguistic repertoire, and not even the most important part. And many of us do not obey the rules even in formal written style: they are too redolent of pedantry, and irrelevant fussiness.

It seems hardly worth saying that the rules of prescriptive grammar are repeatedly broken in casual, informal speech. What we need to do is redefine the notion of grammatical rules, to cover the patterns that in a variety of contexts we actually produce. Such rules must be descriptive ones, capable of explaining, for instance, why 'book the your liked father' is not an acceptable sequence in any variety of modern English. The explanation here would involve principles of word-order; but because as speakers of English we apply rules of this kind so efficiently and unconsciously, we are not aware of them as rules. The irrelevance of prescriptive rules in accounting for basic structural patterns in English can be readily seen when we examine the structures that are produced by second- or foreign-language learners. How do we explain, for instance, that *are you hearing?* seems to many first-language speakers a less acceptable structure in contemporary English than *do you hear?* or *can you hear?* And what about the order of the words in *his nice new leather jacket?* Is any other word-order possible? If not, how do we formulate the rule?

From the above discussion, then, it should be clear that we are using the term rule in the sense of a 'pattern', of a structuring principle that we conventionally use without being aware of it. The rules will vary (at least with respect to surface patterning) according to the tenor of the situation, the dialect of the speaker, and the field of discourse; the rules for newspaper-reporting will differ from those of recipe-writing. And in general, the rules for spoken English will often be different from those of writing. Unfortunately, the association of grammar with the written mode has meant that we often judge speech against writing, and not surprisingly we find the former wanting. Our impressions of the matter are confirmed when we confront transcripts of tape-recorded speech. The following is an extract from an informal conversation between university graduates:

> We – I wanted to – er – you know – go on a bit further but well the – there were six – seven of us I – wait a minute – no – I – well anyway when – my chain broke a bit later – we were going down this hill this really steep hill. . . .

On paper this looks garbled and formless, but it would not necessarily appear so if we were to hear it. This is because we organise our spoken utterances in association with a battery of devices that have no matching counterparts in writing. We use, most importantly, a system of *intonation*; this is the set of 'tunes' into which we embed our every utterance, to distinguish some kinds of questions from statements, and to signal uncertainty, sarcasm, anger, disbelief, and many other kinds of meaning. Intonation, stress, pitch, and tempo are all integrated into the spoken mode, as are the many paralinguistic and extralinguistic features that accompany our speech; we use our eyes and heads, we gesture with our hands, change our voice-quality. In short, conversation involves the whole of our bodies, and is a form of physical behaviour, and thus totally distinct from writing.

In describing the grammar of speech, then, we must take account of the features outlined above, just as in the description of writing we must consider punctuation and the special grammatical devices for achieving emphasis, like inversions of normal word-order. We have said above that we are more used to thinking of grammar in connection with written texts: but the more we examine the wide range of texts that we are quite capable of reading and understanding in the course of everyday life, the less useful the prescriptive rules seem to be. For instance, a recent advertisement has the following structure:

> *The crisp new look of glistening aluminium frames around big bright windows!*

This is not school-English: it contains no verb, and for many it would therefore be incorrect. Such verbless sentences are very common in advertising English, however, so that school-grammar is perhaps not the best tool with which to analyse it. If we continue to view specimens of contemporary English through prescriptive spectacles we often miss the most interesting and innovatory features of particular varieties. While advertising English tries to capture the spirit of informal conversation in its use of verbless sentences, it also innovates by casting words in new roles: as in *the NOW cigarette*, where 'now' is used as an adjective. At the other extreme, the respected, even revered, language of Anglican prayer has a different kind of grammar. In this opening, written to be spoken aloud:

> *Almighty God, our Heavenly Father, who of thy tender mercy didst give thine only Son Jesus Christ . . .*

we find not only the preservation of a pattern common in the early seventeenth century in *didst give*, but perhaps the only use in contemporary English of a *who* clause directly after a noun in direct address, *God.*

So far, we have tried to expose the first two fallacies about grammar on our list, by referring to their origins. We can deal with the next two in a similar way, by remembering that it was the standard variety to which the Latinising, logic-orientated rules of the codifiers were applied. Thus, for many people today the notion of grammatical rules only exists in relation to some notional standard. Rules of grammar are to be found in books about standard English; therefore it is this variety that possesses grammar. From this point it is only a short step to the notion of grammar as a book, to be kept in your desk at school. Whatever is not in the book, moreover, must be ungrammatical: and this will include all varieties of English not acceptable in the schoolroom. Since grammar came to be evaluated, what was ungrammatical must be incorrect, or bad; so that if you spoke a dialect, you spoke ungrammatically, therefore badly, and deserved to be corrected. Once again, we see that the full range of variation in English is not taken into account in popular notions about grammatical rules, in that regional speech is felt to be synonymous with bad grammar.

What was said earlier in this chapter about different varieties of English having their own grammars must apply, of course, to the regional dialects. Unfortunately, the notion that dialects have their own grammars, which their speakers unconsciously apply when they talk to each other, has been the preserve of only a small group of language scholars, the philologists and dialectologists, and only for little more than a century. Rather than formulate rules such as '*I am* is standard: *I be* is south-western dialect', the eighteenth-century codifiers either ignored regionalisms, or listed them as traps to avoid. But while their prescriptions are widely acknowledged, many people persist in using the stigmatised forms and patterns. Some of these, like the cumulative negative construction *I don't know nothing*, are probably used at times by a majority of people in England. Also very common are the use of *them* as a demonstrative (as in *them books*), differences in present and past tense forms of verbs (*he do, he done it*), the pattern in reflexive pronouns (*he's washing hisself*), the form of certain adverbs (*he ran slow*), and the plurals of nouns after numerals (*three mile*). All these examples, many of which will be discussed in the course of this chapter, either preserve patterns which were once more common than they are now, as in the case of the prayer discussed above, or are representative of tendencies towards grammatical change that are very common in the history of English.

SOME CATEGORIES OF GRAMMATICAL DESCRIPTION

The word *grammar* is also used, of course, by linguists, in their attempts to analyse the structures we hear and see around us. To put it simply, grammar for linguists is the level of their analysis of linguistic structure which concerns the organisation of words into sentences. If we are to understand how language works, and how it changes, we must devise some basic categories for grammatical description.

The advertisement for aluminium window frames from which the extract above was taken, contains elsewhere the simple structure *our own experts handle the installation*. Using this sequence as a pattern for our description, we find a group of words in subject position, *our own experts*, consisting of a noun, *experts*, in head-position, preceded by a possessive pronoun, *our*, and adjective *own*. The rest of the sentence is the predicate, and this part must contain the verb, *handle*. The remainder of the predicate, *the installation*, consists of a group of words like that in the subject-position, where *installation* is the noun in head-position, and *the* is an article; here, though, the noun-group is called the object of the verb, so we have the familiar subject–verb–object sequence. We can summarise the structure as shown in Figure 4.1.

The first point we need to make in connection with this structure

Subject			Predicate		
noun-group			verb	noun-group	
our	*own*	*experts*	*handle*	*the*	*installation*
(possessive)	(adjective)	(noun)	(verb)	(article)	(noun)

Figure 4.1 Structure of subject–verb–object sequence

concerns the order of the words: can they be re-arranged, without adding or subtracting anything, to form an equally acceptable sentence in English? If not, then we must conclude that word-order in this sentence is rigid; and, as we shall see, it is a feature of the history of English grammar that the constraints in the system on the ordering of words have become less flexible over the centuries. This aspect of our grammatical system, that of the sequencing of elements, is known as syntax.

We have also just said that two words in our sentence, *experts* and *installation*, are nouns; and the grammarian will be interested in the fact that the form of the two nouns is different, in that the former has the *-s* plural marker. This is the commonest way of marking the plural in English, although as we shall see, there were many other patterns available when the language was first spoken. Grammarians refer to this aspect of grammar – the altering of a word's 'shape' to signal its function – as morphology. Although it is essential to make this distinction between syntax and morphology, we shall find in practice that it is not always easy to discuss one without referring to the other.

It is often convenient, however, to deal separately with those structures associated with the noun – in other words, the noun-groups – and those associated with the verb. How, for instance, do the other words pattern with the head of the noun-group? Is it that the head is pre-modified by words such as articles and adjectives, as in our example, or can we describe it as being post-modified, by the use of structures beginning with prepositions like *in, with*, or relative pronouns like *who*, etc.? Immediately we investigate this area of grammar we see the importance of linguistic variation, particularly the differences between the grammar of speech and writing. A characteristic of many types of written English, for instance, is the so-called heavy pre-modification. Examples from scientific and technical writing abound, such as *Boeing 747 leading edge flap failure alarm mechanism*, where the last word is the head noun. But we also find that newspaper headlines and written advertisements have developed their own characteristic patterns of pre-modification. Such compact language, however, is far less common in casual conversation: for one thing, it is too dense for the ear to process. When it does occur, adjectives are often unremarkable and sequences stereotyped, as in *all those nice little primary schoolchildren*. But in certain types of spoken English, such as the sports commentary, audience familiarity with basic technical terms can lead to structures that are almost as weightily pre-modified as post-modified. The reader can try to find the head noun in subject position in *that running forehand topspin passing shot at full stretch down the line over the high part of the net gives him match point*.

We can make one further point about the subject head in our model sentence. As a noun, *experts* could be substituted by another word if it had already been established that experts were being discussed. We could say *they handle*, where *they* is called a pronoun. Pronouns, like articles and prepositions, are sometimes referred to as grammatical words; they constitute a relatively fixed part of our vocabulary that is less amenable to the kind of semantic description undertaken in the last chapter. Such words, especially pronouns, will accordingly be dealt with here as the occasion arises.

When we analyse verb-groups, the interdependence of morphology and syntax becomes clear. Of great interest are the forms and structures associated with tense. With regard to morphology, an immediate point to be made is that if we were to substitute in our model sentence a singular form of the noun in subject-position (i.e. *expert*), the form of the verb itself would change to *handles*. This addition of -*s* to the verb form marks the agreement of subject and verb: both the *handle* and *handles* forms of the verb mark it as present tense. The system of tense in contemporary English is very complex, and we can only do it scant justice here, but the following paragraphs will make some of the important points.

It is often said that our tense-system comprises two parts, present and past. The most common way of marking a past tense lies in the addition of an -*ed* ending, or inflexion, so that the past tense form of the verb in our sentence would be *handled*. Some verbs, however, form their past tense by changing the vowel in the stem. If the verb had been *break*, the past tense form would have been *broke*. Verbs of this kind, few in number but frequently occurring in most varieties of English, are known as strong verbs. Speakers of English have treated more and more of these verbs over the centuries as weak ones, which means that the ending -*ed* has been added to the base form of the verb, rather than changing the vowel. In other words, -*ed* has been interpreted as the ending that is productive, just as -*s* has become the common marker of plurality; and we can notice how young children, when they are first picking up English as their first language, produce forms like *goed* instead of *went* because they have made a generalisation about -*ed* as the invariant past-tense marker.

This brief account provides us with a broad base on which more complex verbal structures can be built. For English has a variety of means with which to refer to time, past, present, or future. We do this most typically by sequences of verbs which form complex verb-groups. However, as soon as we begin to analyse such groups, we must acknowledge the existence of another system, called aspect, which intersects the system of tense. In general, aspect concerns the ways in which actions in time are viewed – are they habitual, ongoing, or completed? A few examples will make this clear. If our sentence had been *our own experts are handling the installation*, it would have been marked for continuous aspect; that sentence differs from our model in that the action of handling is now seen as something that is going on at the present time, whereas the simple present form *handle* refers to actions which might take place in the future, or which might have taken place in the past. There is a similar distinction to be made between *handled*, and *were handling*, where the action is related to past time; the latter form is also continuous. But aspect can also be perfective; that is, an action can be presented as completed in the past, as in *our experts have handled the installation*, and by combining the elements already cited in these examples in different ways, we can build up verbal groups of greater complexity with regard to tense and aspect like *have been handling*.

Such complex verbal groups consist of a main verb, in this case *handle*, and one or more auxiliary verbs. The auxiliaries mentioned so far are *have* and *be*, and a significant, perhaps even revolutionary part of the history of grammar in English consists of the gradual extension of these auxiliaries into more and more patterns. Today, the complexity of this part of our grammar can be seen by the fact that it is the system of tense and aspect that is commonly re-structured by speakers of some varieties of English beyond the British Isles, and which continues to cause problems for people learning English as a foreign language.

Have and *be*, then, can act as auxiliaries, and another well-known example, *do*, is so important that it will be afforded considerable space below. There is another group of auxiliaries, however, that are distinguished from these three, partly on morphological grounds (they do not have an *-s* ending after *he*, *she*, or *it*), and partly in terms of the kinds of notion (obligation, necessity, possibility, etc.) that they signify. These verbs, such as *can*, *shall*, *will*, *must*, *may*, *could*, *should*, etc., are called modal auxiliaries. The range of meanings associated with their use can readily be seen if they are inserted before the verb *handle* in our model sentence. The importance of two of these verbs – *shall* and *will* – for the present discussion owes to the fact that they are used to refer to actions or states related to future time. Otherwise, the use of the modal auxiliaries can be related to the grammatical category of mood, a category which necessarily overlaps that of futurity, since the future inevitably involves an element of 'possibility'.

We have so far isolated tense, aspect, and mood, with respect to the verb-group. There is one last category to be dealt with in this section, that of voice. The information encoded in our model sentence could have been put in a different way, with the addition of auxiliary *be*, and the preposition *by*, changing the form of the main verb and altering the word-order. Thus: *the installation is handled by our own experts.* The changed form of the verb (it usually ends in *-ed* or *-en*) is known as the past participle, and this kind of construction is called passive. Our original sentence was active. We shall be commenting on some socio-linguistic observations that have been made about voice towards the end of this chapter.

We alluded above to the significance of *do* as an auxiliary, and this part of the chapter will be concluded by referring to two basic syntactic functions which depend, in contemporary English, on the use of *do*. These are negation and the question form. To make our model sentence negative, we insert *do not* between subject and verb: *our own experts do not handle the installation;* and to make it into a question, we start the whole construction with *do*, as in *do our own experts handle the installation?* Both these uses of *do* are relatively new in the history of English. Originally, negation was expressed by distributing negative particles on either side of the verb, so that our sentence might have looked like this:

Our own experts ne handle not the installation.

In other words, the cumulative negative, so often condemned today as illogical, was the usual means of expressing negation. The question form was achieved by inversion of word-order, thus:

Handle our own experts the installation?

We still see this pattern operating when auxiliary verbs are involved: we say *can he run fast?* rather than *does he can run fast?*, but in most cases, *do* is used. We shall be returning to this below.

THE 'SYNTHETIC' GRAMMAR OF THE ANGLO-SAXONS

From the point of view of morphology, there are some striking differences between contemporary English and the language as it was spoken by the Anglo-Saxons. The student of early English is confronted by tables, lists, and paradigms presenting the rich morphology of nouns, verbs, adjectives, and pronouns. Superficially, Anglo-Saxon appears to have more grammar than modern English, and this brings us to the last misconception on our list. Many people think of grammar as morphology, rather than seeing that the latter is included in the former; and since studying Anglo-Saxon requires us to learn a great deal of morphology, we think it must therefore have more grammar. What it does have, of course, is a different *kind* of grammar, and it is for this reason that we can classify Anglo-Saxon as a different type of language.

For the linguist, the significance of the difference between the grammars lies in the fact that in Anglo-Saxon the relationships among words in the sentence are often signalled by inflexions that are put on the ends of words. The shape of a word changes according to whether it is the subject or the object. Thus, it is not so much the order of words in the sentence that determines, say, the subject, as is the case with contemporary English: in theory, words in languages such as Anglo-Saxon can be put in any order, because it is the endings that specify their function. Anglo-Saxon, then, is more like Classical Latin than modern English in this respect, in that syntactic relationships are achieved by what is called synthesis, the building up of the word by adding inflexions to the stem.

A very simple example can show us how a synthetic grammar works. We have seen how there are no possibilities for changing the word-order in *our own experts handle the installation.* In some other sentences in contemporary English, however, word-order can be changed to achieve radically different meanings. In the subject–verb–object structure *the boy killed the bear* the noun-group in final position *can* function as the subject, producing *the bear killed the boy.* Both boys and bears can kill, and we need word-order to tell us who did what. But in classical Latin, word-endings will tell us who did the killing, irrespective of the word-order. Thus, in Latin, the sequence can be *puer interfecit ursum, ursum puer interfecit*, or *interfecit ursum puer*: but in all these examples, we know what the object is, because it has the distinctive *-um* ending. In principle, the same can be said for Anglo-Saxon. The order of the words in *se cnafa of-sloh þone beran* could be re-arranged in a similar number of ways. But we would always know which word functions as the subject because of the ending: *cnafa* (modern 'knave') ends in *-a*, which in this kind of noun is the inflexion associated with subject-position, as *-n* is with that of the object. We should also note how the definite article agrees in form with the noun it immediately precedes; *se* in subject position, *þone* in object position.

What we have been describing is the grammatical category of case, the signalling of relationships among words in a sentence by adding specific endings to the words in question. Above, we saw the association of *-n* with the object, or *accusative* case, with one class of noun, and we saw how the form of the definite article changed. Other kinds of function are also signalled by different case-endings. For instance, a relationship between nouns that might be loosely called possessive is specified by genitive case-endings, of which one, *-'s*, still survives today as in *John's book*. And an indirect object relationship, that of 'to the youth' in *I'll give a pound to the youth*, is often (depending again on the type of noun, etc.) specified by adding *-e*: this is the dative case. Thus, *cniht* (youth) becomes *cnihte*. In general, the Anglo-Saxon case-system is very similar to that of modern German; although the former also has another case, of minor importance and only affecting adjectives, called the instrumental.

The case-system in Anglo-Saxon is considerably more complex than our brief description makes it appear, partly because the cases discharge a wider range of functions than those listed, but also because there is no single range of case-endings that apply to every noun. The student of Anglo-Saxon has to learn to which class of nouns a word belongs before assigning it the correct endings. To some extent, the nouns are also classified according to gender – masculine, feminine, neuter – as in modern German (or as in French, except that it has no neuter).

We can see how a close knowledge of Anglo-Saxon inflexions is needed to understand the kind of language exemplified in this extract from the epic poem *Beowulf*:

Oft Scyld Scefing sceaþena þreatum
monegum mægþum meodo-setla ofteah

We must know, for instance, that the verb *of-teon* (of which *of-teah* is the past form that goes with *he*, *she*, or *it*), 'take away', demands particular case-endings on the words functionally dependent on it: the person deprived must be in the dative case, the object taken in the genitive, rather than the more usual accusative case. Only if we know the system of endings can we identify these parts of the sentence. The object is *meodo-setla*, the genitive plural of *meodo-setl* (mead-bench); the subject, *Scyld Scefing*, a Danish king, has deprived *þreatum*, the dative plural of a word meaning 'troop' (cf. 'threat'), of enemies (*sceaþena*) from many (*monegum*) tribes (*mægþum*). The whole sequence means 'Scyld Scefing often took away the mead-benches from troops of his enemies, from many tribes' – in other words, he brought many of his enemies to heel (the 'mead-bench' is a highly compressed way of expressing the power of the chieftain by referring to his custom of giving mead to his followers). This short extract is not untypical of the language of the longest, best-known, and possibly the best of the Anglo-Saxon poems.

THE LOSS OF INFLEXIONS

We need not conclude from our brief discussion of Anglo-Saxon grammar that our ancestors were splendid linguists, able to write and understand the complex language of the extract above: our own unconscious handling of the modern system of tense and aspect, as described earlier, is no less remarkable. Moreover, it is difficult to know how far such synthetic patterns were representative of ordinary Anglo-Saxon speech. For it is quite possible that Anglo-Saxon poetry consciously preserved, as a form of poetic licence, a kind of syntax that was already archaic at the time the poems were set down in writing. Unfortunately, we have no evidence for the conversational usage of those times, but it would not be surprising if the grammar of written usage were more synthetic than that of the spoken. There is some evidence to suggest that while Classical Latin retained the full range of inflexions in writing, popular spoken Latin had begun to dispense with them.

Even within Anglo-Saxon writing we find that prose, for instance, is in general less synthetic than poetry. In prose sentences where verbs govern direct objects, as in our model, we find that word-order is more often than not the same as in modern English. Thus, the case-endings in *se cnafa of-sloh þone beran* are largely redundant if *se cnafa* is always likely to come first in the sentence: it has no need of distinctive endings to tell us it is the subject. We can conclude, then, that certain varieties in Anglo-Saxon, since the beginning of literacy, were already placing less reliance on the system of inflexions than others.

What we have seen since Anglo-Saxon times is the gradual erosion, in all dialects, of those inflexions. The term which is used to denote this process – *simplification* – does not imply that generations of lazy speakers have merely taken innumerable short cuts in the grammar. The loss of case-endings, for instance, meant that other means had to be found for signalling relations among words in the sentence, since such endings had a syntactic function. Prepositions, like *for*, *of*, *by*, etc., began to serve those functions; and word-order became less flexible. In this, therefore, we see the *quid pro quo* of much linguistic change: while something in the language may be abandoned by its speakers, something else will emerge as a counterbalance.

The dropping of one part of the system of noun-endings occasioned the same process in other parts of the system. The complex classification of nouns according to three genders was simplified, and with it the half dozen or so patterns of plurality which existed in Anglo-Saxon. In the case of plurals we see the selection of just one inflexion as a productive pattern, which is generalised for most nouns. In different dialects, however, different plural inflexions, associated with frequently occurring nouns, became dominant. In the north, -*s*, was selected, whereas in much of the south and south-west, it was -*n*. Today, the system of plurals is still not regularised in any dialect. The codified metropolitan variety preserves fossilised instances of the older range: the -*en* in oxen, the vowel-change in *feet*, *geese*, etc., and the unmarked plural of nouns like *sheep*. Other dialects retain more -*n* forms, as in *een* (eyes) in the north and west midlands, and have extended this pattern to nouns like *house* which originally had no plural inflexion (as in parts of East Anglia and the west midlands). And in 'non-standard' speech generally, the Anglo-Saxon uninflected plural is common in nouns specifying measurement: *three ton of coal*, *three pound of potatoes*, *three mile away*. Thus, the selection of plural endings, and their allocation to particular words, seems to have proceeded in a way that strikes the modern speaker as arbitrary. And most arbitrary, in a sense, is the metropolitan variety, which from the advent of printing has tended to fix its own idiosyncratic selection, while in dialectal speech the process of restructuring has continued.

We cannot say, therefore, that the selection of plural forms in this variety is more logical, or in any way better, than that of other varieties, just as we cannot attribute any kind of linguistic superiority to our different kinds of grammar, inflected or modern. Neither is it appropriate to apply the kind of Whorfian thinking discussed in the last chapter to the process of grammatical simplification, and conclude that such a profound change in grammar must have been accompanied by a shift in the way English people have perceived the universe. Perceptual differences associated with the different kinds of grammar can be discussed at a much more mundane level. The fact that the demonstrative *this*, for instance, was fully inflected in Anglo-Saxon times, meant that every time speakers said *þes* rather than *þis* or *þeos* they were restricting the number of nouns the listener might expect, since *þes* specified masculine nouns, *þis* neuter ones, and so on. Such expectations would have been exploited to the full in literature, so that the modern reader finds difficulty in appreciating all the nuances of meaning in *Beowulf*. But while we may have lost the communicative value of the inflected demonstrative, the loss of distinctive forms for, say, nouns and verbs, could offer enormous syntactic possibilities for a poet and dramatist like Shakespeare. *Lip* is traditionally a noun, but once it has lost its endings, it can be used as a verb, so that in *To lip a wanton in a secure couch* (*Othello*, IV. i. 73) Shakespeare uses it to mean 'kiss lecherously'. Poetic licence for the Anglo-Saxons may have meant the preservation of inflexions; but the loss of them provided poetic licence of another kind

for later poets. It is characteristic of contemporary English that many
words can act as either nouns or verbs, a freedom exploited to the full in
everyday speech, and extended by advertisers – as in the example cited
earlier. Within the last decade or so, nouns like *impact* and *access* have
increasingly been used as verbs in a variety of registers.

It is very difficult to know the why and the how of the process of
morphological simplification. As we said at the beginning of this chapter, it is by no means easy to document grammatical change as it occurs
in our own lifetime. Such study needs, above all, a detailed knowledge
of linguistic variation: and we have little evidence for this in the early
period of English. But one thing we do know about is the erosion of
inflexions as spoken languages come into contact, especially in those
conditions that produce pidgins or cause pidginisation. Pidgins are a
type of language that may be said to have pushed the process of morphological simplification to its limit, by abandoning any inflexions that
might be considered redundant. Thus even the plural ending, which
most English people would probably consider indispensable, is eradicated in a sequence like *di tu big pepa*, 'the two big newspapers' in
Cameroon pidgin. Since plurality is already specified by the numeral *tu*,
it is not absolutely necessary to inflect the noun in this instance.

The notion of redundancy can be readily appreciated when we look
at verbal inflexions, and see how they pattern with pronouns. Taking a
verb like *go*, we can set out the contemporary 'standard' English paradigm thus:

I	go	
you	go	
he		
she	goes	singular
it		
we	go	
you	go	plural
they	go	

We see here that apart from *you*, each pronoun has a different form,
whereas there are only two verb-forms: the third person form agrees
with the *he*, *she*, *it* pronouns by taking the – *(e)s* ending. The inflexion in
the third person is a relic of the fully inflected verb in Anglo-Saxon,
which in West Saxon took this form:

ic	ga
þu	gaest

he ⎫
heo ⎬ gaeþ
hit ⎭
we   gaþ
ge   gaþ
hie   gaþ

Here we find four distinctive forms of the verb, including not only endings but vowel changes. And all the pronouns have distinct forms, including, significantly, the second person ones *þu* and *ge* (modern thou and ye). But when we compare this paradigm with the more highly inflected verb in Latin, we find that pronouns are unusual, and there is maximum differentiation in the forms of the verb:

eo
is
it
imus
itis
eunt

From this comparison of three different paradigms, we can say that languages, or varieties, that have a more fully differentiated system of pronouns which function in concord with distinctive verbal endings can be said to exhibit a greater degree of redundancy than those which have simplified either pronouns or inflexions. Thus, Classical Latin has less redundancy than West Saxon, since it makes do without pronouns in subject position (though pronouns were available for emphasis) and modern standard English points towards the elimination of redundancy by retaining only the *-(e)s* ending. Cameroon pidgin, however, has removed even this:

a   go
yu   go
i   go
wi   go
wuna go
dem   go

The loss of the inflexion in the verb form is compensated for by the plural *you* form, *wuna*, in the pronominal system.

Since West Saxon manuscripts of the tenth century seem to show the merging of unstressed vowels in final syllables, we cannot say for sure that a process like pidginisation caused the abandonment of the Anglo-Saxon system of inflexions. But it would not be surprising if the process was at least hastened in the first instance by contact between the English and their Scandinavian neighbours and subsequently by contact with the Normans. We have already seen how certain pronoun forms arose from such contact with Vikings, suggesting a thorough and close mixing of the two speech-communities. In these conditions, there would have been pressure to level inflexions in the interests of spoken communication. New forms, originating in various parts of the Danelaw and along its borders, could then gradually spread at the level of popular speech. It is noteworthy that the two instances of inflexional change that we have noted – the -*s* plural and third person verbal ending -*(e)s* – arose in areas well away from Wessex, and were gradually adopted into the metropolitan variety.

Today, morphological simplification is most clearly associated with working-class speech. While the metropolitan variety preserves some vestiges of the older pattern, dialects get on with the elimination of irregularity and redundancy. In Norfolk, for instance, we can hear the same verbal paradigm as in Cameroon pidgin. And many dialects make a consistent paradigm of the reflexive pronouns: I wash *myself*, you wash *yourself*, he washes *hisself*, where they are possessive throughout. But as it is in process of consolidating, the metropolitan variety begins to freeze earlier patterns in morphology, and even cultivate variety of form as a mark of education. In short, we are back to the idea that grammar is a matter of morphology.

MORPHOLOGICAL SIMPLIFICATION AND SOCIAL STIGMA

Two other ways in which the morphology of the verb has been simplified involve the conversion of strong verbs to the weak pattern (see p. 93 above), and the simplification of the strong verb itself. The first has resulted in about five-sixths of the 360-odd strong verbs recorded in West Saxon being changed to the weak pattern. Thus, while some verbs, like *drink*, *swim*, *break*, and *bear*, remain strong, and still signal past tense by means of an internal vowel change, many others, like *glide*, *seethe*, *fret*, and *fare*, have adopted the simple -*ed* past inflexion.

West Saxon has seven recorded strong verb patterns. An example, *fleogan* (fly), had five distinct vowel changes in its various tense-forms. As well as a past in *fleag*, and a past participle *flogen*, there were vowel changes *within* each tense: in the present, the form was *fliehþ* after *he*, *she*, or *it*, and in the past, *flugon* occurred after plural pronouns. Today, we find that the number of vowel changes has been reduced to three, so we get *fly*, *flew*, *flown*. But in 'non-standard' speech, we often find a reduction to two forms, so we hear *I flown it*, *I done it*, etc. Here the past participle form is used for marking past tense.

It is customary, among historians of English when describing the evolution of verb morphology, to attribute such changes to the principle of analogy. In using the different forms of a verb like *fleogan*, it is suggested that speakers will be reminded of other verbs which are similar in some parts of the pattern, but not others; thus, verbs originally belonging to different verb classes are blended in the mind of the speaker, and new forms for these verbs, based on parts of the pattern of vowel changes in other verbs, are created. Moreover, the different dialects of Anglo-Saxon may well have had differences in various parts of the strong verb patterns (if they had none at first, they were soon to develop them); and contact between speakers of different dialects would have produced re-structuring in the system. We find in recent dialect speech that variation in verb forms is apparently endless, as different strong verb patterns compete with the dominant weak ones. Finally, it is the presence of that two-part weak pattern, present versus past, that may account for the reduction to two forms in the strong verbs that remain.

It is not only in broad dialect speech that the tendency to reduce strong verb forms to two has occurred. In my own speech, I have noted hesitations about the past tense of *drink*; is it *he drank*, or *he drunk*? The likelihood is that I will simplify the paradigm by using the past participle form *drunk* for the simple past *drank*. Sometimes, however, the process involves the reverse selection: in Jane Austen's narrative, we sometimes find the past tense form used for the past participle, as in *the tables were broke up*, and *much was ate*. Thus, the process of simplification used to be as true of so-called educated speech as it is today of dialect. What has happened is that the tendency to reduce the forms of the verb to two has been stigmatised. There is some evidence to suggest that as early as the sixteenth century new past tense forms in verbs such as *steal* and *break*, possibly arising from the extension of the past participle forms *stolen* and *broken*, were labelled as 'vulgar', and avoided by people with social pretensions. Avoidance of the new *o*-forms as in *stolen*, etc., seems to have led to hypercorrection as well. In sixteenth-century literature, we find that verbs which had long had an *o* in the past tense, like *write*, were written as *wrate* – perhaps the reaction of educated people to a change originating in dialectal, or even merely informal, speech.

It was the eighteenth-century codifiers, however, who legitimised such sociolinguistic stratification by insisting that a tripartite pattern in the strong verb was proper and correct from the linguistic point of view. English, like Latin, they suggested, should distinguish between past tense and past participle. The richer the morphology, the better; and one grammarian, Lowth, thought it essential to restore inflexions, and vowel-alternations, wherever it was possible. English grammar, he declared, was getting too easy, and needed stiffening up.

THE SOCIAL MEANING OF PRONOUNS

In discussing the verb, we have already noted two kinds of change associated with pronouns. One concerns the forms themselves. Many parts of the pronoun system preserve three distinctive case-forms: the nominative, accusative, and genitive, or possessive, *I/me/my, we/us/our, he/him/his, they/them/their*, although other parts have been reduced to two, as in *you/your, she/her, it/its*. As we have seen, some of these forms have arisen from contact with Vikings. Parts of the area formerly known as Wessex, well away from Scandinavian settlement, still use Anglo-Saxon forms. Thus, an earlier accusative or object form of 'he', *hine*, has recently been recorded as *en*, as in *I hit en* (I hit him); and the older form of 'I', *ic*, as *utch*.

The second change concerns the meaning and functions of the pronouns. In our discussion of *you*, we noted that some languages, or varieties, had a number distinction in the second person pronoun: one form for *you* singular, another for *you* plural. This was the case in Anglo-Saxon. Not only was there a singular *þu* (thou) and plural *ge* (ye: later replaced by its object form, *you*), but distinctions could be made between 'you many', and 'you two', 'we many', and 'we two': these are known as dual pronouns. These distinctions have been lost in the metropolitan variety, although some dialects have the form *youse* for 'you many', and other dialects have evolved other patterns of contrast. In parts of the south-west, *us* is sometimes used in subject position as an unemphatic pronoun, while *we* marks emphasis. It is noteworthy that Classical Latin, which as we have seen could manage without pronouns, had a set of pronouns which could be used emphatically; these have subsequently become the pronoun forms in French.

In classifying vocabulary, pronouns are usually said to constitute a closed system, as we explained above. Clearly, there are not many possibilities for adding new pronouns to the system: but we still find that the system changes, because the use of pronouns is so closely bound up with the process of social interaction. Pronouns occur very frequently in speech – one reason, perhaps, for the continued use of the dialect forms – but more important is the fact that from time to time they arouse our social sensitivities. Recently, the lack of a neutral pronoun unmarked for gender, to signify third person singular, has been an issue raised in the cause of sexual equality. Many women understandably resent the airy use of *he* in reference to unspecified people of either sex. In earlier centuries, however, it is the second person pronoun, the pronoun of address, that is at issue; to such an extent that the Revolution in France in the eighteenth century and the Russian Revolution in the twentieth both stimulated legislation on the matter, so central did linguistic usage in this respect seem to be to the creation of equality.

We saw in the last chapter how Elizabethans could address each other with *thou* or *you*. These pronouns had different social meanings. Someone you did not know well, with whom you might want to establish a relationship of neutral, respectful distance, could be addressed with *you*. And you could expect *you* in return. For someone you felt especially close to, either emotionally or socially, a reciprocal *thou* might be appropriate. The equality of these relationships was underlined by reciprocal pronoun usage. But in unequal relationships, different pronouns would be given and returned. It was necessary to address a superior by the use of *you*, and *thou* would be expected in return. Moreover, you could be defiant, or insulting, by breaking this code: using *thou* to a superior, or to someone of equal standing who had no reason to expect it. And heightened feelings could be registered – sympathy, tenderness, anger, reverence – by switching from *you* to *thou* in the middle of a conversation.

This system of pronominal address, inherited by the Elizabethans, can be represented in a diagram as shown in Figure 4.2. Anyone with a

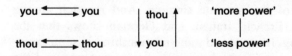

Figure 4.2 System of pronominal address

knowledge of modern European languages like French, German, and Italian will see similarities between this system and pronoun usage in those languages as it was almost until today. What we have to account for in English is the widespread loss of *thou*, and with it the means of 'power-coding' relationships by addressing someone as *thou*, and getting *you* in return. Of particular interest is the displacement of the original second person singular pronoun by the *you*-form, which originally indicated plurality.

The use of the plural pronoun *you* as a respectful marker of address was a change led by the most powerful social groups. Originating in the Latin of the later Roman Empire (there were two Emperors, so to address one was to address the other as well) the custom of using, and demanding, the polite plural pronoun spread into many European languages during the Middle Ages. Once established in French, it was adopted by the Francophile English aristocracy. At first, *you*, as a marker of special esteem, was rare, an emblem of courtly custom; but gradually, relationships such as parent/child, lord/servant, husband/wife were power-coded, in that the former in each pair demanded *you*, and returned *thou.* By about 1500 it seems that this practice had been copied by the middle class, and *thou* was becoming the 'marked' form. It could be used for special effects; moreover, it was the reciprocal pronoun of the lower class.

In that *you* was emblematic of upper-class manners, as *thou* was of working people, the widespread adoption of *you* in the course of the seventeenth century may be said to represent the triumph of middle-class values. More difficult to explain is the abandoning of the non-reciprocal pattern of power-relationships. In general, this pattern persists in societies where rank and status are relatively fixed and transparent. When social relations become more fluid, however, specific relationships are liable to be re-interpreted, and reciprocal pronouns used instead. In many European languages, relationships involving social class or rank, such as customer/waiter, officer/soldier, employer/employee, have been resolved by the use of the plural pronoun of distance and respect; whereas differences of status in the family, as between parent and child, for example, have been interpreted as meriting the mutual use of the intimate singular. And research among younger speakers of French, Italian, and German shows that the system is still changing. In more and more relationships, in some countries more than others, solidarity is winning out over power, and the equivalent to *thou* in those languages is being extended. In short, people are rejecting a linguistic expression of inequality and at the same time excluding the reciprocal expression of respectful distance. The pronouns of intimate equality are felt by young people in Europe today to be the best means of expressing democratic sentiments.

We do not have the evidence to reconstruct such a shift in sixteenth-century England. We do not know whether it was parents and children, or masters and servants, who initiated the rejection of power-coding. But it is interesting that while the merchants, tradespeople, and professions were aping upper-class manners, they abandoned the means of marking power relationships with those below them. It has been suggested that this was motivated by an egalitarian ethic. More likely was it a reflex of middle-class insecurity. In sixteenth-century urban society, particularly that of London, social relations were not fixed, which perhaps explains the Elizabethan obsession with them. With power and influence increasingly identified with the entrepreneur, there was no means of knowing who was entitled to *you*, and who to *thou*. The best solution was to stick to *you*, which would not offend, and rely on the more open-ended set of address terms discussed in the last chapter. For such terms can be avoided altogether, whereas pronouns cannot be. This, after all, is the way we handle the issue in contemporary English. Athough we can still upset people by being over-familiar when they are unable, or do not wish, to respond in the same way, we at least are able to avoid committing ourselves in address by choosing not to use names, titles, and Christian names, or expressions of hail-fellow-well-met familiarity at all, at least until we are sure of our ground.

The retention of *thou* in dialect may have been motivated by covert prestige. It is noteworthy that it is still heard in northern England where the desire to maintain a regional identity is strong. Whatever the reason, dialect speakers who use the pronoun enjoy a clear advantage over speakers of the metropolitan variety. For the former, *thou* can be the norm; *you* can be a special pronoun to establish social distance with outsiders (thus inverting the sixteenth-century middle-class pattern). Or *thou* can be used to signal extra intimacy. The gamekeeper in *Lady Chatterley's Lover* takes full advantage of these possibilities.

Finally, it is worth commenting on the selection of *thou* (sometimes *thee*) as the mutual pronoun of address among the Quakers. In that they chose the pronoun of lower-class solidarity, the Quakers of the seventeenth century could be said to have anticipated the future development in the other European languages. *You* was apparently too loaded with connotations of class superiority: English people had managed with mutual *thou/thee* for centuries, and why should they not continue to do so? Moreover, the pronoun had a long, unbroken history of use in the domain of religion (as it still does). It was perhaps this insistence of the Quakers, who were not then considered to be as respectable as they have since become, that helped to stigmatise *thou/thee* in the minds of many people. If *thou* was the pronoun of religious fanatics, subversives, and stable-boys, sensible people might be wise to forget it!

SYNTACTIC ELABORATION AND SOCIAL PRESTIGE

In the examples above, we have seen that changes in grammar may be introduced, or extended, by upper-, middle- or lower-class usage. The same is true for the process of syntactic elaboration, particularly in the extension of use of the auxiliary verbs. Lower-class speech, for instance, seems to have promoted *do* as a 'dummy' auxiliary (see above, p. 95). Already used as a *substitute* verb in Anglo-Saxon (as in *swa hie ær dydon*, 'as they before did', where *dydon* stands for a previously-mentioned lexical verb *ricsian*, 'rule'), *do* came to be used in questions: it is not difficult to imagine how a sequence like this could be queried with *did they*? This pattern probably spread from the south-west, where it is recorded first; and by the sixteenth century, do-questions were a feature of lower-class London usage. In Shakespeare, it co-exists, as a marker of popular speech, with the older, upper-class inversion pattern, as in *go you?*. At this time, also, *do* was spreading into the negative construction. Originally, *I don't go* would have been *Ic ne ga (noht)*; from this arose *I ne go not*, then *I go not*, then *I don't go*. Perhaps this use of *do* was originally emphatic, as it is used today in declarative sentences – *I DO go and see him!*; from there it may have been over-used, in the way described in the last chapter, and subsequently become the norm. Today *do* is usual in questions and negative constructions except where other auxiliaries like *have, can, are*, etc., are present; and even then one of these, *have*, is yielding to the process of extension. In the USA, *do you have a pen?*, *no, I don't* is more common than the *have you (got)* . . ., *no I haven't* pattern heard in England, although here the do-pattern is also gaining ground among the young.

Another development of *do* seems to be associated with the written English of the sixteenth and seventeenth centuries. We find it used in declarative sentences, as in *she doth go*, where no special emphasis seems to have been required. But the rise of this pattern is both dramatic and short-lived, since it had begun to die out by the following century. The explanation for this may be that *do* could be used to mark the tense of verbs which had no morphological distinction between present and past, like *put* and *cast*; and also of those verbs borrowed from Latin, like *illuminate* and *imitate*, which at that time were entering literary English in enormous numbers, and at too fast a rate, it seems, to become rapidly assimilated to the English tense-system.

Other extensions in the use of auxiliaries are also associated with writing. And as we saw earlier, a great deal of writing in English has evolved in the shadow of other literary traditions, notably those of Latin and French. The earliest English writing appears to show the influence of Latin structures. While Latin had verbal inflexions which marked future tense, Anglo-Saxon had not, so scholars had to find other ways of translating Latin future tenses into English. One solution was to extend *sceal* (modern *shall*), a modal verb meaning 'be obliged', for this purpose. Similarly, the Latin pluperfect tense came to be expressed using the past tense of the verb *have*, as in *he had said*. Originally this meaning in Anglo-Saxon would have been conveyed *lexically*, using an adverb with a simple past tense; so that *he had said* would have been *he sæde ær*, 'he said previously'.

Such constructions were not only copied, or adapted, from Latin; increasingly they came to be seen as 'better' than the corresponding English ones. The prestige of Latin as a written, and above all, codified language, was projected on to its structures themselves. By the end of the eighteenth century the native English pattern of negation, as in *I don't know nothing*, where negatives are used cumulatively, had been stigmatised, since it did not conform to the Latin pattern. Further sticks were found to beat it with. The cumulative negative was declared illogical, and speakers who used it must learn to tighten up their thinking. These ideas are still influential in the educational system. In the 1960s in the USA, language programmes aimed at Black school children were trying to eradicate this construction from their speech, and replace it with the 'logical' standard one.

Such attempts to link certain grammatical structures with patterns of thinking are reminiscent of the ideas of Whorf, discussed earlier in this book. We find these ideas, conscious or otherwise, in the work of many contemporary educationalists, sociologists, and psychologists. Some linguists also have applied them, notably in connection with structures larger than any we have discussed so far in this chapter. For instance, the various ways in which sentences – and those sentences within sentences that are usually called clauses – are joined, have been differently evaluated.

In Anglo-Saxon, the joining of clauses and sentences relied less on specific conjunctions like *when, before, although, while*, etc., than on *then (þa)*, and *and*; and often, such units were not linked at all, but merely juxtaposed. We can demonstrate this by using different ways of presenting much the same information:

(a) *I was tired: I went to bed.*
(b) *I was tired, and I went to bed.*
(c) *Because I was tired, I went to bed.*

Of these, (c) is sometimes described as being more explicit, in that the relationship between the two ideas – tiredness and going to bed – is made logically dependent: the first idea is subordinated to the second. *Because I was tired* can thus be called a subordinate clause, and this kind of structure is much more typical of Latin-based style than the other two examples. Of these (a) leaves the readers or listeners to work out the relationship between the juxtaposed clauses for themselves: it is less explicit. This kind of construction, called *parataxis*, is very typical of Anglo-Saxon, as is also the second, which can be called simple co-ordination.

We can use all three models today, but it is the last one, (c), that is often more highly valued than the others, because of the notion of explicitness alluded to above. Thus, the ability to use subordinate clauses has been related to more abstract, more sophisticated kinds of thinking. Parataxis has sometimes been dismissed as vague or even naive. But the prestige attaching to subordination really derives from its association with writing. This kind of sentence-linking is much less common in speech: we are back to the second misconception on our list, that grammar is something applicable to the written word rather than the spoken.

Failure to recognise this has contributed to the wide currency enjoyed by recent hypotheses relating language and educational success. Subordination is one of the features associated by Basil Bernstein with the so-called elaborated code – the kind of language capable of conveying individual perceptions to a universal audience. In Bernstein's works of the late 1960s and early 1970s, syntactical subordination, or more properly, the capacity to use syntactical subordination, is considered to reflect logical thought; therefore working-class children are disadvantaged at school because their speech makes small use of this kind of grammatical pattern. When we inspect the other grammatical habits that working-class children are alleged to use – short, simple, often unfinished sentences, simple repetitive use of conjunctions (*and, then*, etc.), rigid, limited use of adverbs and adjectives, use of the active rather than passive voice (see p. 95 above) – we find a list of features characteristic of all speech, irrespective of education or class. Speech is necessarily less 'discriminative' than writing, since the ear can best process a much less 'dense' kind of language than the eye. The ability to command the elaborated code – in the sense of being able to use the features Bernstein lists for it – is really the ability to use the structures of written English in your speech.

Even now our argument is in danger of forgetting that written English, like speech, varies. We are more likely to find the passive used in reports of chemistry experiments than in narratives. And since subordination is typical of formal, expository prose, we often find that twentieth-century novelists, like Hemingway, try to cultivate a style which avoids it. By being less explicit, a paratactic style also can be said to respect its readers by demanding that they themselves share the burden of interpretation. In the traditional ballad, for instance, we find the paratactic principle extended, so that line and stanza, narrative and dialogue, action and scene, are juxtaposed without comment. Moreover, the proverb, with its simple structure (*more haste, less speed*) is no less capable of expressing complex, even abstract thoughts than more explicit, less elliptical language. The tendency for subordination to replace parataxis as a dominant style should be seen for what it is: a matter of style, not linguistic progress, whatever that might be.

5 Pronunciation

The extent of regional variation in the pronunciation of English is universally acknowledged and often remarked on. In this chapter, we shall see how an awareness of such variation can help us understand the process of change. First, however, we need to examine some general misunderstandings about the nature of pronunciation; in particular, its relationship with spelling, and the ways in which notions about correctness, and the view that some forms of pronunciation are slovenly, have been influenced by the prestigious Received Pronunciation (RP) accent. Then we shall look at sounds themselves, and see how they can be described independently of our spelling system, by describing first some of the RP consonants, and then the vowels. RP itself will be seen to vary, according to the level of formality of context, and also with respect to the age, sex, and even social attitude of its speakers: and we shall see how such variations reflect changes in the recent past. We shall then see how three consonant pronunciations, formerly common in upper- and lower-class speech, have subsequently been stigmatised, especially in urban accents. Three widely-known regional pronunciations will then be described, and their origins traced; and we shall see how in two cases they preserve sounds that were once more generally used. Finally, we shall examine the evidence for the series of momentous vowel changes known as the Great Vowel Shift, and assess the role of social factors in the adoption of the new pronunciations that resulted.

Contrary to what many people think, regional pronunciations in England are not dying out. Although in some respects they have changed quite dramatically within living memory, the direction of change has by no means always been towards RP; the accents of the big cities – London, Liverpool, Birmingham, Newcastle – have if anything intensified certain phonetic differences across the generations. Moreover, we cannot speak of the existence of a national norm of pronunciation; some regional features are so deeply embedded in the speech of all but the most privileged social classes, that it is possible to speak of *regional* norms in areas of England that are well away from London and the south-east. And although RP still provides an important point of reference in matters of pronunciation, it has lost a great deal of its prestige in recent years.

Contemporary variations in pronunciation provide us with the best introduction to changes which have taken place in the sounds of English since Anglo-Saxon times. Unlike words and meanings, and grammatical forms and constructions, the sounds of the past cannot be fully reconstructed by examining written texts. Anything we say on the subject can only be guesswork. In the past, however, historians of English have been most concerned with the interpretation of rhymes, the so-called phonetic spellings of handwritten manuscripts, and the comments of codifiers and other observers. Present-day regional pronunciations at least have the virtue of attestability, even though we can never be sure how far they may throw light on the usage of the past.

It is possible that the changes in pronunciation that have occurred during the last 1500 years are no greater than the range of regional variants that can still be heard today. But although it is likely that regional pronunciations have diverged increasingly over the centuries, it is not necessary to assume they derive from a single source. About the Anglo-Saxon dialects we know little, but it is at least conceivable that in some respects they had distinctive systems of pronunciation. By the fourteenth century, as we have seen, differences among the written manifestations of the dialects are so radical that it would be surprising if significant variations did not exist also at the phonetic level.

The history of English sounds has much to do with the spread of features from one region to another. But geography is not the only source of variation. Everybody's pronunciation varies according to the formality of a situation; and a variant developing in, say, casual style, may spread to other styles as well. Finally, new variants may arise from contexts where emphatic, or forceful, styles of speech are used. Pronunciation is infinitely variable and constantly evolving.

The spread of new variants is often dependent on social factors. For example, we must take account of the prestige enjoyed by the group with which a particular pronunciation is associated. This is especially relevant in towns and cities, where dialects of many areas are brought into contact. Often this results in the erosion of sharp differences; but new patterns are often created as different social groups strive to maintain their linguistic identity, or distance themselves from others.

The spread of prestigious pronunciations throughout the countryside may be attributed to middle-class speakers in the towns. More contro-versially, dialect surveys, and sociolinguistic investigations of urban speech, suggest moreover that it is women who most actively try to identify with prestigious pronunciations. Men who worked in trad-itional rural occupations tended to preserve dialect pronunciations to mark membership of the male peer-group, while in the towns those variants stigmatised by the education system still enjoy a *covert* prestige among working-class men for the very reason that they are considered incorrect.

It is not easy to perceive general trends in the history of English pronunciation. It seems likely, however, that the consonant system has remained relatively stable for the past 1500 years. As we shall see, this has much to do with the nature of consonant sounds themselves. Vowels, on the other hand, seem particularly subject to change. While the short vowel system may in many respects resemble that used by the Anglo-Saxons, the long vowels and diphthongs exhibit immense changes, just as they can be seen to be especially variable in contempor-ary regional pronunciation. In this chapter, we shall see the significance of three trends, involving the lengthening, raising, and diphthongising of vowels.

Changes in pronunciation cannot be attributed to a general careless-ness on the part of speakers. While such a notion might recommend itself to those who take an apocalyptic view of linguistic change, it is only in some cases that economy of effort, making short-cuts in the articulation of sounds, can be specified as an important factor. Neither is it appropriate to explain the adoption of new pronunciations on the grounds that they are 'easier to say' than other variants. In general, what we find easy to say is what we are used to saying, just as we have difficulty in mastering the sounds of a strange language. We shall see the relevance of these observations in the next few paragraphs.

POPULAR IDEAS ABOUT PRONUNCIATION

Since spelling is the only widely-known system of representing sounds, it is not surprising that people often refer to letters, not sounds, when they are discussing pronunciation. The extent of this spelling-consciousness can be seen in the common misconception that English has five vowels – *a*, *e*, *i*, *o* and *u* (whereas most varieties of the language have at least four times that number). We find constantly that spellings are cited in support of various pronunciations: the *h* should be sound-ed, because it is there in the spelling, and people should avoid saying *lawr and order* because there is no *r* in *law*. Such ideas are so firmly held among certain social groups that in 1979 the BBC set up a panel to monitor the pronunciations (and also, incidentally, the grammar, words, and meanings as well) of its broadcasters, so persistent had been the letters of complaint.

There is a related misconception that not only should each letter be given a pronunciation, but it should also be given one pronunciation only. In other words, the fallacy that letters 'have pronunciations' is given a further twist, in that each letter is supposed to have a correct pronunciation. Thus, the *t* sound in *later* should be pronounced by touching the tongue-tip against the teeth-ridge behind the upper front teeth; the glottal stop, which involves a closure in the area of the throat known as the glottis, will not do. Such arguments express the relationship between sounds and spelling the wrong way round: we speak with sounds, not letters, and linguists must therefore find a way of categorising sounds independently of their written representation.

It is often thought that RP conforms most closely to such spelling-based models of pronunciation. But while it may be true that an RP pronunciation of a word like *later* respects the arguments expressed in the last two paragraphs, in other ways that accent does not match up to spelling. Both t's are not sounded in a word like *hotter*, for instance, and neither is the *r*, which is also preserved in the spelling of innumerable words, such as *car*, *card*, *starter*, where it is given no realisation in sound. Thus, RP does not distinguish between pairs of words like *fort* and *fought*, unlike those accents which pronounce *r* in all positions in the word. For this reason, there is no substance in those arguments that seek to justify RP as a superior accent on the grounds that it can make more distinctions in the pronunciation of words than other accents. Thus, while it may be true that an accent that pronounces *h* can distinguish between, say, *arm* and *harm*, other accents can differentiate *meet* from *meat*, *horse* from *hoarse*, or *no* from *know*, which RP, for one, does not.

Pronunciations which do not seem to conform to either the canons of spelling or RP are often referred to as careless or even slovenly. The essential point here is that every single first-language speaker of English uses such pronunciations, for the simple reason that we can only be 'correct' when we are conscious of how we are sounding. Sociolinguistic research suggests that when people are immersed in the telling of a story, for instance, their pronunciation is not the same as when they are reading aloud from a list of individual words. In certain situations, for instance formal ones, we tend to adjust our pronunciation towards some norm of correctness, or at least, what we assume or imagine our audience will find most acceptable or persuasive; but in casual speech, where communicative intent is more relevant than form, we regularly make even those sounds that in conscious moments we would stigmatise. And if many people find this argument hard to accept, it is because they automatically turn to the carefully controlled, or monitored pronunciations they would use in formal contexts whenever they are asked to consider their own speech. But it is a fact that can be demonstrated if people are tape-recorded in unguarded moments. Not only will first-language speakers say *I'm going to go and pick some raspberries* differently from the way they would say it in casual style, they will probably find it very difficult to tell how they would say it if they did not have the words in front of them.

The point made in the last paragraph will become clear if we remember that sounds, like words, do not occur in isolation. They are produced in conjunction with other sounds: and the articulation of one sound may affect that of another. Thus, the *d* consonant of *bread* in first-language English is usually pronounced further back in the mouth than in *breadth*, where the dental articulation of *th* often influences the position of the preceding consonant. The sound represented by the letter *d* is not, therefore, always made in the same way: and we shall find this is true of all other sounds as well. Just as the pronunciation of consonants is affected by neighbouring consonants, so are they by neighbouring vowels; and vowels are often conditioned by the consonants that immediately precede or follow them. In other words, we must learn to look at sounds as part of a sequence; which is, after all, how we hear them in connected speech.

THE ANALYSIS OF SOUNDS

Sounds do not occur in isolation, but a scientific description of the ways in which they are produced in the mouth requires us to take them one at a time. And since sounds are subject to such widespread regional variation, we can also only describe one accent at a time. It is customary for linguists to start with RP, and this is what we shall do here: not because it is in any way superior or even desirable, but because it is widely understood. A great deal of what we shall find, moreover, is relevant to all first-language speakers of English, at least in England. And, since we have said that the sounds of any accent vary according to situation, we must specify that it is the formal style of RP that provides the basis of the following account.

The study of pronunciation involves more than just the accurate analysis of articulatory movements. For we ought to be able to explain why most first-language speakers of English do not need to be aware that the *d* sounds in *bread* and *breadth* are different. One reason for this is that these sounds can never bring about a change of meaning; they are therefore felt to be the same sound. To use another example: the initial sounds in *car* and *key* are different, articulated in slightly different places in the mouth, but many speakers of English may not be able to perceive this. If we substitute a *b* sound for the initial sound of *car* we get *bar*, which clearly not only involves a different sound but also creates another word with an entirely different meaning. The initial sounds of *car* and *bar* are therefore to be called different phonemes, a term we have already met, and defined, in chapter two. The different kinds of *k* sound in *car* and *key* can be called *allophones*, or different realisations, of the same phoneme.

The phoneme can be seen either as a family of sounds, or as an abstract concept encompassing a number of phonetic realisations. While these may be very large, the number of phonemes in most varieties of all languages is fixed and relatively small: many accents of English have about forty-four. Central to the notion of the phoneme is that it is a sound capable of bringing about a change of meaning. As such, it contrasts with all other phonemes in a particular accent: and together they constitute a system. A system is a structure of interdependent units, and if a change occurs with respect to one unit (phoneme), it is likely that some re-structuring of other parts of the system will occur.

This rather theoretical exposition will become clearer as more examples are cited. Many people will have direct experience of the kinds of misunderstanding that occur among speakers with different accents, where someone fails to locate the specific place of a sound in the system of another speaker. For instance, the Cockney vowel in *but* makes that word sound like *bat* to a northerner: in isolation, the vowels in both words may sometimes be considered to be the same. But though the vowels may be phonetically similar, it is quite clear that they have different places in the systems of different accents. To simplify, the vowel in Cockney *but* occurs in many words spelt with *u*, as in *cut*, *fun*, and *numb*, with *oo* as in *blood* and *flood*, *ou* as in *country* and *young*, and sometimes with *o*, as in *son*, *nothing*, and *London*. In many northern accents, a similar vowel occurs in words spelt with *a*, as in *cat*, *fan*, and *land*. Each accent, however, has its own way of making distinctions among words, distinguishing, for instance, between *but* and *bat*, *but* and *bet*, *bat* and *bet*, and so on. Every accent has its own system, and the functioning of the parts must be established before adequate comparisons can be made among them.

There is a final point to make about the patterning of sounds. Some phonemes – like the medial consonant in *measure* – occur much less frequently than others in speech. This is partly because the number of positions in which they occur is limited: some consonants, for instance, do not occur in initial position; others may be restricted to that position. Such sounds may be said to occupy a less central place in the system than others.

THE CONSONANTS OF RP

Consonants, unlike vowels, can be broadly characterised as sounds which involve contact or near-contact between the organs of speech – the tongue, lips, teeth – and parts of the roof of the mouth – soft palate, hard palate, and teeth-ridge. Because such contact can be felt or sensed by the speaker, consonant sounds are more likely to remain stable than vowels, their variants more amenable to codification and stigmatisation.

The RP system has twenty-four consonant phonemes. These can be subdivided into groups according to *how* they are produced; in other words, the kind of contact involved. We shall concentrate here on only three major groups, the plosives, fricatives, and nasals, the members of which together comprise eighteen of the total number of consonants. The first class is that known as *plosives*. These consonants are made when certain organs of speech are brought into short, sharp contact, and then smartly released. There are six plosive consonants in RP, and they can be shown to distinguish the following words, all of which have the termination *-ill*:

| pill | till | kill |
| bill | dill (the herb) | gill (of a fish) |

English-born speakers of English will probably recognise that this sub-system of sounds constitutes a meaningful way of distinguishing the words listed. The arrangement of the words in pairs introduces another dimension of description: the *place* of articulation. We need to specify which speech organs are involved. /p/ and /b/ – the slanting brackets indicate that we are talking about *phonemes* – are made by bringing the lips together and then quickiy emitting the build-up of air-pressure from the lungs by opening the lips. /t/ and /d/ are made by bringing the tongue-tip against the ridge behind the upper front teeth – the *alveolar* ridge – and then releasing it; and in the case of the final pair, the back of the tongue makes a similar kind of contact with the soft palate at the rear part of the roof of the mouth, the *velum*. Thus, the vital positions for the plosives are bilabial, alveolar, and velar. All first-language speakers of English, regardless of their accent, make these distinctions, although they sound, or realise them, in many different ways. And readers can check the accuracy of the foregoing by conscious observation of their own articulation.

It remains to explain how the members of each pair – /p/ and /b/, for instance – are distinguished. All the plosives are articulated in the manner described, but accompanying the production of the bottom series /b d g/ is a vibration of the vocal cords, folds of tissue situated in the larynx which we are capable of opening and closing. Such vibration is called *voicing*. We now have a system of description for the consonants: we can speak of the initial sound in *bill*, for example, as a voiced bilabial plosive; that in *kill*, as a voiceless velar plosive. These labels can be used in the description of any language, and their immediate value for us is that sounds can be discussed independently of the spelling system.

With its three well-spaced places of articulation, and the paired oppositions between voiced and voiceless, the system of plosives seems symmetrical and neat. It is presented quite simply in Table 5.1.

Table 5.1 System of plosives in RP

Lips	Alveolar ridge	Velum	
p	t	k	Voiceless
b	d	g	Voiced

With the next group of consonants, the *fricatives*, a similar pattern can be detected. These consonants depend on a different kind of contact, one producing turbulent air. The air from the lungs passes through a narrow passage as the speech organs almost, but not quite, close the oral cavity at some point. These hissing and buzzing sounds can be maintained as long as breath lasts, in a way that is not possible for the plosive sounds. We find a different series of articulatory positions for the fricatives, but there is among all but one the same contrast between voiced and voiceless. Teeth and lips are involved in *feel* and *veal;* teeth and tongue in *thigh* and *thy;* teeth-ridge, hard palate, and tongue with *Confucian* and *confusion;* and glottis, that part of the vocal tract where the vocal cords are situated, with *heat*. Finally, the alveolar ridge, where the initial sounds of *seal* and *zeal* may be distinguished from their plosive counterparts /t/ and /d/ by virtue of the friction that occurs between tongue and teeth-ridge. Table 5.2 shows the positions. As the table indicates, /h/ has no voiced counterpart that can bring about a change in meaning.

Table 5.2 Articulatory positions for fricatives

Teeth + lips	Teeth + tongue	Alveolar ridge	Palato-alveolar	Glottal	
*f*eel	*th*igh	*s*eal	Confu*c*ian	*h*eat	Voiceless
*v*eal	*th*y	*z*eal	confu*s*ion		Voiced

The third group of consonants we shall examine are the *nasals*. These are articulated in the same way as the voiced plosives /b d g/ except that the oral cavity is kept closed at some point and the air passes out through the nose: thus *rib* is distinguished from *rim*, *red* from *wren*, and *rig* from *ring* by the feature of nasality associated with the last sound in the second word in each pair. The nasals therefore have the same places of articulation as the plosives, but there is no significant contrast between voiced and voiceless. They are symbolised as /m/, /n/, and /ŋ/.

The latter sound, the velar nasal in *ring*, calls for further comment. Such is the influence of spelling that many people regard this not as a single sound, but as a sequence of the sounds /n/ and /g/. But it is only in some accents – notably those of the west midlands and north-west – that a /g/ is sounded in words like *ring*. In RP, however, and many other accents, *ring* is pronounced /rɪŋ/; the back of the tongue comes into contact with the velum or soft palate, as for /g/, but air escapes through the nose rather than the mouth.

So far, we have described two-thirds of the consonants in the RP system. The other six – the initial sounds of *chore*, *jaw*, *roar*, *law*, *war*, and *yore* – will be dealt with when and if the occasion arises (see Table 5.3). Space prevents us from analysing all the consonants in detail, neither can we do justice to the wealth of phonetic variants for each phoneme. But we need now to look a little more closely at that part of the system we have described. As we inspect it, we shall find that it is a little less watertight and elegant than at first appears.

We saw above that /h/ stands out from the other fricatives in that there is no significant voiced fricative in the glottal place of articulation, as there are in the other places. /h/ stands out in other ways as well. Whereas we can usually put other fricatives in initial, medial, and final position in a word – /f/ as in *fish*, *heifer*, *off*; /v/ in *veal*, *ever*, *give* – there are no words in any accent of English where /h/ is in final position; and the only time it occurs medially, in words like *behind* and *adhere*, it is at the onset of a syllable that is stressed.

Part of the description of a sound, then, is the range of positions it can occupy. This is known as its incidence. To take another example, the velar nasal /ŋ/ likewise has incidental peculiarities. This occurs, as we have seen, in final position, where it is frequent in the verbal termination -*ing*, as in *walking*. We also find it before the positionally-related velar plosives /k/ and /g/ in *think* and *finger*, and medially between vowels, as in *singer* (which in RP, and most southern accents, does not rhyme with *finger*). But the sound virtually never occurs in initial position, and certainly not in formal styles of pronunciation. We shall see the relevance of these observations later in the chapter.

RP VOWELS

Vowels are in general more difficult to describe than consonants since we often cannot feel the movements of speech-organs involved in their articulation. Of paramount importance in the description of vowels is the shape of the tongue as it moves or stays momentarily in a fixed position in the mouth. In particular, we need to know which part of the tongue – front, centre, or back – is raised towards the roof of the mouth. Also important is the shape of the lips: whether they are rounded or spread. Finally, we shall need to distinguish those vowel sounds where the tongue moves during the process of articulation – these are called diphthongs – from those where the tongue stays still; and within the latter class, we need to be aware of the *duration* of the vowel, whether it is long or short. We can now move on to describe the RP vowel system.

There are seven short vowels in RP, seen in *pit*, *pet*, *pat*, *pot*, *put*, *putt*, and the final vowel of *patter*. *Pit*, *pet*, and *pat* have front vowels: the front of the tongue is raised towards the palate; higher for *pit*, lower for *pat*, between the two for *pet*. Thus we can distinguish between the vowels in those words by referring to the height of the front of the tongue in the mouth. With these sounds also, the lips are spread: they adopt a 'smiling' position. The vowels of *pot* and *put* are *back* vowels: the back of the tongue is raised, higher for *put* than *pot* (it is difficult for us to feel this, but X-rays show this is so). With these two vowels, the lips are rounded, or slightly pursed.

The vowels of *putt* and pat*ter* require careful explanation. In RP the vowel in *putt*, *nut*, and *cut* is different from that in *put*, *good*, and *bush*, a distinction not made in some accents, especially in the north and midlands. Like *pot* and *put*, *putt* has a back vowel, but one that is unrounded, and therefore made with spread lips. The social significance of this vowel – symbolised as /ʌ/ – will be discussed below. Lastly, the final vowel in *patter* is unlike the other vowels in this series, in that it is the centre of the tongue that is raised when the vowel is articulated. It is also distinguished by the fact that it never occurs – in formal style, at

Table 5.3 The consonants of RP

		Voiceless				Voiced		
			Initial	Medial	Final		Initial	Medial	Final
A **Plosives**									
	bilabial	1/p/ as in	pin	dipper	lip	2/b/	bin	rubber	rib
	alveolar	3/t/ as in	tin	bitter	bit	4/d/	din	rider	rid
	velar	5/k/ as in	kin	pocket	sick	6/g/	gate	bigger	big
B **Fricatives**									
	labiodental	7/f/ as in	fin	leafy	leaf	8/v/	vine	never	leave
	dental	9/θ/ as in	thin	ether	wreath	10/ð/	this	worthy	seethe
	alveolar	11/s/ as in	sin	fussy	fuss	12/z/	zoo	razor	gaze
	palato-alveolar	13/ʃ/ as in	shin	fishy	rush	14/ʒ/	gigolo	measure	rouge
	glottal	15/h/ as in	hen	behave	–				
C **Affricates**									
	palato-alveolar	16/tʃ/ as in	chin	kitchen	rich	17/dʒ/	gin	rigid	ridge

In the consonants below, the voiced/voiceless contrast is not significant

D Nasals

		Initial	Medial	Final
bilabial	18/m/	man	gammon	ram
alveolar	19/n/	nose	sinner	sin
velar	20/ŋ/	–	singer	sing

E Lateral

	21/l/	love	colour	fill

F Frictionless continuant

	22/r/	run	hurry	far away

G Semi-vowels

		Initial	Medial	Final
palatal	23/j/	yes	–	–
bilabial	24/w/	win	away	–

any rate – in syllables that are stressed. Thus, the first syllable of *about*, and the second of *opportunity* have the same vowel as the last syllable of *patter*; hence, as the commonest vowel of unstressed syllables, this sound is the most frequently occurring vowel in any variety of English. If this comes as a surprise to many people, it is because the sound in question – called *schwa* by linguists, and symbolised as /ə/ – is represented by many different spellings.

We can sum up this account of the short vowels with the aid of a simple diagram, which represents a schematised side-view of tongue-positions within the mouth (see Figure 5.1). We have italicised *putt*

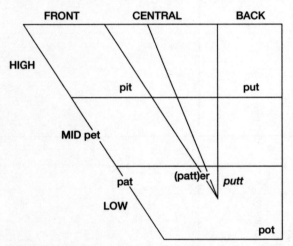

Figure 5.1 Positions of tongue in pronunciation of RP short vowels

because it is outside the front-spread versus back-rounded symmetry of the RP short vowel system.

The five long vowels in RP are heard if we choose words beginning with /b/: *bee*, *bar*, *bore*, *boo*, and *burr*. Only one of these, that of *bee*, is a front vowel; it is made with spread lips, with the front of the tongue high in the mouth. The vowel in *bar* is also made with spread lips, but in RP it is an open back vowel. *Bore* and *boo* both have back-rounded vowels; the back of the tongue is higher in *boo* than in *bore*. Finally, the vowel of *burr* is a long central vowel, with a similar tongue-position to /ə/. It will be noticed that many of the words cited have an *r* in the spelling, which has no realisation in RP pronunciation. We shall see the significance of this below. Our system of long vowels can be summarised as in Figure 5.2.

The diphthongs, of which RP has eight (but sometimes nine) are

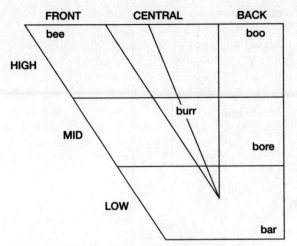

Figure 5.2 Tongue-positions for RP long vowels

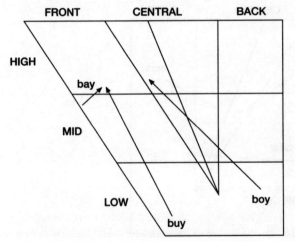

Figure 5.3 Tongue-positions for diphthongs gliding towards /ɪ/

more difficult to describe than the vowels so far introduced. Many people are surprised to be told that the RP vowel in *bait*, for instance, is a diphthong; but we have to be able to specify how that word is distinguished from *bet*, *bit*, and *beat*. In the RP pronunciation of *bait*, the tongue moves from a position similar to that of the vowel in *bet*, to one like that of the vowel in *bit*. In other words, the tongue is progressively raised in the course of articulation, and this can actually be felt if the pronunciation of *bait* is slowed right down, so that the glide from /e/ to

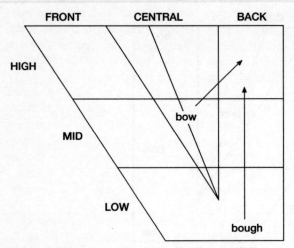

Figure 5.4 Tongue-positions for diphthongs gliding towards /ʊ/

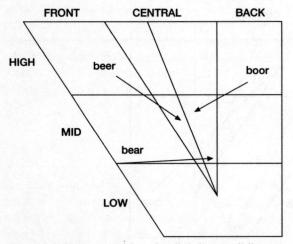

Figure 5.5 Tongue-positions for diphthongs gliding towards /ə/

/ɪ/ can be appreciated. A glide in the same direction also occurs in *buy* and *boy*, from the low-front-spread, and low-back-rounded starting-points respectively. These diphthongs can be shown as in Figure 5.3. The diphthongs in *bough* and *bow* (as in bow and arrow), and in *beer*, *bear*, and (sometimes) *boor*, move in different directions. *Bough* and *bow* move towards the /ʊ/ of *bush*, the last three towards /ə/. Figures 5.4 and 5.5 will make the starting-points of the diphthongs clear.

There are two points to be made about our description of the RP vowel system. The division drawn between long and short vowels, although traditional, is not meant to be absolute, since there are many grades of length. In fact, those vowels we have described as long are distinguished from the short vowels as much by quality as length. And within the long vowels, length is conditioned by the nature of following consonants. For instance, the long vowel in *leaf* is even longer in *leave*, and longer still in *leaves*. It is the voiced consonants immediately following the vowel, and combinations of them, that appear to have exerted a lengthening influence. Voiced consonants also affect the character of one of the short vowels. In RP, and in other southern accents, the /æ/ vowel before voiced plosives, as in *bad* and *bag*, for instance, is longer than in *bat*, and *back*. These examples show the importance of phonetic environment in the study of pronunciation.

The other point concerns the vowel of *boor*. Although we have described it as a diphthong, this pronunciation of the word is actually rather uncommon. Many speakers of RP do not distinguish between *boor* and *bore* (and, for that matter, *boar*); they use a long vowel in all three. What is happening here is that one diphthong is gradually being eradicated from the system. That diphthong, /ʊə/, is only used in words of rather infrequent occurrence, such as *tour* and *moor* and occasionally *sure;* and in those words, especially *tour*, it is often replaced by the vowel of *tor*. In sum, the *distribution* of the diphthong – its occurrence in particular words – is contracting: it is becoming marginal to the system. If it is lost altogether, there will be one phoneme less in the system (see Table 5.4).

VARIATION AND STYLE

It is when we examine connected speech that we see just how fluid our pronunciation is. This is particularly apparent in speech that is rapid and casual, and is as true of RP as any other accent. Whole words are reduced to what seems to be a minimal form, or changed almost beyond recognition. And even in RP, variants are regularly used that are commonly castigated as 'slovenly'.

In our discussion of /ə/, we noted the relevance of stress. Not all syllables in a word are given equal weight: in *hotter*, for instance, the *hot* part is pronounced with more stress. In connected speech, moreover, whole words are given less stress than others. Frequently-occurring 'grammatical' words like *and, but, from, for, shall, must*, have an unstressed pronunciation with /ə/, so that *what's for dinner?* becomes /wɒts fə dɪnə/. And in the most rapid and casual styles the vowel /ə/ is a common realisation of some of these words such as *are, her, or*, and *of*,

Table 5.4 The vowels of RP

I   Simple Vowels

    A   Short vowels. These do not occur in stressed syllables unless before a consonant in final position.

1	/ɪ/	as in pit	⎫
2	/e/	as in pet	Front vowels, lips spread
3	/æ/	as in pat	⎭
4	/ɒ/	as in pot	⎫
5	/ʊ/	as in put	Back vowels, lips rounded
6	/ʌ/	as in putt	Back vowel, lips spread
7	/ə/	as in patt*er*	Central vowel, lips neutral

    B   Long vowels

8	/iː/	as in bee	Front vowel, lips spread
9	/ɑː/	as in bar	Back vowel, lips spread
10	/ɔː/	as in bore	⎫
11	/uː/	as in boo	Back vowels, lips rounded
12	/ɜː/	as in burr	Central vowel, lips neutral

II   Diphthongs

13	/eɪ/	as in bay	⎫
14	/aɪ/	as in buy	Front-closing
15	/ɔɪ/	as in boy	⎭
16	/aʊ/	as in bough	⎫ Back-closing
17	/əʊ/	as in bow	⎭
18	/ɪə/	as in beer	⎫
19	/ɛə/	as in bear	Centring
20	/ʊə/	as in boor	⎭

---

as in *what are you thinking?*, *he left her stranded*, *more or less*, and *one of the best*. Consequently, in those grammatical words like *he*, *him*, *his*, *her*, and *had*, where /h/ is pronounced in formal styles, or when these words are strongly stressed, it is dropped in rapid speech.

Other kinds of reduction, known as elisions, are made in casual style. Consonant-clusters are simplified when they occur at word boundaries. Thus, in *last night*, an RP speaker is unlikely to pronounce the /t/ in *last*. Moreover, the final consonant of a word like *gone* may change in anticipation of the initial consonant of the following word. Thus, it may be /n/ in *gone riding*, but /m/ in *gone bicycling*, and /ŋ/ in *gone gliding*. This process is known as assimilation, since the articulation of one consonant is assimilated to another. Thus, the /b/ in *bicycling* is made with the lips, so the /n/ in *gone*, an alveolar nasal, is replaced by a nasal also made with the lips. Similarly, the velar position of /g/ in *gliding* determines the same position in the preceding nasal. In sum, the number of articulatory movements is minimised, and the process can be described as one that seeks 'economy of effort'.

Another kind of assimilation involves consonants that we have not yet introduced. One of these is the vowel-like palatal consonant that occurs initially in *yore*, *yet*, *yeast*, etc. Its phonetic symbol is /j/. In sequences such as *miss you*, this palatal consonant combines, in effect, with the consonant immediately before it. A new sound is created in the process. Out of *miss you* comes /mɪʃuː/, in which the medial consonant is the voiceless fricative in *shin*, *shoe*, etc. (The transition to the 'sh' sound can be felt if the sequence from /s/ to /j/ is speeded up.) Similarly, the sequence *got you* becomes /gɒtʃə/ (spelt *gotcher*, or *gotcha* in comics, etc.). This 'tch' sound belongs to a class of consonants, two in number, known as the *affricates*. The initial sound of words like *chin* and *chore* combines the characteristics of both plosive and fricative consonants, by starting like /t/, and ending like the /ʃ/ sound in *shoe*. The /tʃ/ sound has a voiced counterpart, the initial sound in *jaw*, or the final sound in *edge*, with the symbol /dʒ/.

So far, we have seen how the phonemic structure of a word may change in accordance with the words that occur with it. We must now consider how the pronunciation of an individual phoneme may vary in different phonetic environments. The phoneme we shall choose in illustration is the voiceless alveolar plosive /t/. In rapid, informal pronunciation, this sound is not always articulated in the manner we have described above. When in final position, as in *right*, the sound is usually accompanied by a closure in the glottis, which produces the well-known glottal stop or plosive. This is known as glottal reinforcement. And when /t/ is followed by certain consonants, as in *sit down, football*, the glottal closure becomes dominant, and there is either only very weak contact between tongue and alveolar ridge, or none at all.

Two other variants of /t/ will be discussed here. In the speech of many RP users, and of others as well, the tongue does not come away sharply from the alveolar ridge, but tends to vibrate after contact is made. Thus, a plosive articulation is immediately followed by a fricative one, and a 'ts' sound is produced. *Great*, then, has a slight /s/ at the end of the word. /t/ can therefore be said to have an *affricated* variant in certain positions. The other variant only occurs between vowels. In words like *butter*, but more particularly, perhaps, across word boundaries, as in *got away*, the /t/ often has a voiced variant, so that we hear *budder, god away*. The voicing occurs because vowels are usually accompanied by vibration of the vocal cords; and in these instances, the vibration carries across the intervening consonant, and includes it.

It is as pointless to condemn as 'slovenly' these glottal, affricated, and voiced variants of /t/ as it is to say that weak forms, simplified consonant-clusters, and assimilations are the marks of incorrect pronunciation. There are so many involuntary articulatory movements involved in speech that we can never be conscious of how we sound on all occasions, especially when our speech is at its most rapid and relaxed. And as we shall see, some of the phonetic tendencies we have described have been operating in the language for centuries, and may even be as old as English itself.

VARIATION AND CHANGE

Our description of RP is by no means yet complete. No accent is monolithic: and RP, as well as varying according to situation, also has variants associated with age. We have already noted that some speakers differentiate *tour* and *tor*, while others do not; and in general, it is older speakers who keep them apart. Some older people make a further distinction: certain words, like *shore*, used to be pronounced with a diphthong, to sound like *shawə*, so that a three-way distinction could be made between *shore, Shaw*, and *sure* (with /ʊə/). This diphthongal pronunciation of *shore* (arising, as we shall see, from the loss of *r*) is now so rare that we can speak of a systemic difference between those types of RP that use the diphthong, and those that do not.

It might be thought that a further systemic change is under way, in that /ʊə/ is gradually being eliminated from the system. But that process has been checked, it seems, in those words which have the palatal consonant /j/ immediately preceding the diphthong. In words like *lure* (pronounced /ljʊə/) *curious, pure*, etc., the high tongue-position needed for the /j/ sound influences that of the following diphthong, which also has a high, though back, tongue-position. The distribution of /ʊə/, therefore, is to a large extent conditioned by the nature of the preceding consonant.

It is not easy to specify the reasons for these changes. One suggestion is that there are not enough oppositions of the *shore/Shaw* type to make the diphthongal pronunciation of words like *shore* seem worth preserving. In other words, a rare diphthong gives way to a common one. Similarly, the infrequency of /ʊə/ tends to undermine its position in the system. While systemic pressures of this kind are of great importance, we must not forget that a social value often attaches to particular variants. We can illustrate this with a recent change of a different type. Younger RP speakers often pronounce the vowel in words like *cat* and *back* with a lower vowel than their elders. The older pronunciation, often heard in British films of the 1940s and epitomised more recently in the speech of the tennis commentator Dan Maskell, sounds to many ears more like /e/ than /æ/ (*metch* rather than *match*). In contrast, the younger RP sound is much closer to the lower vowel common in the north and midlands, and it is conceivable that this is its origin. Northern pronunciations have recently enjoyed a temporary prestige, and perhaps the older realisation of /æ/ had become a stereotype of an RP that was felt to be archaic and even quaint. Social attitude, then, may underpin this example of a *realisational* change.

RP, of course, is not the only variety of pronunciation that is changing. Any accent, at any point in its history, is in process of change, as variants associated with age, sex, or style, become either dominant or recessive. Our examples so far, however, have been changes that are only recent. Changes in the more distant past can be explained when we turn to the processes we have described for informal style. A development as significant as the rise of new phonemes depended to some extent on the voicing of consonants between vowels. It seems likely that the voiced fricatives in *love* and *thousand* were not phonemes in Anglo-Saxon, but were merely phonetic realisations of their corresponding voiceless fricatives, /f/ and /s/, when these occurred in medial positions between vowels. There were no pairs of words like *razor* and *racer*, *waver* and *wafer*, the meanings of which are dependent on the voiced/voiceless contrast in medial position; so the Anglo-Saxon scribes did not need to mark the fact that *s* in, say, *þusend* (thousand) was voiced, any more than we indicate the different articulations of /k/ in *key* and *car*. Contact with French, however, increased the incidence of the voiced sounds. A great many French words had /v/, for instance, in both initial and final position, so that oppositions like *vine* and *fine*, *serf* and *serve*, arose. In words of French origin, /z/ occurred finally (so *cause* could be kept apart from *course* after loss of /r/); and to a lesser extent, in initial position, hence *zeal* beside *seal*. Thus, a phonetic tendency within the language was reinforced from outside, enabling the French sounds to be absorbed into the English consonant system.

Many pronunciations also derive from assimilations that took place in the past. Modern *fetch* arises from Anglo-Saxon *fetian*, and the place-name Stamford originally had *stan* (stone) as its initial element. Most English people today probably say *samwich*, not *sandwich*, but both assimilated and unassimilated pronunciations co-exist in words like *Tuesday*. Many people may avoid /tʃuːzdeɪ/ as 'incorrect', and there is evidence that some assimilated pronunciations were once quite common in educated speech, but have since been stigmatised. Three centuries ago, *injun* for *Indian*, *shewer* for *sewer* (deriving from /sjʊə/) seem to have been quite common, but survive only in accents other than RP.

Even today, some people think it more correct to avoid pronouncing *racial* as /reɪʃəl/.

In *fetch*, *injun*, and *shewer*, the consonants arising from assimilation are not new additions to the inventory of phonemes: /tʃ/ occurred in Anglo-Saxon *ceorl* (churl), /dʒ/ in *ecg* (edge) and /ʃ/ in *scip* (ship). In other words, the frequency of occurrence of these sounds was increased by assimilation. Another consonant, however, virtually owes its place in the English sound-system to this process. The voiced fricative /ʒ/ from assimilation of /z/ + /j/ can occur at the boundaries of words of Anglo-Saxon origin, as in *how's your father*? Medially, it occurs in words like *treasure*, *occasion* and *usual*: *treasure* would once have been /trezjər/. A significant fact about these last-mentioned words is that they are all of French or Latin origin; and when we inspect the incidence of the sound in other positions, we find it only occurs – and very rarely – in words of similar source. In initial position, the sound is limited to *gigolo*; and in this word, it is likely to be replaced by the native affricate /dʒ/, as it is when it occurs in final position, in the French words *beige*, *prestige*, and *garage*. But people with pretensions to refinement are more likely to retain the 'French' pronunciation, and this is most noticeable, perhaps, in the pronunciation /gərɑːʒ/, with the fricative, beside the Anglicised /gærɪdʒ/. In sum, the sound in question occupies a marginal place in the English consonant system, especially outside RP; and even within that accent it is the least common of the consonants, its occurrence in initial and final positions conditioned historically by the desire to display the refinement attaching to the sounds of a foreign, and prestigious, language.

THREE STIGMATISED CONSONANT PRONUNCIATIONS

We saw above that certain assimilated forms that are now dialectal were once also used by upper- and middle-class speakers. Similarly, these social groups used pronunciations that are now quite heavily stigmatised. One of these involves /h/, which we have seen is often dropped in words like *he*, *him*, and *her* in unstressed position in rapid, informal style. Like the medial /ʒ/ sound in *treasure* discussed above, /h/ has a restricted incidence; but unlike /ʒ/, its position in the consonant system is much less strong than it was 1500 years ago.

In Anglo-Saxon, /h/ could occur in initial position as it can today, but it could also occur in medial position, as in *hliehhan* (laugh) and finally, as in *heah* (high). In these latter positions, the phoneme probably had a variant similar to the final sound of the Scottish word *loch*, the velar fricative /x/. /h/ also occurred in consonant-clusters, its realisation again being dependent on the position of such clusters in the word. *hn, hl, hr*, and *hw* occurred initially, as in *hnappian* (to nap), *hlaf* (loaf), *hring* (ring) and *hwæt* (what). *ht* was found medially and finally, as in *ahte* (owned) and *niht* (night); and in some post-Conquest texts, like *Sir Gawain and the Green Knight*, it is spelt with the symbol ʒ.

By the fourteenth century, it seems that the sound had been largely eliminated from initial clusters: at least, this is what spellings suggest. This process of simplification may have been motivated by systemic pressures, as in the case of *Shaw, shore* discussed above: there were not enough words depending on the opposition *hn* versus *n*, etc. Since simplification of consonant-clusters is common today in contact varieties of English, however, it may be plausible to attribute the source of the process to Anglo-French bilinguals, for whom clusters of this kind were strange. But one of them, *hw*, still survives in the speech of some older, principally female, RP users in words like *what* and *which*. These pronunciations, whose existence today has probably been reinforced by the spelling, are also found in Scots and in the speech of some New Zealanders.

The *loch* variant of the sound, which is articulated in the velar – or sometimes uvular – region of the throat, survives also in Scots, as the popular stereotype *bricht moonlicht nicht* suggests. In Scotland, its presence has perhaps been reinforced by the occurrence of a similar sound in Gaelic. But the sound has also been recorded recently in *light* and *night* along the border of Yorkshire and Lancashire; and in final position, in *thigh*, in the Pennine village of Heptonstall. In these positions, however, the sound has otherwise been lost entirely, or replaced by another fricative, as in *cough* and *enough*. In some dialects, this tendency can also be found in other words (*pluff* for plough is recorded in parts of Yorkshire) and may be viewed as the replacement by a common sound of one that is becoming infrequent – as in the case of *beige*, etc., discussed above.

Today /h/ is firm only in initial position, so it is not surprising that it is often eliminated in regional pronunciation. It seems that this was also true throughout English society from the Middle Ages, when manuscript spellings suggest its absence in pronunciation, right up to the eighteenth century, when the influence of spelling reinforced its use, and it is now the most famous shibboleth in English pronunciation. But in dialectal pronunciation, it is sometimes retained as a marker of emphasis, so we might hear *honions* for *onions;* and similar pronunciations are heard, but for different reasons, by those anxious to avoid the shibboleth, but who are unaware of the distribution of the sound. This phenomenon, known as *hypercorrection*, accounts for the initial /h/ on the pub-sign 'The King's Harms' depicted in the painting on the cover of this book.

The presence of the velar nasal /ŋ/ in the -*ing* of *going*, *seeing*, etc., also owes more to the recommendations of the codifiers than to the natural preference of speakers of English. Originally, this consonant was probably no more than a phonetic variant of /n/ before velar plosives, as in *þanc* (thank) and *tunge* (tongue). Gradually in words like *tongue* the /g/ was lost in many accents (but not those of the west midlands and north-west) so that the velar nasal itself became phonemic, enabling words like *sin* and *sing* to be contrasted by the final nasal consonant alone. The incidence of the sound had increased by the fourteenth century as the verbal terminal -*ing* developed, displacing earlier -*inde*, -*ande*, etc.; but in this, the /g/ was often lost, and the velar nasal replaced by the more frequently occurring /n/. Pronunciations like *goin'* and *seein'* have been dialectal, it seems, for at least 500 years. During the sixteenth and seventeenth centuries this pronunciation was also in use among the upper class, and has remained so in the speech of the aristocracy at least until the 1930s. *Huntin'*, *shootin'*, and *fishin'* is the linguistic stereotype of a class whose status has been secure enough for it to remain unmoved by the eighteenth-century doctrines of correctness.

Our third stigmatised pronunciation is the glottal variant of /t/. The phenomenon of glottal reinforcement, which we have seen is associated with informal RP style, is found in many English dialects; and outright replacement of the alveolar articulation by the glottal one is not uncommon in the eastern counties, especially those directly to the west of London. What is just a tendency in RP, then, has become a well-established variant in the dialects. And in the working-class pronunciation of many big cities, notably London and Glasgow, it has become the norm in final and medial position between vowels. It is in the latter position that the sound is most strongly disparaged. A glottal plosive in *butter* stands out more than in *late*, and we find that in London, Cockney women often try to avoid it in this position (preferring the affricated variant 'ts').

Since the glottal stop in English is only a variant of /t/, and not a separate phoneme, we should not be surprised if little explicit reference was made to it by observers in the past. We do not know how long the sound has been a common feature in the speech of London, for example. But it is difficult to resist the impression that stigmatisation actually promoted the use of the glottal plosive. What all the pronunciations discussed here have in common is that they seem to be spreading, especially among working-class men. In Norwich, for instance, the dropping of *h* is regular among this group, although Norfolk is an area where /h/ is traditionally sounded. And the glottal plosive is now found in many big cities, although it may be resisted in those which, like Liverpool with its heavily affricated /t/, /k/, and /g/, already have a clear regional variant. Moreover, the use of glottal pronunciations among young middle-class speakers is often cause for comment. Not only is it for this group a marker of informality, but it is also, perhaps, an emblem of values which they identify with the working class.

Use of the glottal stop is perhaps the most salient feature of an emerging regional norm known as Estuary English. Associated with the south-east of England (Estuary refers to the Thames Estuary) this accent also includes a fully vocalised final /l/, which sounds like /u/, in words like *fill* and *film*. It is becoming widespread in many professions, especially perhaps the mass media, and is often cited as evidence of linguistic decline by conservative observers in the press who apparently favour the retention of RP.

THREE REGIONAL INDICATORS

Many first-language speakers of English in England, particularly those from the north and the midlands, will have noticed at once that the system of pronunciation described for RP is different, in some important respects, from their own. We shall look at just three sounds that arouse regional sensitivities: the vowels of words like *nut* and *fun*, *pass* and *path*, and the consonant *r*. Of these, the vowels are indicators of social class as well, in that they fallaciously epitomise 'northern' pronunciation, part of a stereotype of ignorance, backwardness, and poverty still dominant in many southern minds, not least those of journalists on so-called national newspapers.

In much of the north and midlands, there is no distinction between the vowels of *put* and *putt*, *could* and *cud*. All four have the short, high, back-rounded vowel that characterises only *put* and *could* in RP. We can therefore speak of a systemic difference between accents: RP has one more short vowel–phoneme. It is worth pointing out, however, that in some accents, distinctions are made that are unknown in RP: much of Lancashire, for instance, distinguishes *look* from *luck* by having a long vowel, that of *soon*, in the first word of the pair.

From observations made by scholars during the seventeenth century, it seems likely that the current northern pattern was once much more general than it is today. Shakespeare's London audience would probably have said *nut* like today's northerner. In the south, the vowel has subsequently been lowered and unrounded, not only in RP, but in other southern dialects as well. Thus over much of southern and eastern

England, we find the possibility of a *put/putt* contrast; but the /ʌ/ vowel is, not surprisingly, realised in different ways. In Cockney, as we have seen, it is often no longer a back vowel at all, but a front one, so that *nut* sounds like *gnat* to a northerner.

We do not know how, or where, the change began. But the first thing we can establish is that there was, as it were, space in the vowel area involving the back of the tongue. We assume that the short vowel system in Shakespeare's time was as shown in Figure 5.6. There are only

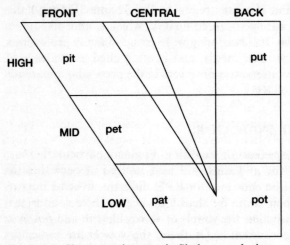

Figure 5.6 Short vowel system in Shakespeare's time

two back vowels, with a lot of space between them compared with the front vowels, where any movement up or down might bring the vowels too close together to maintain a distinction. Apart from *putt*, then, this system is much the same shape as the contemporary RP one we have described above. The vowel /ʊ/ may have developed a lower variant after certain consonants, perhaps in rapid and informal style. Indeed, there may have been a set order of consonants exerting a lowering influence. Recent research in the USA suggests that the raising of the /æ/ vowel in words like *ham* to sound like *hem* is dependent on such an order, so that only in some regions is the vowel raised before all consonants. In RP, the change seems to have been checked in words with initial lip-consonants, as in *put, bull, full*, which keep the rounded vowel also found in northern accents. But there are exceptions: *but, pun*, etc., have /ʌ/, whereas *cushion* and *sugar*, which have no initial labial consonants, do not. This complicated distribution of the sounds makes it extremely difficult for northerners to learn this part of the RP system.

In the words so far listed, the new sound can be regarded as merely a phonetic variant of /ʊ/, since its occurrence is determined by the nature of preceding consonants. But the possibility of a new contrast was emerging. Words spelt with *oo* were in process of shortening, from the vowel of *soon* (cf. *look* in Lancashire today) to its short counterpart /ʊ/. Thus the historically different sounds in *put* and, say, *stood, book*, etc., were now the same; hence *stood* versus *stud, book* versus *buck*. But when we examine the dialects, we find the lowering and unrounding process has affected even the *oo* sounding words, so that *soot, cushion, put*, and *sugar* have /ʌ/. The distribution of sounds in the south-East Midlands and East Anglia seems to be entirely unpredictable.

On the basis of this evidence, we may postulate the following origin and spread of the new /ʌ/ sound. It arose in a dialect contiguous to London, perhaps in informal style, and became associated in the city with immigrants from the area in question. In the mixing of dialects characteristic of London at this time, certain variants were associated with different social classes, each striving, consciously or otherwise, to maintain identity or distinctiveness from other social groups: what sociologists call the flight–pursuit mechanism. At some point, the new variant became prestigious with an influential social group. It was eventually adopted by the London elite, but in time became the norm in the capital, which in its turn began to influence the surrounding countryside.

Social prestige and dialect mixture may lie behind the adoption of the long, back vowel in words like *path* and *pass*. As in the case of /ʌ/, this is a change originating in the south-east; but unlike it, there is no systemic difference among accents involved. The reason for this is that two features are associated with the RP vowel: length, and a back quality. Most northern accents also have a long vowel, but a fronted one that contrasts with a short front vowel. Thus, in both north and south there is long–short opposition but the quality of the long vowel is different, and the *distribution* of long and short vowels is different. These differences are summarised in Table 5.5.

The lengthening of the originally short *a* sound in *cart* and *calf* in

Table 5.5 The distribution of long and short vowels in RP and northern accents

	RP		North		
LONG (+ back)	cart,	calf	cart,	calf	LONG (+ front)
	path	pass			
SHORT	cat,	map	cat,	map	SHORT
			path,	pass	

both RP and the north is associated with the loss of the following consonants, /r/ and /l/ (on which, see below). But in much of southern England, the vowel was lengthened before other consonants, notably the voiceless fricatives, as in *path*, *pass*, and *after* (and also before nasals followed by other consonants, as in *dance*). Both long and short vowels co-existed, it seems, in London speech from the seventeenth century; but their social values were still fluctuating well into the nineteenth century. In 1836, Walker wrote that the short vowel was 'polite', the long one 'vulgar', although the latter had formerly been fashionable. But Walker may have been fighting a rear-guard action, based perhaps on the spellings. For the long vowel eventually won out, developing the characteristic 'far back' quality – as some northerners aptly describe it – it shares with Cockney. Even today, fluctuation occurs in some words, such as *elastic*, while others, such as *gas* and *daffodil*, retain the short vowel. This may be why northerners who otherwise try to modify their accent in the direction of RP tend to retain the short vowel in *path*, *pass*, etc., whereas they often try to accommodate to the /ʌ/ versus /ʊ/ distinction by using an /ə/-type vowel: thus *nut* sounds like /nət/.

The situation in early nineteenth-century London concerning the vowel of *path* may have been similar to that of words like *cloth*, *cross*, and *off* in more recent times. The consonants in these words had also lengthened the preceding vowel in many southern dialects, so that *cross*, for instance rhymed with *horse*. This lengthened sound was also adopted into RP, but has since become something of a stereotype of an old-fashioned kind of RP. But the more recent preference for the short vowel may have been motivated by a desire to avoid a pronunciation that has also been a characteristic of Cockney. Or the pronunciation may have been influenced by the spelling.

We mentioned above that in many accents, the vowel in *cart* is long. The lengthening is associated with the loss of the /r/ sound before a consonant; and in many accents, including RP, /r/ is also lost in word-final position, as in *far* and *shore*. It seems likely that all varieties of English used to pronounce the /r/ in all these positions, as is suggested by the spelling. But by about the middle of the eighteenth century, scholars had recorded its decline in the speech of the prestigious, except where it occurs before a vowel. It is still pronounced in all positions, however, in the south-west of England, in parts of Lancashire, Yorkshire, the north-east, Scotland, South Wales, and Ireland; and also, of course, in North America.

The high incidence of /r/ in most of the accents listed is not a feature that attracts much social comment. But its south-western realisation, with the tongue curled right back, is often used as a regional stereotype, one that evokes the rather comfortable associations of life in a pleasant cider-drinking countryside. In the United States, however, it is more commonly a prestige feature. We see here the arbitrary way in which social values are attached to certain sounds: while dropping the *h* in a lower-class accent is stigmatised, few people notice that RP speakers regularly drop the *r* except before vowels.

Accents differ, then, with respect to the incidence of /r/. But the sound is also realised in many different ways in different regions. In Liverpool speech, the tongue-tip often *taps* the alveolar ridge; and in parts of Northumberland, a 'burr' is made in the back of the mouth, rather like the French /r/ we are taught in school. This sound is a uvular fricative. Moreover, '*r*-pronouncing' has profound implications for the sound-system. Not only can pairs like *lore* and *law*, *sort* and *sought* be distinguished, but it seems that the sound has had, and continues to have, a marked effect on the preceding vowel. So that when /r/ is lost after vowels, we find compensatory re-alignments in the vowel system, of which the development of a diphthong in *shore*, as mentioned above, is one example.

It is not unreasonable to assume that the precise phonetic character of /r/ was as variable in the past as it is today. Thus, it is difficult to know exactly how different *r*'s have affected preceding vowels. But modern pronunciations give us clues. In the north-east, the burred /r/ may be rare today, but its influence can still be heard in the back quality of many vowels in words such as *first*, which sounds a bit like *forced*. Similarly, the strongly retracted tongue-position of /r/ in many American accents has tended to obscure preceding vowels, so that in *hurry* and *very*, for instance, they sound alike. It seems probable that in Shakespeare's time, a similar obscuration of the vowel in words like *fern*, *shirt*, and *spur* was occurring. Originally, these would have had sequences of /e/ + /r/, etc., as the spellings suggest; but with the loss of /r/, the preceding /ə/-type sound was lengthened. In RP today, these words have the long central vowel, a sound unknown in accents which preserve /r/ in all positions. But in dialects which, like RP, have reduced the incidence of /r/, we find a radically different vowel-pattern in these words. Often the vowels are short. *First* is *fust* in parts of the south and East Anglia; and in Nottinghamshire, Lincolnshire, and parts of Yorkshire, we hear *bod* and *chotch* for *bird* and *church*.

Another development affecting a vowel before /r/ has acquired a social significance. The short /e/ vowel in words like *clerk* and *Derby* was lowered in some dialects to an /æ/ sound like that of *pat*, which, after loss of /r/ and lengthening, became identical with the vowel of *cart*. In sixteenth-century London, such *ar* variants co-existed with *er* ones (in one case, a variant pronunciation of *person*, *parson*, eventually became a new word). Until the eighteenth century, *ar* variants were fashionable, as in *sarve* and *varmin(t)* (vermin), but many of these were eventually stigmatised; perhaps the *er* spelling, fixed long before by the printers, was felt to match the other pronunciation better. But *clerk* and *Derby* retain *ar* in RP; and if these are often pronounced with *er* in working-class speech, it may be because many people have reacted against the stigmatised *ar* forms, and *hypercorrected* their pronunciation. Alternatively, the *er* pronunciations in those words may derive from the more usual development of the vowel before /r/, which may also explain their presence in the speech of the United States.

Space prevents us from dealing with less well-known, but otherwise more ancient features of traditional dialect pronunciation. In the area formerly known as Northumbria, for instance, an older front-type vowel in words like *stone* is preserved, as in the Yorkshire place-name Stainmore, 800 years after a rounded, back vowel had started to develop in such words in dialects of the south. It is assumed that this vowel is closer to the Anglo-Saxon one in *stan*, but it also seems likely that the northern pronunciation was reinforced by the Scandinavian form of the word (*steinr*) during the Viking Age. As we shall see, this Anglo-Scandinavian culture area preserved other sounds which help us to understand changes in the more recent past.

THE GREAT VOWEL SHIFT

During the fifteenth and sixteenth centuries, it seems that there were radical changes in southern pronunciation. The vowels in words such as *tide* and *house*, originally long ones, became diphthongised. Those in words like *meet* and *moot* were raised to the position formerly occupied by *tide* and *house*. Many words with *ea* spellings like *meat*, whose pronunciation had been kept separate from those spelt *ee*, were raised to the same /iː/-type vowel as in words like *meet*. And other words with *a* spellings, like *mate*, were at first raised, and then diphthongised. This generally upward movement among the vowels occurred too late for the changes to be recorded in spelling. The decisions of the printers had been made, so that our modern spellings preserve the patterns of 500 years ago.

The details of the shift are notoriously difficult to work out. We often have to contend with the puzzling, even contradictory, observations of contemporary scholars. Recent attempts to reconstruct the chronology of the changes have often, moreover, disagreed among themselves. And only in very recent times have linguists tried to suggest a motivation for

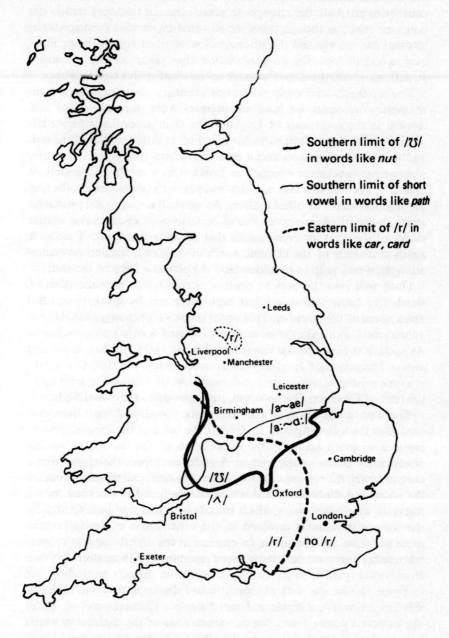

Southern limit of /ʊ/ in words like *nut*

Southern limit of short vowel in words like *path*

Eastern limit of /r/ in words like *car, card*

• Leeds

• Liverpool

• Manchester

Leicester

Birmingham /a~ae/

/a:~ɑː/

• Cambridge

/ʊ/

Oxford

/ʌ/

Bristol

London

/r/ no /r/

• Exeter

Figure 5.7 Three traditional pronunciation variants in England

the shift that is rooted in a social context. Scholars in the past have been content to attribute the changes to some inherent tendency within the language itself, as though it possessed some mysterious predisposition towards the raising and diphthongisation of front vowels. Here, however, we shall look for an explanation that takes account of social stratification and the desire to mark social identity through language.

The sixteenth- and early seventeenth-century observers whose contemporary accounts we have to interpret were men who lived and worked in the south-east of England. We shall accordingly locate the origins of the Vowel Shift in Tudor London, as different dialects mixed, and as self-consciousness about class and status intensified. As a new prestige pronunciation emerged in London as a result of the shift, it gradually spread outwards and downwards in the social scale, affecting the sound-systems of other dialects. As we shall see, regional pronunciation today often preserves sound-patterns that characterise earlier stages of the shift, or even sounds that pre-date it entirely. If we look again at dialects of the extreme north of England, we find pronunciations that may help us to understand the *phonetic* basis of the shift.

Until well into the present century, a traditional pronunciation of words like *house* and *mouse* has been preserved by speakers in rural areas north of the Humber. This vowel is not a diphthong, as in RP, but a long vowel, more like the stereotyped *hoose* of Scottish pronunciation. As such, it is closer to the vowel in RP *moon* and *soon* than *house* and *mouse*. Historians of English have assumed that a vowel of this northern type existed in words like *house* over most of England, at least up to the time of Chaucer. The *oo* vowel, then, pre-dates the Vowel Shift.

The diphthongisation of this long back vowel, /uː/, may have proceeded in the following way. Instead of the back of the tongue remaining at a constant height in the articulation of the /uː/ sound, raising began at the centre of the tongue. A glide developed, therefore, from a central vowel, /ə/, towards the /uː/ vowel. We shall call this Stage one of the process. A diphthong of this type can be heard in Cockney speech today, in words like *spoon*, which sounds a bit like *spur-oon*. Gradually the tongue movement involved in the articulation of *house* became more pronounced. The initial /ə/ element in the diphthong lost its neutral quality and took on a back vowel resonance, as in modern RP, or a front vowel quality, as in many south-eastern dialects (sounding, for instance, like *heouse*, with the initial vowel similar to *bet*). We shall call this Stage two. *The Linguistic Atlas of England* (Sanderson *et al.*, 1978) shows over a dozen distinctive pronunciations of the diphthong which have evolved in the dialects; and the sound is particularly susceptible to regional variation in the United States.

The vowel of *house* was not the only one to be diphthongised. Words like *tide* may once have sounded like /ti:d/, with a long, high front vowel similar to that found in RP *bee* and *feed.* As in *house,* a glide from the centre (but moving frontwards) may have characterised the first stage of diphthongisation. Gradually the diphthongisation has spread through all words of this class, except in certain cases. For instance, words like *night* and *right* in many northern counties retain the earlier *ee* sound, as in *it'll be reet* (right). This is because the *gh* in the spelling registers the presence of an earlier velar fricative /x/, which in these areas has been lost relatively recently, as is explained above. The fricative kept the preceding vowel short, but when it was lost, the vowel was lengthened long after other /i:/ words had been diphthongised.

We assume that a process of diphthongisation such as we have described took place in words like *house* and *tide* in southern England. The origins of the process may be sought in a casual, informal style of speech, perhaps involving the development of a 'lax' pronunciation of the diphthongs as a means of economising on articulatory energy. Alternatively, the conditioning effect of following consonants, perhaps in a set sequence (nasals, say, before fricatives, before plosives, etc.) may afford the explanation: it has been claimed that dialect maps of northern England show that in certain areas diphthongisation is still in process of occurring before certain consonants. The fortunes of *tide* and *house* are summarised in Table 5.6.

Table 5.6 Process of diphthongisation in *house* and *tide*

	Front		Back
HIGH	/ti:d/	monophthong	/hu:s/
MID	/tǝɪd/	Stage one: first element of diphthong is /ǝ/	/hǝʊs/
LOW	/taɪd/ in present RP	Stage two: first element of diphthong is a low vowel	/haʊs/ in present RP

Once the vowels of *house* and *tide* had been diphthongised, there was room for the other long vowels to move upwards. Originally, the vowel of *meet* may have been pronounced with a vowel like the *é* in the French taught in school. We can symbolise this as /e:/. The vowel in words like *moot* would have been a long back vowel of similar tongue height, /o:/. By about Shakespeare's time, it is probable that the vowels in these words were much the same in quality as they are in contemporary RP.

So far, we have described only that part of the shift where high vowels are concerned. While it is conceivable that the process began at the 'top end', it is now more usually thought that it was the raising of low vowels that triggered it. To illustrate this, we shall need to look more closely at the long front vowels, which at this time were much more numerous than is the case with contemporary RP. The vowel in *meat*, as the spelling suggests, was different from that of *meet*. *It* may have been like that of *met*, but with a longer vowel (/ɛ:/). Finally, there was *mate*, with a low, fairly front vowel, a bit like northern *mat*, only lengthened (/a:/). Our illustration now appears as shown in Table 5.7.

Table 5.7 Long front vowels in the Great Vowel Shift

		Front
HIGH	*tide*	/i:/
MID-HIGH	*meet*	/e:/
MID-LOW	*meat*	/ɛ:/
LOW	*mate*	/a:/

It was the pronunciation of words like *mate* that seems to have been crucially important in sixteenth-century London. At first this was a short vowel, which was lengthened as the final *e* (a relic of the obsolescent inflexional system in the grammar) ceased to be pronounced; its phonetic quality would have differed from region to region. In some south-eastern dialects, notably those of Kent and Essex, it seems to have developed a relatively high pronunciation. Such a raising may be associated with forceful styles of speech, since it has been found that increased articulatory energy tends to raise front vowels. We do not have any knowledge of other sounds in these dialects at this time, but it is possible that if *mate* had a fairly high vowel, then either it had merged with *meat*, or *meat* had been raised to merge with *meet*. We can see here, then, the possibility that the Great Vowel Shift involved the 'pushing upward' of the long front vowels by the development of words like *mate*.

If we compare our diagram above with those representing modern RP earlier in the chapter (Figures 5.2 and 5.3), we find that *meet* has been raised to the high front position formerly occupied by *tide*, and *meat* now has the same vowel as *meet*. The vowel in *mate* has been raised, to the position formerly occupied by *meet,* but has since (by about 1800) been diphthongised. In regional pronunciations, however, we find different patterns. Some dialects of the north midlands have a diphthongal pronunciation of *meat* (sounding like *mate* to RP ears) which keeps it distinct from *meet.* And in many regional accents of the north, the vowel in words like *mate* is not diphthongised, but retains the character of the vowel in the south before diphthongisation.

We have now outlined most of the changes involved in the shift. But we have yet to suggest the mechanism. As we have seen, a relatively high variant of the vowel in *mate* was associated with the speech of Essex and Kent, and as we saw in chapter two, Kentish was a stigmatised dialect. The London bourgeoisie, then, would want to distance its own pronunciation from that of the lower class, which was constantly being swelled by immigrants from these areas. One way of doing this was to raise the vowel of *mate* even higher than that of the lower-class variant; and raising of the lowest vowel in the system would necessitate raising all the vowels above and, ultimately, pushing the vowel of *tide* into a diphthong. It seems that in the speech of the bourgeoisie, the vowel of *mate* was raised to a height close to that of *meat,* so that some observers actually recorded a merger of the two sounds. It is arguable whether this actually occurred; but what the contemporary observers in the six-teenth century seem to have recorded is a picture of enormous complex-ity, with three competing systems in this area of long front vowels. The aristocracy, now no longer able to distance itself with the use of French, seems at first to have kept *mate*, *meat*, and *meet* distinct. At the other extreme, a third system had merged *meat* and *meet*. It appears that this was the lower-class pattern: and the fact that it is this that eventually formed the pattern for the future prestige accent need not surprise us. As is often the case, the unacceptable yesterday becomes the acceptable today.

Part III

Imposition and spread

6   The imposition of English in the British Isles

It is possible to argue that in the course of the last four centuries the minority languages of the British Isles have been undermined by English political and economic power, the policies of English governments, and English attitudes, both official and unofficial. The opprobrium cast on the regional dialects of England has been visited, on a grander scale, and with far-reaching consequences, on the speech of regions diverse in language and culture, and situated far away from the metropolitan south-east. In this chapter we shall trace the long and complicated history of English as a dominant language throughout the British Isles. We shall see how a northern variety of English was developed as the language of an independent Scottish state, and how that variety was displaced in official domains by metropolitan English after the union of parliaments in 1707. Next, we shall consider how the Celtic languages have been maintained, and even promoted, despite generations of linguistic domination. In Ireland, we see a version of English colonialism, and the only territory where a Celtic tongue has become an official language. We shall then consider the maintenance, first of Gaelic in the Scottish Highlands, and then of Welsh, the object of a recent and vigorous campaign of promotion. Finally, we shall discuss two cases of what has been termed language death, the abandoning of Cornish and Manx as the first languages of the local Celtic communities.

With one important exception, the languages with which we are dealing are Celtic, and therefore structurally distant from English. They represent two branches of the Celtic language-family. The Gaelic of Ireland, and its implantations in the Scottish Highlands and the Isle of Man, form one branch. Welsh and Cornish, together with the Breton of north-west France, are more closely related to the British Celtic that was displaced during the Anglo-Saxon settlement, as described in chapter one. While the two branches had diverged considerably, rather as, say, Swedish, Norwegian, and Danish have done, there was contact between the languages of each branch, at least until English domination severed the links. Such contacts ensured a degree of mutual intelligibility between Gaelic-speaking Irish and Scottish Highlander, and between Welsh and Cornish; but since the imposition of English, the absence of a centre in either branch of Celtic has precluded any tendencies towards standardisation and hastened the proliferation of regional varieties. However hard it may be to speak of a 'standard' English, it is even harder to speak of a standard Welsh, or a standard Scottish Gaelic.

Before we deal with the one exception mentioned above, it is necessary to point out that the story as outlined in this chapter so far represents a particular point of view. It has been told from the perspective of the Celtic communities themselves; more particularly, from the perspective of Celtic nationalism. In the sense adopted here, nationalism is based on the premiss that the most potent symbol of cultural uniqueness and political autonomy is the possession of a distinctive 'native' language. So that any weakening of the bond between people and language – a bond nationalists see as natural – is seen as an erosion of self-esteem and communal integrity.

It should already be clear that this view of language may be difficult to square with what we have seen elsewhere in this book of actual behaviour in bi- or multilingual communities. In the course of both this chapter and the next we shall see how far this nationalist perspective can explain the language-behaviour of people who live outside England, how far it remains an issue only for the middle-class intelligentsia, amongst whom it has flourished for less than two centuries, and, indeed, how far it is possible to describe the spread of English in neutral terms.

The exception yet to be dealt with is Scots. In origin a variant of the Northumbrian dialect of the Anglo-Saxons, Scots has been spoken in south-eastern Scotland almost as long as in England. But outside Scotland, it has rarely been accorded the status of a separate language, partly because attitudes to it have been governed by purely linguistic criteria, and partly because English people have often found it convenient to forget that Scotland was not politically united with England until 1707. This political factor inevitably complicates assessment of the current status of Scots; in fact, it constitutes one of the best examples of the difficulty of drawing the line between a dialect and a language. As we shall see, our stance on this issue will depend on the relative weight we attach to different kinds of criteria.

Whatever status we accord Scots, we must acknowledge that English has most successfully been imposed throughout the British Isles.

Aggression and expansionism have emanated from England since Norman times. This stance was part of a wider European process known as internal colonisation, in which peripheral areas of Europe were increasingly dominated and exploited by the centre. Thus, by the twelfth century, Norman nobles had buttressed southern and eastern Wales with great castles, and had established a presence in Ireland. The Welsh aristocracy was finally defeated in the thirteenth century; and in time, Ireland was to become the first English colony, its land confiscated for the benefit of outsiders. Scotland alone withstood military conquest; but by the early eighteenth century English domination had been achieved through political ingenuity. Thus, though their language has never figured in census returns like the Celtic ones, many speakers of Scots have felt, and still feel, that they themselves are a linguistic minority whose linguistic traditions have suffered at the hands of the English.

Unlike the imposition of Latin in Europe, the spread of English was not dependent on military victories. Nor did it confront oral vernaculars; Wales and Ireland both had developed languages and traditions of literacy as old as the English, and Scots, in the later Middle Ages, was also used for literary and legal purposes. But in other respects, the story is familiar. English in most cases has had a long time to take root; it has acted, and still acts, as a lingua franca. And, there have been obvious material advantages in learning it: industrialisation, and the consequent disruption of life in rural areas, has meant that many people have had to learn English to get employment.

As an imposed language, English has had a symbolic value clearly different from that of the minority languages. On the one hand, as the official language of a power often regarded as alien and remote, it has often been redolent of authority and high social status. It also became of course, the language of social aspiration and economic advancement. On the other hand, it has often been felt to lack those virtues of warmth, sincerity, and local dignity associated with the minority languages. We see here a replication of the symbolic values accorded to those varieties perceived in England as local, versus that perceived as 'standard'. Throughout the British Isles, therefore, the latter has often been seen as useful, but impersonal; effective, but neutral and cold.

The history of English outside England has two major strands. We must first describe how varieties of English – often local ones – were established in the early Plantations of English settlers such as those in Wales and Ireland, and how those varieties developed in the relative isolation of their new locations. Second, we must trace the imposition of metropolitan English as the language of administration, law, and education, a process associated with the Tudors but in the case of

Ireland begun in the late Middle Ages. This task is impossible to do without reference to the sociolinguistic history of the minority languages themselves. Thus, we must know something about the functions of those languages in the past, how they have been maintained, and how they are being promoted, just as we needed to explore, in chapter one, the factors involved in language imposition, maintenance, and shift in the period of Anglo-Saxon settlement, and beyond. The history of *relationships* between speakers of different languages, then, cannot just involve the history of the dominant language.

So far, we have used the term *minority* in reference to the languages under discussion. Logically a minority language should be one spoken by only a minority of the population in a given area. Here we are using it differently, in the sense of a language quite widely spoken, but subordinated to a *dominant* language, in this case English. Only in Eire has the minority language been declared a 'national', official one – but there we need to distinguish between its declared status and its actual use among the mass of the population. The other surviving Celtic languages have varying functions and sociolinguistic profiles. Formerly discouraged by England, their status in recent years has been at best that of tolerated languages, although governments in London tended to ignore their existence. More recently still, they have sometimes been *promoted*, not by central government, but by local agencies often concerned to advance the cause of nationalism. Interest in the languages has been kindled, especially among the middle class, and increasingly they have been learned as second, or additional languages. The best known instance of such newly engendered language-loyalty is the recent campaign to promote Welsh, a language which has also, like Gaelic in Ireland and the Highlands of Scotland, been maintained as the first language of some small, isolated local communities. But interest in minority languages has also occurred in the absence of any native speakers at all, as in Cornwall and the Isle of Man. And it has affected the attitudes of speakers of Scots. During the past three decades in particular, Scots has become a focus for language-loyalty, particularly in Scotland's universities.

The imposition of English throughout the British Isles is a process of such length and complexity that it is difficult to make generalisations that are valid for all territories. Nor is it always possible to respect national boundaries and sensitivities. Scotland, for instance, has been split culturally, ethnically, and linguistically for well over a thousand years; this means that we must deal with its Scots-speaking community quite separately from its Gaelic one, for the simple reason that linguistic history only indirectly follows the history of nation-states. In addition, the special relationship between English and Scots must be explored within a framework different from that of contact between English and the Celtic languages.

Two broad generalisations about the process of imposition may perhaps be made. First, we shall see the significance of the Tudors – who were, ironically enough, of Welsh descent – in helping to shape official attitudes towards minority languages in the rest of the British Isles. Although the Tudor monarchs, like some of their Continental counterparts, clearly saw the importance of language as an instrument of political and social control, it is unlikely that they had a coherent policy of language suppression, even though that may ultimately have been an *effect* of their actions. This, incidentally, had profound consequences for Scots, even though neither the Tudors nor their successors were likely to have seen it as a separate language. Second, it was the educational system that everywhere was instrumental in disseminating a taught variety of English. And after the introduction in 1870 of universal primary education, no other language was even recognised in the schools. Significantly enough, in the twentieth century it is in education that campaigns to promote the minority languages have found both a focus, and some notable successes.

THE DEVELOPMENT OF SCOTS

The split in the cultural traditions of Scotland goes back at least as far as the seventh century AD. By then, the Anglo-Saxons of Northumbria had extended their kingdom to roughly where Edinburgh now stands, adding to the original Celtic population. From the west, Gaels from Ireland had established a kingdom over most of Scotland north of the Forth. By the eleventh century, Scotland had a Gaelic dynasty, its kingdom stretching from the north-west Highlands to the area of the present border with England, although the Outer Isles and parts of the extreme north-east had yet to be wrested from the Norwegians. But the Northumbrian dialect of south-east Scotland was still spoken; and links with England were strengthened by the arrival of refugees from the Norman Conquest. The court and church were Anglicised; land was granted to men from England (some of whom spoke Norman-French) and many English-speaking people settled in Scottish towns. Gradually the influence of Gaelic contracted to the Highland area while southern Scotland, with its Northumbrian admixture developed a culture that was partly Germanic, partly Celtic.

Scotland was at first successful in resisting the territorial ambitions of the English kings. After Bannockburn in 1314, Scotland enjoyed

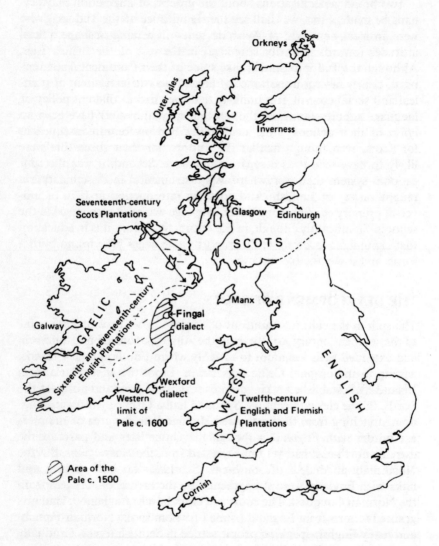

Figure 6.1 The imposition of English in the British Isles

some form of independence from its expansionist neighbour for nearly 400 years. During this period, the Scottish court cultivated contacts with France, and developed its own educational institutions, parliament, law, and literature. And in the opinion of many, the Scottish variant of the Northumbrian dialect was developed as the language of these institutions, to the point where we can speak of Scots as a language separate from, though related to, English.

The centuries of independence saw Scots emerge as a developed vernacular. We see a process of functional elaboration, similar to that described in relation to English in chapter two, except that it was Latin, not French that was replaced in official domains. In 1390, Scots was first used for parliamentary records; and the laws were translated into it in 1425. Moreover, an impressive literature was written from the fourteenth century onwards. The relationship between the literary Scots of this period and that of English can be judged from lines like these, taken from William Dunbar (?1460–1521):

> lut schulderis and luttard bak,
> Quhilk natur maid to beir a pak,

where *lut* means 'bent', *luttard* 'stooping', *quhilk* is a Scots spelling of 'which', *beir* of 'bear'. Interestingly enough, we witness during the sixteenth century the same kind of agonising about the suitability of Scots for literary purposes as we saw in our discussion of English.

The cultivation of Scots was not, it seems, accompanied by a consciousness that it was, or should be, different from English. Such language-consciousness dates from the late eighteenth century, with the origins of modern nationalist thought. Even though a section of the Scottish nobility purported, like modern nationalists, to speak on behalf of the entire population, patriotism in medieval Scotland was based on antipathy to England, much like the anti-French patriotism of the English themselves. Sections of the Scottish bourgeoisie probably also favoured greater contact with England for economic reasons. The replacement of Latin by Scots was probably seen as a question of vernacularisation rather than of the explicit promotion of a 'national' language. Although contemporary observations are almost entirely lacking, the process of standardisation is most clearly seen, perhaps, in literature: a literary norm was emerging, for poetry, and more crucially, for prose. To sum up: by the end of the sixteenth century Scots may be seen as the language of an independent Scottish state and a large section of Scotland's population. It could have become what today is called a national language if its subsequent development had not been dominated by the imposition of English.

The undermining of Scots was not the result of decrees and proscriptions, but of the gradual weakening of independent Scottish institutions. The Reformation, which played such a key part in Tudor policy, had its strong adherents among sections of the Scottish bourgeoisie, so there was no need for the English to impose it. Elsewhere in the British Isles, the language of religion has often proved an important factor in language maintenance; but in southern Scotland, it does not seem to have been an issue. Scots accordingly never became the language of prayer books and Bible in Scotland, and this seems to have been vital in exposing Scottish people to the metropolitan language of England. This variety was also disseminated in a great deal of printed literature at this time. Scotland had its own presses, but these printed English forms alongside those of Scots. Other Scottish institutions were soon to be eroded. In 1603, the Union of Crowns meant that a Scottish king was on the throne of England; but it was at London that he held his court. Gradually the most privileged and powerful class in Scotland adopted the language of England.

Finally, the Act of Union in 1707 ensured that Scotland's laws and administrative arrangements were determined in London, and therefore in English. By the eighteenth century Scots had become the Low language, and metropolitan English was now the medium of law, administration, education, and religion. And in language, as well as politically, it was 'the end of an auld sang', as was said in Scotland at the time.

From the eighteenth century onwards, the gentry of Scotland tended to receive an English education. This meant that all ideas about the best or most correct usage were articulated with respect to English; no variety of Scots was codified. Scots, therefore, came to be seen as a dialect, to be disparaged; there was a proliferation of books listing Scotticisms to be avoided in polite company. The first Scottish Members of Parliament, finding their accents derided in the English parliament, strove to sound like Englishmen. Like the dialects of England, Scots lost all social status, and its use in school was punished after the 1872 Education Act.

Unlike the dialects of England, however, Scots was never reduced to a patois. A literary tradition was maintained, by people such as Burns; and in the nineteenth century Scots was used to record versions of ballads and folk-songs as they were found by assiduous Scottish collectors. In the twentieth century, attempts have been made by poets like Hugh MacDiarmid to promote Scots as the medium for a serious and tough-minded poetry that was international in character without losing its Scottishness, but which was unencumbered by the traditional associations of Burns. The maintenance or re-creation of a literary prose tradition has been more problematic, since continuity was interrupted in the sixteenth century. There are few models for serious, expository prose, and even in the novel, Scots has gone the way of English dialects in that writers have tended to use it in depictions of regional or lower-class dialogue only. Modern Scottish novelists must cultivate their own literary language, as MacDiarmid had to do for poetry; but it is worth noting that one writer, Lewis Grassic Gibbon, achieved this in the 1930s with *A Scots Quair*.

Outside imaginative literature, however, a Scots prose tradition was maintained in popular Scottish newspapers, particularly those of the north-east, where there is a strong loyalty to the local form of Scots. And in 1983 a Scots translation of the New Testament appeared, a work hailed as a monument of prose style and literary achievement, even as a turning-point in the fortunes of Scots. Since then there have been numerous experiments with written Scots within what has become a vigorous literary culture in Scotland.

The notion that Scots is at most a dialect of English has been communicated to most Scottish people. With no census returns to remind them of the number of speakers of Scots, and no classical texts to give them a sense of historicity – save, perhaps, the *New Testament* – many Scottish people, like some speakers of English-based creoles, may feel that their tongue is not different enough from English to justify calling it a separate language. In other words, it is linguistic criteria that are uppermost in their minds (as they are in the minds of most English people in their attitude to Scots): Scots sounds, grammar, and vocabulary are close to those of English in a way that those of Gaelic, say, are not. But purely linguistic criteria are not enough in settling demarcation disputes of this kind. Speakers of Dutch dialects, say, on the border with Germany, may understand speakers of neighbouring German dialects better than they can the speakers of Dutch dialects on the other side of Holland; but the conventional wisdom is that people who live in Holland speak Dutch, and that Germans speak German. To call Scots a dialect of English is to ignore its development during Scottish independence, and to reduce its status to that of the regional dialects of England, unless we use the term *dialect* in a more specialised sense, to refer to regional varieties with their own traditions of writing (as we speak of the dialects of English in medieval times). In sum, the terms *dialect* and *language* are not fine enough to apply unequivocally to Scots.

Opponents of the view that Scots and English are separate languages are likely to argue that many alleged Scots usages can be found in northern dialects of English. Boundaries between usages, for instance, do not by any means always run parallel with the border. Even if they do at present, it can be shown that certain usages alleged to be Scots, like *gaed* (went) and bellies being *sair* (sore) instead of aching, used to be heard either in Northumberland or Cumbria and have only recently been replaced by a less localised English form. Geographical patterns of usage are often complex: sometimes areas on each side of the border share a form unknown outside dialectal English, such as the Anglo-Saxon word *heck* (hay-rack), and occasionally the border divides forms that are also dialectal, like Scots *pook* (to pluck) beside northern English *ploat*. Relationships of this kind are typical of the border areas between dialects; but so they are between different though related languages.

Differences between Scots and English are often therefore not absolute, but may be expressed in terms of general tendencies and frequencies of items. But we can still point to some items that seem characteristic Scots usages. We find a different selection of loan-words north of the border, as in *gar* (make), *gowk* (cuckoo) from Scandinavian. Many Scots loans from French, such as *dote* (endow), *vivers* (victuals), *howtowdie* (young hen) are not found in England because they were adopted during the early sixteenth century, at a time of close political contact with France. Some Gaelic words, such as *tocher* (dowry) and *clarsach* (harp) are not well-known in England. Modal verbs are sometimes used differently: *will I push it?* instead of the usual English use of *shall*.

Differences in pronunciation are striking. Above all, they are often of a clearly systemic kind. Not only is there a different system of vowels before /r/ – *fern*, *fir*, and *fur* often have /e/, /ɪ/, and /ʌ/ respectively – but there is a significant point of divergence from all varieties of English in that vowel *length* is a contrastive feature of much less importance. It has been suggested that Scots vowels are to be regarded as short except in certain positions: finally (as in *see*), before /r/ (*seer*), and before voiced fricatives (*seethe*). Elsewhere (in *seat* and *seed*, for instance) the vowel would be short. We find a similar pattern with diphthongs. /aɪ/ is longer in *drive* than *ride*, and each diphthong may be regarded as a separate phoneme. Distinctions are also conditioned by morphology: *tied*, the past tense of *tie*, is pronounced differently from *tide*. These patterns of length are so pervasive that the pronunciation of most Scottish people must be described independently of any English sound-system. Even those who adopt an accent that is close to RP will tend to merge distinctions usually made in England: *pull*, *pool*, and *boot* often have the same, short vowel, as do *cot* and *caught*.

Other, more well-known features of Scots pronunciation we have already noted in our description of northern dialect sounds in chapter five. The stereotypes *there's a moose loose aboot the hoose* and *it's a braw bricht moonlicht nicht the nicht* testify to the retention of the undiphthongised vowel in words like *house*, and of the fricative in *night*. Other pronunciations, such as the unrounded vowel in words like *hame* (home) are reflected in traditional Scots spellings. But within Scotland, many of these pronunciations are regarded as broad, and often stigmatised, just as other features (including words and grammatical patterns) are marked regionally, and stylistically. It is for this reason that the study of Scots in many Scottish universities has tended to promote the idea that it is a language separate from English, with its own history, its own dimensions of regional, social, and stylistic variation, and to some extent its own norms.

Recent studies of sociolinguistic variation in southern Scotland tend to suggest, however, that in many respects local speech is *exonormative*: English norms are highly influential. As we have seen, Scotland's upper class had begun to adopt the standards of the London elite during the eighteenth century; more recently, the middle class has moved in the same direction. This is partly a means of avoiding the heavily stigmatised speech of the working class in the big cities, such as the Edinburgh use of tags like *ken?* (do you know?) and the Glasgow use of the glottal plosive. Many middle-class speakers are over-anxious to adopt an accent similar to RP: the somewhat archaic stereotypes known as the Kelvinside and Morningside accents (after certain districts in Glasgow and Edinburgh) may be regarded as attempts to preserve a kind of RP similar to 'refayned' pronunciation used by people – older women, especially – in various cities of England. The diphthongs in these accents appear to be hypercorrect: in words like *side*, the first element of the diphthong is raised almost to the /e/ of *set*, so that it sounds like *sade*. In pronunciation, therefore, it is helpful to distinguish between Scots, which itself exists in regional dialectal variety in different parts of Scotland, and which is characterised by those features, among others, listed earlier, and a so-called educated Scottish accent, which is much closer to RP. The latter is one of the most prestigious regional accents of English.

Scots usages are most consistently found among working-class speakers. While a middle-class Scot may say *I'll not be going home* – a construction not uncommon in the north of England also – a farmworker might say *I'll no be gaun hame*. But in the big industrial cities, usage is changing, just as it is in England: and sometimes it may be described as moving away from a base in Scots. Thus, while a recent recording of an Edinburgh schoolboy shows the retention of the traditional vowel in *house*, research in the same city shows that among the working class, especially young men, pronunciation of *r* is very different from the 'trilled' or 'tapped' variants stereotypical of Scots, and is so weakly articulated that the accent of this group has actually been described as *r*-less.

Whatever linguistic changes are under way in Scotland, commitment to Scots has increased in recent years. In part this is a reflection of growing nationalism, seen in the electoral successes of the Scottish National Party (although that party has shown little interest in Scots, as distinct from Gaelic). Language-loyalty has also been inspired by the example of the Welsh Language Society's vigorous campaign. Nationalism, however, tends to obscure divisions of class and ethnic group but those issues surface, in rather subtle ways, when commitment to a particular language is espoused. Many younger, middle-class Scots resent what they see as the Anglicisation of their culture, and their loyalty to Scots may be a belated assertion of ethnicity. They want to see themselves as Scots, not citizens of the United Kingdom; and within the last decade, there has been a widespread demand for political autonomy. But since it has in general been the lower class that has maintained the minority languages, commitment to those languages is also, in part, a commitment to the values of that class. Similar motivations, incidentally, may underlie attitudes to Welsh. It has been persuasively argued that the group most loyal to that language are the heirs to the Welsh tradition of political radicalism that earlier in this century manifested itself in trade unionism and Labour Party politics. University- and college-educated sons and daughters of miners and steelworkers see their national identity as an emblem of class, and of the older, co-operative and collective values of the community.

Feelings of language-loyalty must be taken into account in any consideration of the sociolinguistic profile of Scots today. Many Scottish people feel justifiably bitter at finding their linguistic inheritance relegated to a paragraph or two in histories of English, and dismissed as just another dialect of English. So recent Scots language activism has focused on the teaching of Scots in the education system, the status of Scots as a minority language within the European Community, and the issue of representation in the 2001 census. But nationalist feeling is also apt to inspire arguments that are clearly manipulative. Scotland deserves independence: independent nations have their own language: therefore Scots must be a different language from English. This view places a high value on the Scots literary tradition as markedly different in language from the English one, and as having survived the Middle Ages, unlike in any other regional variety of English.

The current status of Scots may accordingly be defined in two different ways. If we accept the view that English is an international language, the property of no single nation, then we can view Scots as the first *national* variety of English outside England, just as American English is a later one. This view respects national sensitivities, and also the linguistic similarities between all varieties of English. Alternatively, we can see Scots as a *deposed* language, which would have enjoyed the kind of relationship to English as, say, Portuguese to Spanish, if the dominant language had not been imposed in Scotland. Our choice between these alternatives may depend to a large extent on which side of the border we happen to live!

LANGUAGE IMPOSITION IN THE CELTIC TERRITORIES: SOME GENERAL CONSIDERATIONS

We have mentioned the importance of the Tudors in the formulation of policy towards England's neighbours. It was they who took the first steps towards formal unification with other territories, and therefore towards the imposition of English as the official language throughout the British Isles. Religious uniformity was one instrument of hegemony, and this meant carrying the Reformation to the linguistic minorities. But supremacist attitudes towards minority languages could undermine the ideal of religious conversion: an effective way of achieving the latter was to make translations of the Prayer Book and Bible into the minority languages, and populate the Church in those lands with priests who could preach in them. Ironically enough, the survival of Scottish Gaelic and Welsh may have depended, to a large extent, on this 'historic blunder': those languages gained prestige by remaining the parlance of the Church.

The ambitions of the Tudors, and in particular of subsequent governments, may be compared in this respect with those of the other centralising European monarchies, particularly France and Spain. It is noteworthy that nations where power is devolved on a federal basis generally have a more tolerant attitude to linguistic minorities, as in Switzerland. But in France, the Celtic-speaking Bretons have been subjected to centuries of oppression; and in Spain, the Catalans in the east of the country suffered under the dominant Castilians until power was devolved to the regions following democratisation in the late 1970s. Wherever we find this linguistic imperialism, we find a similar ideology expressed by the dominant power: bi- or multi-lingualism is incompatible with a unified 'nation' and a free people, therefore the minority languages are associated with 'the enemy' – either secular, or religious; therefore to use them is to identify with the opponents of the State.

Spuriously benign arguments are often advanced to justify the process of suppression. Gaelic in Scotland, after all, was in the eighteenth century the language of 'savages'; English was therefore a civilising force. And in nineteenth-century Wales, it was even suggested that the use of Welsh was a *cause* of poverty: if people would only learn the right language, they could better themselves.

A number of techniques, of varying degrees of subtlety, were used by the English to impose their language. The various Celtic communities have therefore felt different effects at different times. The Cornish were an early casualty of Tudor centralisation: their language ceased to function as a community medium by the end of the eighteenth century. In Wales Anglicisation was begun in the sixteenth century by weaning the sons of noblemen away from their subjects by educating them in England. This removed the source of patronage for vernacular poetry and song, which subsequently became a culture of the lower class. Furthermore, the introduction of English as the language of government and law broke local traditions of prose. By the early seventeenth century, a similar process of weaning had begun among the Gaels of the Scottish Highlands; and by then, the Irish chieftains had been defeated. This broke the cultural and linguistic links between Gaelic speakers in Scotland and Ireland, just as contacts between speakers of Welsh, Cornish, and Breton had already been destroyed. In the case of the Scottish Highlands, however, the full force of linguistic oppression was not felt until after the middle of the eighteenth century.

In Ireland, the picture is complicated by religious division. The Tudors encountered great difficulties in extending the Reformation to Ireland, and the Irish chieftains proved resilient in defence of their lands. Since England was at war with Catholic Spain, it could not afford to have an unreformed Church on its doorstep. Treatment of Ireland and the Irish, therefore, was characterised by brutality and paranoia. Ireland became England's first colony, its ancient local culture overlaid by a Protestant English-speaking one. Settlers from England and Scotland were planted on land confiscated from the Irish, and merchant companies in London were given a free hand to plunder its resources. Like Wales, Ireland had been colonised by small numbers of English-speakers during the twelfth century; but unlike Wales, Ireland was to endure a further, much more significant plantation under the Tudors and Stuarts. Irish Gaelic has therefore had eight centuries of contact with English of one kind or another; yet alone of the Celtic languages, it has become the official language of an independent nation-state. We shall accordingly be treating Ireland in more detail than the other Celtic communities.

Throughout the Celtic British Isles, the education system was a powerful agent in the imposition of English. One result of the processes discussed above was that standardisation in any Celtic language had been difficult to maintain, and the breaking of links among Celtic peoples had undermined the sense of historicity that plays such an important part in forming people's attitudes to their own language. Even if opportunities had been given, the use of the Celtic languages even as media of instruction would have been accompanied by great problems. But the education system overwhelmingly favoured English. Even before the Education Acts of the 1870s, schools in Ireland had been used to promote English, although Wales had maintained traditions of Welsh teaching in the Circulating Schools of the eighteenth century. But after the introduction of compulsory schooling in the last quarter of the nineteenth century, teachers punished children if they spoke their first language, and denied them opportunities of reading and writing in them. Older, first-language speakers of Welsh, for instance, today often cannot write a letter in their own language. Not only was education often punitive from a linguistic point of view, it was also Anglocentric, in that children learned about the history and culture, not of their own societies, but of the English and their empire, in the English language. The role of the education system was summed up very well in the nineteenth century by the MP who said: 'a band of efficient schoolmasters is kept up at much less expense than a body of police or soldiery'.

The survival of the Celtic languages was also threatened by economic factors. In general, the Celtic communities are situated well away from the centres of technological development: for this reason they are often insultingly referred to as the Celtic fringe. They have tended to be over-dependent on a small number of traditional industries, such as farming, crofting, and fishing, and therefore offer limited opportunities for employment today. In the past, the local economy in two areas has been especially vulnerable to upheavals which have had profound and lasting effects on demographic structure. In the Scottish Highlands, massive depopulation followed the unsuccessful Rising of 1745. By the early nineteenth century, the Highland lairds had been so successfully weaned away from their subjects that they preferred the profits from sheep, and later, deer, to the overseeing of the local communities. Gaelic speakers were evicted in their thousands, many emigrating to the industrialised cities of southern Scotland and also to Canada (where today, in places like Cape Breton Island, Gaelic is still spoken). Land once cultivated yielded to the wilderness. In Ireland, the potato famines of the 1840s hit hardest the Gaelic speakers of the west: death or emigration

reduced Ireland's population by one-quarter. Such population movements have tended to unbalance many communities with regard to sex
and age: it was often the young, able-bodied men who were lost to the
large towns. And where urbanisation has occurred, such as in south
Wales, the Celtic tongues have failed to compete as first languages with
English, the language of commerce, and of the employing class.

The psychological effects of centuries of cultural and linguistic
imperialism on speakers of the minority languages have been severe.
The processes of government and law, enshrined in an alien language,
have often been disorientating, if not totally mystifying, to the community. A sense of powerlessness undermined the feeling of local identity. This has often been exacerbated by the education system, where
success at first was equated with proficiency in English, and later with
working far away; discouraged and demoralised, those who remained
in the local community often awaited and expected initiative and lead-
ership from 'incomers'. At the more personal level, many speakers of
each minority tongue were often made to feel ashamed of their first
language. Linguistically insecure, and therefore nervous, if not sullenly
defiant in their use of English, children in the schools of Scotland and
Wales were often judged 'inarticulate', like their Black counterparts in
the USA.

It is not surprising that there has been a substantial language shift
towards English in the Celtic areas over the last century and a half.
Indeed, some pessimistic observers have predicted extinction for some
Celtic languages by the end of the next century. The census returns to
some extent speak for themselves. First-language speakers of Scottish
Gaelic amounted to about 5 per cent of Scotland's population ninety
years ago; today, it is only about one-third of that figure. In Ireland,
native speakers of Gaelic were estimated at about 23 per cent in 1851;
forty years on, the figure was 14 per cent. Welsh proved more durable:
the period of language shift is the present century. But in 1900 perhaps
half of the population of Wales could speak Welsh; since 1971 the
figure has stabilised at around one-fifth. And in the course of the present century, Manx has been abandoned as a first language altogether.

Yet in some important respects, these figures do not speak for themselves. How do they relate to different social functions, differences of
age and sex, and of town and country? Can people read and write in the
minority languages? Data on these issues is often lacking for the past.
Today, however, we know that the figures quoted for Scottish Gaelic
need to be balanced against the fact that in Harris, in the Outer Isles,
over 75 per cent of the population can speak the minority language. We
need to know about the users of these languages, since the symbolic

value of a language derives in part from its association with certain social groups and contexts. Such knowledge can also help explain how languages are maintained and promoted and how, why, and where English is learned.

The census figures also obscure another important fact. At first, native speakers of Celtic languages would have learned English as a second language. Such bilingualism would be diglossic, with English as the High language. Since the end of the nineteenth century, however, nationalist campaigns have been mounted in Ireland, the Scottish Highlands, and later Wales to arrest the decline of the Celtic languages by teaching them as second languages. In the course of the present century, therefore, English has become the first language of increasing numbers of people in Celtic areas, while it is the Celtic tongues that have been learned as second languages. So knowledge of Scottish Gaelic has risen; and in the Republic of Ireland, Gaelic is generally taught in school. But there, first-language speakers are outnumbered by ten to one; and as we shall see, the second-language speakers of all the Celtic tongues tend to be different kinds of people from those who maintain Celtic as first languages in the more remote, less fertile areas.

A minority language can be maintained as the first language of the local community if there is little incentive to replace it with the dominant one. In the Outer Hebrides, and parts of the west of Ireland, isolated communities that are dependent on traditional industries, such as crofting, have maintained Gaelic as a community language. While emigration from these areas has been constant, it has still been possible for a small number of people to continue living much as their ancestors did. But since job opportunities for young people remain scarce in such a limited economy, the pull of English has been strong. In such an environment Gaelic has been maintained among the crofting class despite the absence of overt expressions of language-loyalty on the part of its speakers. All the same, Gaelic is seen by them as a symbol of group identity, even if it is rarely articulated in these terms. The language binds the community together in defiance of the values associated with the wider, urban, commercial world where English is spoken.

While the towns and cities have generally been the bastions of the English language, they have also been the only refuge for people unable to find subsistence in the countryside. In what often seem inhospitable and alien surroundings, immigrants from the Celtic-speaking areas have sometimes retained and subsequently promoted the minority language, as a symbol of their identity and their past. It has been said that Glasgow – which in 1971 for instance had 12,000 Gaelic speakers – is the place to hear Gaelic spoken in Scotland, and in Ireland, Belfast. Thus, it is among such emigrés that the potential for feelings of language-loyalty, of expressions of commitment to the minority language, have normally developed.

It is in the towns and cities too, that people have been stimulated to learn minority tongues as second or additional languages. This trend is most noticeable among younger people, often from middle-class backgrounds. The most vociferous expressions of language-loyalty have perhaps been those of the Welsh Language Society; but such activism has also spread to Scotland in more recent years. The campaign on behalf of Gaelic has intensified, and as we have seen, Scots has also been involved. The intellectual origins of such campaigns are complex, but stem in part from the notion that language is the crucial symbol of nationality. From the end of the eighteenth century, but especially after the 1840s, struggles for independence in Europe and beyond have often been inspired, or justified, by the fact that a particular group speaks a language different from that of a dominant or conquering power. It is unlikely, however, that this language-loyalty was ever much in evidence amongst the first-language speakers of the Celtic tongues during the nineteenth century, such as the Irish peasantry of the west or the working class in newly-industrialised South Wales. Amongst these, language attitudes were probably much more instrumentalist, a matter of *choosing* English for its usefulness, and of gradually abandoning the Celtic languages which for them lacked a positive symbolic value.

The long-term survival of the minority languages will depend on more than just the declarations of language-loyalty among college-educated activists. Such attitudes are not uncommon when a language is under threat, even among monolingual speakers of English. Neither are these languages likely to survive if their only speakers are situated on the depopulated, infertile peripheries. The decisive factor may be their ability to function as community languages in the towns and cities, where most people live and work. Also important may be the presence of a communal hostility to central authority, especially if the latter is clearly associated with the English language. And at the very least, sustained and active support in a number of official institutions may be necessary. Experience has shown that it is one thing to pass laws to promote a minority language, and quite another to implement them.

An issue facing minority languages everywhere is that of standardisation. If, say, Gaelic is to be learned in Highland schools, which variety is to be taught? In general, there are no varieties which approach that of a spoken standard, and when particular *written* varieties are promoted as standards learners have to face the problem of too narrow and too archaic a range of texts. In particular, minority languages must be cultivated as media for serious and functional prose. Language activists maintain, however, that none of these problems are insuperable. They were overcome in Belgium, Switzerland, Finland, and many other European nations.

Many people in England may feel doubtful about the usefulness of such language-promotion. If English is widely available, why not just let people learn it, and save the effort and expense? It is unlikely that any minority language could compete with English in the domain, say, of commerce, so why bother with them when jobs might be at stake? These arguments are powerful, but they forget, or ignore, at least three issues. First, people will learn a language if communal experience has shown that it can guarantee a job, or at least offer the possibility of getting one. But in a period of increasing unemployment, knowledge of English will no more secure a job, of any kind, than will the acquisition of a more prestigious variety by speakers of regional types of English. Second, language means other things to people than mere utility. Different languages in a bilingual society have different social values, and these are of great personal importance to the people who speak them. Third, there is no reason why people should not be competent in both languages, as we have argued elsewhere.

We may conclude this section with a few general remarks about English as it is spoken in the Celtic territories. We must not forget that some form of English has been spoken in parts of those areas for many generations; this kind of English will accordingly differ in character from that more recently acquired. Some of the more obvious features are associated with pronunciation; a salient aspect to English ears is their intonation patterns, the way in which the pitch of the voice rises and falls, or lilts, to use the popular term. Since we have not dealt with intonation in this book, we cannot define this aspect in technical terms here; but other features of accent are widespread. These varieties tend to be *r*-pronouncing, in the sense established in the last chapter. This may be because English was introduced to these areas when the pronunciation of /r/ before consonants and in word-final position was more general in English, or because contact has been maintained with *r*-pronouncing dialects of English (and, in the case of Highland English, Scots). Neither must we discount the reinforcing influence of the Celtic languages, which tend to pronounce /r/ in all positions. The latter influence may account also for the treatment of *l* after vowels and before consonants. In many varieties of English, including RP, the *l* of *lip* is pronounced differently from that of *pill*. The final consonant in the latter has a back vowel resonance, and is accordingly called 'dark *l*' whereas in *lip* it is described as 'clear'. A 'clear *l*', however, is common in all positions in many of the varieties described here. Finally, the vowels in words like *mate* and *home* are often less clearly diphthongised than in RP, and have the /eː/ and /oː/ type vowels described in chapter five.

In vocabulary, naturally, we find words of Celtic origin. Some, like *ptarmigan* (the bird) in the Scottish Highlands, refer to local objects or affairs, but others, like *shannach* (chat) in Ireland, are words for very general concepts. More striking changes have been made in grammar, in the system of tense and aspect. Often this reflects the influence of the grammars of the minority languages. In Scottish Gaelic, for example, the present tense has come to be used in reference to future time only; consequently, present time is indicated, very roughly, by using verb-groups. So in Highland English, the present continuous forms are used where English speakers use the simple present: *you put that there* becomes *you're putting that there*. Similarly, many people in south Wales use continuous forms to specify habitual aspect: *they are going to chapel every Sunday*. And in some varieties of Hiberno-English, a habitual present, as in *I do be*, has been created.

In general, the English of Wales, the Highlands, and to some extent Ireland enjoys relatively high prestige among many people in England. The prestige derives from the fact that these Englishes still have the hallmarks of a *taught* language; and nowhere is this more true than in the speech of the Scottish Highlands, often acclaimed by English people as the home of the 'best' English. Where such local varieties bear the imprint of other dialects of English, or of the Celtic language, they are often evaluated in a rather patronising way, as quaint, disingenuous, or fresh. It is not uncommon to hear these sentiments expressed about the English of Ireland. The sources of these attitudes may be many, but one of them may have to do with an unconscious desire to atone for the imposition of English. It is characteristic of conquering powers that they only 'discover' the culture of the conquered peoples when the material basis for that culture has been destroyed, and is beginning to disappear.

LINGUISTIC COLONIALISM IN IRELAND

The first English spoken in Ireland was that of settlers of the late twelfth century. In Henry II's rather piecemeal campaign of internal colonisation, a company of English (mainly, it seems, from Somerset), Welsh, and Flemings from south-west Wales was established on the coast of south-eastern Ireland under the direction of Norman knights. The variety of English they spoke became known as the Wexford or Yola dialect. Later settlements were made in the area of Dublin, which was captured from the Irish; and the dialect spoken just to the north of that city, known as Fingal, lasted until about 1800.

The native culture, however, was largely untouched by these early settlements. The Irish were heirs to a monastic tradition that had surpassed all others in Europe, and their literature was one of the richest and most ancient. It was to this culture that the Normans adapted, just as their kin in England were to become Anglicised. Thus, though they controlled two-thirds of Ireland by the middle of the thirteenth century, the area of English hegemony, known as the Pale, had contracted by the 1490s to a small part of the east coast around Dublin. The Gaelic chieftains were still in arms, and many Norman families, now Gaelic in law and language, were degenerate subjects in the eyes of the English kings. A royal Proclamation of 1541 urged that 'the King's true subjects in Ireland' should use not Irish but the English language.

The ensuing Tudor campaigns against the ruling Irish families were long, costly, and bitter. Military victories were followed by confiscations of land, expulsions of Irish people by the planting of English settlers; the first of these colonised the south-east midland area of Ireland from the 1550s. By the beginning of the seventeenth century, the last vestige of Irish resistance – involving mainly the chieftains of Ulster – was crushed. The Gaelic nobility fled – an event known as the Flight of the Earls – and large tracts of Ireland were given over to London companies as resources to exploit.

It might be said that the Reformation in Ireland was achieved not by conversion, but by Plantation. Although by 1603 the Prayer Book and New Testament were translated into Irish Gaelic, Ireland remained a bastion of Catholicism. Protestants were accordingly planted in large numbers in the eastern half of Ireland, originating from England and, in the case of Ulster, from Scotland. The Catholic Irish, denied the right to own land, became tenants of the new Protestant owners, and many were forced to live in the infertile west. Sectarian violence was common, and Catholic rebellions were put down with the ruthlessness and arrogance that have characterised English attitudes to Ireland for the last 300 years.

By the beginning of the eighteenth century, it seems that language in Ireland had become a clear indicator of social class. Gaelic was a marker of rural, Catholic poverty; English was associated with Protestantism, ownership, and the towns (although some towns, like Galway and Drogheda, had a sizeable Gaelic-speaking working class until well into the nineteenth century). Increasingly, however, use of the English language was not synonymous with allegiance to the English crown. The Irish ruling class – known during the eighteenth century as the

Protestant Ascendancy – found, like its counterpart in the American colonies, that governments in London were thwarting its attempts to exploit Ireland's economy: and many English-speaking Protestants were active in the unsuccessful independence movements of the 1790s. In 1803, an Act of Union made Ireland part of the United Kingdom; and henceforth the Ascendancy became Anglo-Irish, its sons educated in England, its horizons now determined by the dominant culture of the English.

At the time of the Act, perhaps half the population of Ireland used English as a community language. By the end of the nineteenth century, it was the language of the great majority. Gaelic had no official champions. Neither the Catholic church nor the variety of schools of the eighteenth and nineteenth centuries promoted it. On the contrary, every circumstance and condition favoured the use of English. Gaelic culture, now only kept alive by poets and priests, had no centre: regional variations had intensified, so that English could act almost as a lingua franca. Moreover, education for ordinary people meant learning to read and write English: the Irish schoolmasters themselves were the keenest to punish the speaking of Gaelic in school. And literacy in English was a necessary weapon in the growing campaign for independence – now the concern of Catholics only – and in the agitation against the abuse of absentee landlords. The enemy spoke English, and had to be fought in a language with unbroken traditions of literacy and political discussion. Finally, hundreds of thousands of Gaelic-speakers died in the potato famines of the 1840s, in which a quarter of the population was lost through death, or emigration to America, where of course English was spoken. The incentive to abandon Gaelic was now overwhelming.

A movement to promote the minority language did not emerge until 1893. The Gaelic League set up classes to teach it, and the language became a symbol for the cause of independence, though not a vehicle of it. In 1921, however, Gaelic was declared the national language of the new Free State, and it has since been promoted in the educational system. For most people in what is now the Republic of Ireland, Gaelic is a second language, learned in school; they may not speak it very well, but a majority express loyalty to the language when questioned directly. In contrast, Gaelic has been maintained as a community language in pockets of the remote west; and younger people have been encouraged to stay in some of these Gaeltacht areas by means of generous economic aid. While in the west Gaelic symbolises a traditional way of life, elsewhere it is associated with social mobility. Certain jobs, such as those in the civil service, depend on a knowledge of Gaelic, and language-loyalty is therefore stronger among professional groups than it is, say, among business people. Efforts are being made to promote the language in the capital, Dublin: all-Irish primary schools have been trying to develop social contacts among Gaelic speakers, who tend to be scattered over a wide area.

Several varieties of Hiberno-English have emerged from the long and complex involvement of the English with Ireland. Usages originating in the dialect speech of the early settlers have in turn been influenced by the more recent, and more standardised English of the Irish ruling class. Patterns vary between south and north, where many Scots speakers were planted; and between east and west, where the acquisition of English is relatively recent. In general, however, Hiberno-English often preserves features that were once more common in England, as contacts with English models have weakened. *Cog* (cheat) was once fairly general in sixteenth- and seventeenth-century English, while an /eɪ/-type diphthong in *easy*, *tea*, etc. preserves a pronunciation once current among the Protestant Ascendancy in the eighteenth century, one that became a stock joke among the London literati. Such a pronunciation suggests the merger of *meat* and *mate*, discussed in chapter five, which was no longer the fashionable pattern in eighteenth-century London.

Gaelic influence on Hiberno-English can be seen in all levels of structure. Consonant-clusters unknown in Gaelic, such as *lm*, as in *film*, are pronounced in accordance with Gaelic patterns of vowel and consonant combination; hence, /fɪləm/. The grammar of tense and aspect has also been re-structured. A habitual present is realised as *I do be*, and the perfect is modelled on Gaelic: the present tense of *be* is linked to the *-ing* form of the following verb by *after*, as in *he is after writing* (instead of *he has written*). The verb-group *have been* is therefore rare: *how long are you here?* refers to past, not future time. And Gaelic-influenced structures are also found in written usage. Literal translations of idioms, such as *we were going to put the fight upon the rebels*, and of figurative expressions, such as *'tis an aise to the gate they to be married* (said of a couple who have been busy courting by a certain gate), are found in the work of writers such as Synge, Lady Gregory, and Douglas Hyde, at a time when the nationalist movement was urging the cultivation of the English of Ireland as a literary medium.

The linguistic profile of the north is strikingly complex. The sources of different groups of colonists can still be traced today. A traveller moving from the Ards peninsular, on the coast east of Belfast, towards the north-west coast of Donegal on the other side of Ireland, will first encounter what were originally Plantations of Scots; then English ones from the midlands of England; then the Gaelic community of the Tyrone area; then midland English again; then the Scots Plantation of the Laggan, now in the Republic; then the Gaelic of Donegal. To some extent the traditional speech of each community preserves its ancestry. In areas originally settled by the English, we sometimes find pronunciations like those of the seventeenth-century prestige accent of English. The vowel in words like *side* is /əɪ/, which is the kind of diphthong associated with Stage one of the Great Vowel Shift. Traditional Ulster Scots, which has many of the Scots features discussed earlier in this chapter, tends to be influenced by this Ulster English; thus *bag* for *udder* is replaced by Ulster English *elder*, a form still used in the midlands of England. Other forms, such as *thole* (endure), from the Anglo-Saxon, might derive from the usage of settlers from either England (where it is now archaic) or Scotland, where it is still used in certain areas.

Since the early nineteenth century, industrialised Belfast has drawn immigrants from different parts of Ulster. Protestants from the north and east, with a linguistic background in Ulster Scots, have often been ghettoised in the Protestant working-class communities, while immigrants from the south and west have settled in Catholic ghettos. Recent research has revealed the heterogeneity of Belfast speech, where variations associated with class, age, and sex are complicated by religious differences. Catholic children tend to be educated in schools run by their church, while most children of Protestants attend state schools – and thus in this respect too, their communities remain separate from one another. Innovations in working-class speech show little influence from models that can be broadly described as RP. Thus, while words like *bang, back, that*, and *bad* have the same vowel in RP and in middle-class Belfast speech, they often have different vowels, conditioned by neighbouring consonants, in working-class pronunciation. Furthermore a change in the pronunciation of these words is in process of crossing the sectarian divide. A back vowel is becoming more common among the Protestant working class in the east of the city, and it is spreading, via younger Catholic women, into the communities of the west.

In Northern Ireland, as in many other parts of the United Kingdom where minority languages are spoken, there seems to have been during the last decade or so a growing awareness of language as a symbol of political or ethnic affiliation. The census returns of 1991 show that Irish has been strongly maintained predominantly amongst the Catholic population, with over a third of its speakers under the age of 25. And in 1992 the Ulster-Scots Language Society was formed 'to promote the status of Ulster-Scots as a language', with its own magazine Ullans (modelled on Lallans, a journal devoted to Scots in Scotland). Since then Belfast City Council has called for Ullans to have 'complete parity of esteem' with Irish, and Ulster-Scots is now represented on the UK Committee of the European Bureau of Lesser-Used Languages. Whereas the dominant political discourse has tended to polarise the situation in Northern Ireland as 'Irish' (nationalist) versus 'British' ('loyalist') this new development may be a sign that the latter affiliation is being re-examined.

BILINGUALISM AND LANGUAGE MAINTENANCE IN THE SCOTTISH HIGHLANDS AND WALES

In the Scottish Highlands, the assault on Gaelic has been more recent than in Ireland, and in some ways more dramatic. At the Union of Crowns in 1603, Highland society was still organised in clans, each owing allegiance to a chieftain, the local economy still being dependent on cattle and the cultivation of crops where soil and climate permitted. All affairs were conducted in Gaelic, a common literary form of which was shared with Ireland. And of great concern to governments in London, their agents in southern Scotland, and the Lowlands in general, was the fact that Highland society was still in arms – something they had to put up with until the middle of the eighteenth century.

In the course of the seventeenth century, attempts were made to undermine the allegiance of the clans to their religion, and to stigmatise their language. One effect of the Reformation was to remove the single institution uniting southern Scotland with the Highlands, the Catholic church: so Protestant ministers were sent among the clans. Attachment to Gaelic – seen as a chief cause of 'barbaritie and incivilitie' – was weakened among the Highland nobility after the Statutes of Iona decreed in 1609 that the sons of chieftains be educated in the south. Gradually, the Scottish Society for the Propagation of Christian Knowledge established schools in the Highlands, in which Gaelic was retained for worship, but English was the medium of instruction. It seems, however, that these early attempts at Anglicisation were not successful in promoting a shift away from Gaelic.

Highland involvement with the Stuart Pretenders to the throne stimulated the most ruthless repression of clan life, customs, and language, by forces loyal to the crown. After the rising in 1745 the clans were crushed militarily, their weapons confiscated, and their language proscribed. The destruction of social organisation was followed by the erosion of its economic base, as thousands of Highlanders were evicted from their homes and forced to emigrate in the course of the nineteenth century. In the crofting communities that remained, people went to school to learn English; and since then, many achieving success at school have been educated at secondary level in schools requiring residence away from home, and consequently in an environment favouring English. All the same, Gaelic has been maintained in some of the more isolated communities; in Lewis, for instance, availability of secondary education since the beginning of the present century has meant that Gaelic has also been taught there.

The depopulation of the Highlands stimulated the expression of loyalty to the Gaelic language. In Glasgow, emigrés set up schools where Gaelic was used as a teaching medium, and books and newspapers were published in the language. An Comunn Gaidhealach was founded in 1891 to promote Gaelic, and in 1918 it succeeded in securing an Education Act that required local authorities to provide for the teaching of Gaelic wherever there was a demand. Since then, literature in Gaelic has been cultivated, the language has been taught in some schools, universities, and further education, particularly at evening classes, and there have been numerous campaigns to promote Gaelic in the mass media.

A century of language-activism has checked the steady decline in numbers of Gaelic speakers. In the decade after 1971 such activism was on the increase: in 1980, for instance, parents on Mull agitated for their children to be educated in Gaelic. Furthermore, it tended to become politicised: a Scottish Nationalist MP, Donald Stewart, introduced in 1981 a parliamentary bill demanding parity with Welsh. This was unsuccessful, but after further activism fluency in Gaelic was officially recognised as a marker of British 'nationality' in 1982. This trend contrasts with the essentially apolitical nature of An Comunn Gaidhealach's activities, which eschewed involvement in issues such as crofters' rights, and which failed to identify with any kind of nationalist movement, either cultural or political.

A study of language use on the island of Harris in 1977 suggested some grounds for optimism about the future of Gaelic. The Outer Hebrides were now officially bilingual, and it was the schools that were promoting the minority language. And now that secondary education was available on the islands, children could study Gaelic as a subject at that level, while in the primary schools they were taught in the language. Textbooks were published in Gaelic, even in scientific subjects, and, significantly, bilingualism was now something achieved by first-language speakers of English, as well as of Gaelic.

Outside the education system, Gaelic had been introduced into business transactions, notably by the Post Office. And while the language was not used in such a wide range of functions as Welsh – political debate, for instance, tended to be in English, even when local issues were discussed – it was significant that younger people were re-interpreting the appropriateness of Gaelic in certain situations. Thus, while older, working-class crofters testified to the importance of Gaelic to the home, religious worship (the Bible had been published in Gaelic by 1801), and to the traditional dance and song session known as the ceilidh, younger islanders were more likely to use the language on the telephone, or in the bank, where their parents would tend to use English as a marker of politeness or social distance. For the older generation, Gaelic was often a symbol – albeit covert – of older, traditional values, while younger people seemed to have more faith in the *vitality* of the language.

The position today, however, seems less hopeful for the future of Gaelic. The 1991 census shows a further retraction westwards and a sharp decline in numbers of speakers. It seems that the activism and promotion of the 1970s was associated with Hebridean people returning to live in the islands, a process which has now declined. The fall in numbers is especially marked among young people, in contrast to the returns for Irish in Northern Ireland and Welsh in Wales, where one-third of the speakers of the minority languages are under twenty-five.

We must now turn to Welsh. To a large extent, the great tradition of Welsh literature survived Plantations of the twelfth century, and military defeats of the thirteenth. Although in 1284 the law in Wales was to be administered in English, no attempt was made to proscribe the use of Welsh in the law-courts. But in parts of south-west Wales, the language was eradicated. During the early twelfth century, pockets of English settlers were established in the fertile areas to the west of the Gower peninsula. It was from these that the Flemish farmers, woollen manufacturers, and traders, planted later in the same century in what is now south Pembrokeshire, gradually learned their English. The original Welsh inhabitants were displaced, and this part of south-west Wales retains an Anglicised character to this day.

The imposition of English was formalised by the Tudors. The Act of Union in 1536 demanded that Wales be ruled in English, and that all holders of high office use the dominant tongue. This meant that the sons of the Welsh gentry were to be educated in England, depriving Welsh culture of official patronage. Access to English, however, remained limited. The increasing use of English in law meant that for many ordinary Welsh people, justice was a mockery. They continued to use their own tongue, while legal arrangements were made for them, and argued about, in another, incomprehensible language.

The Reformation, however, gave the Welsh what it had given the

English – a text which came to be regarded as classical. In 1588, the Welsh Bible was published. Throughout the next three centuries, Welsh was maintained in the religious domain; and in the dramatic rise of Nonconformism in the eighteenth century, it played an important role in symbolising the values of Methodism as opposed to those of the hieratic, and English, Anglican church. And not only did this religious revival stimulate the production of a sacred literature, it also gave rise to the Circulating Schools, which taught reading and writing to over half the indigenous population. Today, language-loyalty is strong in those remote, rural parts of Wales where Nonconformist values are still held.

It has been suggested that the language of the Welsh Bible exerted too strong an influence on the literary Welsh of succeeding centuries. As its functions in other official domains were limited, written Welsh lacked models of its own other than the Bible. Sixteenth-century written usage was also codified to some extent, in that a dictionary and grammar of Welsh were produced; and these, too, were greatly influential. While written Welsh was felt to be fixed, and certain forms and structures, even pronunciations, were taught as correct, the spoken Welsh of ordinary people continued to change and diverge. The only standard available for Welsh was therefore a sixteenth-century written one, and so the relationship between written and spoken usage may be described as potentially diglossic.

Two developments in the nineteenth century assisted the spread of English. First, much of south Wales, principally Glamorgan, was industrialised. The extraction of coal and iron ore depended on massive immigration into the industrialised Valleys, at first from surrounding Welsh counties, then from the south-west of England. After about 1850, the population increase in Glamorgan was second only to that of London. Although mining areas in the northern valleys were initially strongly Welsh in culture and language (in 1851 about 90 per cent of Merthyr Tydfil's population was Welsh-speaking, and the town was an important publishing centre in the language), the influx of English-speaking newcomers was too large to be assimilated to that culture. Since then, the trend in south Wales has been towards English monolingualism. The second development was the extension of universal education after the Acts of the 1870s. Industrialisation favoured the use of English among the working class in the south: and that process was formalised in the education system, which ignored the existence of Welsh altogether.

In the twentieth century, however, it is in education that Welsh has made most headway. Since the 1930s, Welsh has been taught in primary schools in the strongly Welsh-speaking areas, and since 1950 there have also been bilingual secondary ones. The Ministry of Education has approved a policy of bilingual education for all Welsh children, and it is as a teaching medium that the language is used in over 650 schools in both urban and rural areas. And for the language-loyalists, one of the most encouraging trends, perhaps, is the way in which many parents, including monolingual English-speaking ones, send their children to Welsh-speaking nursery schools.

Most English people cannot fail to be aware of the more newsworthy attempts by the Welsh Language Society to promote the minority language. With an ideology clearly articulated by its founder, the playwright and lecturer Saunders Lewis, the predominantly young membership of the Society has been seeking to promote Welsh, not only in education, but in other official institutions. Since the Welsh Courts Act of 1942, defendants are entitled to use their own language, and since 1975 the Post Office has submitted to the demand for bilingualism in its transactions. But perhaps the most spectacular advances have been made in the broadcast media. In 1981, the government was forced to restore its original pledge to establish a Welsh television channel.

The spoken English of Wales reflects not only the influence of Welsh and the English taught in schools. In parts of the south, as we have seen, varieties of English have been spoken for centuries, and Welsh English may also reflect features originally widespread in England, but now dialectal, and from the non-standard speech of immigrants into the industrialised south. Welsh word-order underlies *saw him yesterday, I did* and *it's happy I am*, Welsh pronunciation the quality of the /r/ sound, which in many parts is made by tapping the tongue-tip rapidly against the alveolar ridge. The pronunciation of words like *blew* and *threw* may reflect earlier, or dialectal English. In parts of south Wales these words, which are often kept distinct from *blue* and *through*, belong to the class of /juː/ words such as *Tuesday, due, duke*, and *feud* discussed in chapter five. Up to the seventeenth century these words were pronounced in the prestige accent of London with a short /ɪ/ before the /uː/ sound; gradually the /ɪ/ became more dominant, to be replaced by /j/ (to give /tjuːzdeɪ/ etc., from which the assimilated variant /tʃuːzdeɪ/ derives). In contemporary RP, however, the /j/ has been lost after /l/ and /r/, so that *blew* is /bluː/, identical to *blue*; while in these parts of Wales, this loss has not occurred, and the earlier /blɪu/ pronunciation is retained. A diphthong of this kind can also be heard in parts of England such as Berkshire, so that a source in English dialects is also possible.

LANGUAGE DEATH: CORNISH AND MANX

Cornish and Manx have been abandoned as community languages, the former in the course of the eighteenth century, the latter in the course of the present. In Shakespeare's time, however, Cornish was quite widely spoken in much of Cornwall, while Manx was almost universally known on the Isle of Man. In each case, they seem to have survived as first languages among lower-class speakers from peripheral rural areas. These two examples of language death invite consideration of the factors involved in the successful maintenance of minority languages.

A recent study of the decline of Gaelic in a part of north-east Scotland has attributed the cause of language death to the destruction of traditional economic and social life. A minority language can therefore be said to lose vitality as its community of speakers is threatened. When we consider the language of Cornwall, we find that it survived longest in the fishing and mining communities, whose traditional forms have not survived the social and economic changes since the eighteenth century. Similarly, urbanisation in the Isle of Man has been seen as an influential factor in the demise of Manx. But such factors are not the only ones. Language-loyalty tended to surface too late, education and religion were too unsympathetic, or too powerless to maintain them, and there were too many opportunities for contact with speakers of English (unlike, say, in the Highlands of Scotland), and too few for contact with other Celtic languages. The literary traditions of both Manx and Cornish were likewise too fragile to sustain a sense of historicity. We can see the importance of these as we examine each language in turn.

Cornish derives from the British Celtic that was displaced by the Anglo-Saxons. Before its demise as a community language it had been used in certain High domains: in church services until 1678, and as the medium for oral drama, especially during the fifteenth and sixteenth centuries. The period of overt interest in the language, however, corresponds with its decline as a community language. Antiquarians translated parts of the Bible into Cornish in the course of the seventeenth century, and in recent years a revival movement has developed among sections of the middle class. Mebyon Kernow (Sons of Cornwall, founded in 1951) won seats in the 1968 local elections, and has been agitating for bilingual education in schools.

Since the Anglo-Saxon invasions, Cornwall has from time to time rebelled against English authority. Deprived of political autonomy in the tenth century, Cornwall became an earldom; and after the Norman Conquest, an English-speaking bailiff class served the needs of French-speaking landowners. When the Tudors introduced the Prayer Book in 1547, the Catholic Cornish rebelled, but were treated in much the same ruthless way as were the Irish; and the demand for a Cornish Bible and Prayer Book was refused. Bilingualism increased rapidly during the seventeenth century. There is evidence, however, that after its demise in the community Cornish was maintained by what have been termed semi-speakers – individuals who, for a variety of reasons, show interest in learning a language when it is in process of being abandoned by a community. Such speakers survived into the nineteenth century, and have provided a tenuous link with the efforts of the revivalists, where the only other source is the written language.

Manx is a variety of Gaelic, which took root on the Isle of Man when it was conquered by the Irish in the fourth century. After a period of rule by Scotland, control passed to certain English families in the fourteenth century. English has been the official language since then, although formal absorption of the island by the English monarchy did not take place until the eighteenth century. Today, Man has its own parliament, and some economic autonomy, but the language has never been identified with self-government. Manx plays only a symbolic role in government ceremony.

As a community language, Manx died out in the course of the present century. It had been maintained by speakers in the rural areas, whose populations have been declining since the growth of towns in the eighteenth century. Immigration from England at that time made the towns centres of English influence. It is only since the beginning of the seventeenth century that the language has had a written form: the Prayer Book was translated into it, as was the Bible in the eighteenth century, along with some verse. Manx continued to be used in church services until the nineteenth century, when formal education began to undermine it.

In the 1940s there were still some speakers who remembered Manx as a language they had used with parents and grandparents. And since then, there has been some interest in learning the language on the part of some islanders. While Manx flourished, its fortunes seem to have been attended with indifference; now that it no longer has a function in the community, it is a cause for revivalists. It remains to be seen whether Manx, or Cornish, are successfully revived as community languages. Before we write them off, we should remember that a number of languages around the world, like Hebrew, have been raised from the dead.

7 English as an international language

As a first language, English is now spoken by over 300 million people in North America (including Canada), Australia, New Zealand, the Caribbean, and South Africa. Hundreds of millions of others, especially in Africa and southern and south-east Asia, speak it as a second language. In this chapter we shall see how the spread of English beyond Europe is associated with four centuries of colonialism. Three different strands of colonial expansion will be distinguished. First, we shall see how the activities of trading companies brought speakers of English into contact with people in many different parts of the world, and how such contact with West Africa in the sixteenth century gave rise to the Atlantic slave trade. One result of this was the formation of English-based pidgins, some of which subsequently became the creoles of the Caribbean. Second, we shall discuss colonial settlement, and how new varieties of English were established in America, Canada, Australia, New Zealand, and South Africa. The extent to which standardisation has occurred independently in these countries will be explored, and we shall discuss in some detail how American English developed, and its status in the world today. Third, we see how nineteenth-century imperialism institutionalised English in certain older colonies, such as India, and newly-acquired ones, principally in Africa. The spread of English in the education system in these areas will be traced, and we shall assess the development and status of second-language varieties of English, with the main focus on Africa. Finally, we shall examine some of the language planning problems of ex-colonies which have chosen English as an official language.

   It need hardly be said that such a vast topic, spanning four centuries across four continents, should be the subject of a very large book, or series of books, rather than a single chapter of this length. Not only are the issues highly complex, involving a great variety of cultural settings and changing political, social, and economic circumstances, but also controversial: the terms *colonialism* and *imperialism* themselves are good examples of words whose meanings depend on the loyalties of the user. But the student of English is entitled to ask some very basic questions about the spread of the language today. How long has it been used in a certain territory? Who took it there? How did people learn it? We can sketch the answers to some of these questions, but we can also pose others of a more general sociolinguistic character. What relationships do the overseas varieties have to the different Englishes in England? Do they show the same kinds of patterning with regard to region, social class, sex, and age as we associate with speech in England? How do English people regard them? What problems do they pose for those wishing to write literature? How much do their distinctive features owe to particular dialects of English spoken in the British Isles, how far have they arisen independently, since the era of earliest settlement? The answers to these questions must at the moment be fragmentary, since research on particular varieties is often not only very recent, but unevenly spread. But it is essential for any student of English today to be aware of them.

We can deal with only a few examples, and offer only a few insights, in the course of this chapter. But some rather crude generalisations may help the historian of language. In dealing with English involvement with the world beyond Europe, we do not see a concerted, systematic policy during the last 400 years. Different types of colony were established, for different reasons, in different areas, at various times. We are dealing moreover with a number of impulses and movements, with a focus that is at times more economic than political, or vice versa. It has been said with justification that the flag often followed trade: commercial exploitation, as in India, preceded any kind of co-ordinated attempt by government to lay claim to a territory and then administer it. When governments tried to do this their policies were often ignorant of local conditions, their functionaries having to work from hand to mouth. As we shall see, colonial policies and practices may at times have worked in opposite directions. Finally, England was not the only adventurer into the New World, still less the first. Its exploits were often governed by political rivalries, at first with Spain, later with the Dutch, later still the French and Germans. European wars were fought on colonial territories in different parts of the world, and colonies subsequently changed hands often; they became like the commodities – spices, oils, or sugar – they were often plundered for, to be bought, stolen, or tricked from other European powers.

English came into contact with an enormously wide range of languages and cultures during this period. Moreover, it was virtually always in a position of dominance. In general, this was as true of the languages of other European colonists – Spanish, French, Dutch – as it was of the previously unencountered languages of Native Americans, Africans, Mogul princes, Australian bushmen. Some of these were oral vernaculars; some had long traditions of literacy; others, like Hindi and Arabic, were the languages of great religions. English gradually came to symbolise Christianity, military and administrative power, and modern technology. But because it was introduced over areas of great linguistic heterogeneity, English was widely adopted as a lingua franca, like Latin during the Roman Empire.

Throughout the period of colonisation, English has had a reference point in the metropolitan variety of England. The early colonists were of diverse social and regional origins, yet their speech continued to be influenced by the prestige norms of their country of origin. It was 'Standard English' that was taught in and by the schools and colleges of the old colonies, and that was spoken by the administrators of these territories. But while attachment to the norms of England was strong, the process of standardisation has often taken a different course. The best example is that of the United States of America, which not only has the most speakers of English in the world today, but whose variety has also been increasingly influential in many parts of the world, like the Caribbean, Canada, and Australia. We shall accordingly be treating the English of the USA in more detail than other national or areal varieties of the language.

EARLY TRADE IN THE ATLANTIC, AND ITS LINGUISTIC CONSEQUENCES

By 1600, England had made trading contacts in three continents. Fishing expeditions off Newfoundland were to open up a trade in fur; the quest for ivory and gold established contact with parts of the west coast of Africa, which led to the trade in African slaves; and one of the most famous trading companies of all – the East India Company – had gained a foothold in India, from which it continued to enjoy a monopoly on India's wealth for over two centuries. The trading companies were run by bourgeois entrepreneurs, who were granted concessions to exploit certain areas by the government in return for the right to tax profits. The activities of these companies lasted throughout the colonial period, and their importance for the history of English is that they brought speakers of English into contact with people throughout the world.

A more immediate linguistic consequence can be seen in certain areas. Contact with people in parts of West Africa, for instance, some-

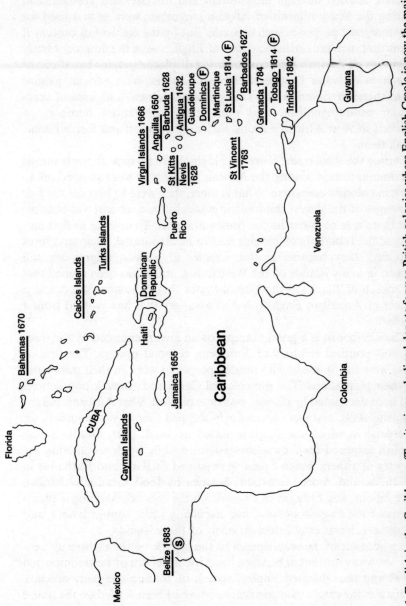

Figure 7.1 English in the Caribbean. (Territories underlined denote former British colonies where English Creole is now the major language spoken. When they are known, dates of acquisition by Britain are given. S and F refer to Spanish and French, which are still spoken in territories formerly possessed by Spain and France.)

times gave rise to English-based pidgins. These simplified varieties of English, learned through intermittent and unsystematic contact, and bearing the heavy imprint of African languages, were at first used for only marginal purposes such as trade. But by the eighteenth century it seems that such pidginised varieties of English were the dominant trade languages on Africa's west coast, having displaced pidgins based on the languages of other European colonial nations. West African pidgins could therefore function as a kind of lingua franca in an area of spectacular multilingualism; and even today substantial numbers of speakers in West African nations, such as Cameroon and Sierra Leone, speak them.

During the slave trade, however, pidgins were perhaps the only means of communication among the African people who were shipped off to work in colonies elsewhere. What is more, they were to become the *first* languages of the slaves' children, or grandchildren, since it was possible that there was no other lingua franca available. To operate as first languages, the functions of pidgins had to be elaborated, their structures amplified: they became *creoles*. Creoles of various origins are still spoken in many islands of the West Indies, and it has been argued that the speech of Blacks in the United States should be analysed not as a dialect of American English, but as a variety that has evolved from a creole.

The Caribbean is a good example of an area dominated by the trading and political rivalries of European colonial powers. The first of these were the Spanish, who needed people to work in their mines and on their plantations. The pre-colonial Carib and Arawak populations had been decimated by disease, war or expulsion. West Africans had the requisite skills, and were accordingly shipped over in vast numbers, an enterprise in which the English played no small part. Gradually the English acquired their own possessions, usually by dismembering the empires of others. From Spain were gained St Kitts and Barbados in the 1620s, and, more important, Jamaica by 1660. Gradually African slave labour was brought in to work on the tobacco and sugar plantations of the English possessions, displacing white convict labour, and creole speech was established on many of those islands.

An account of Jamaica speech in the middle of the eighteenth century shows a continuum between the African speech of newly-imported slaves and the educated English speech of trading company officials. There was the creole of those Blacks who had been settled on the island for some time, the less strongly creolised speech of freed slaves, the speech of poor whites, the English dialect speech of newly-arrived servants from the British Isles, and the 'Jamaica accent' of some planters and merchants. Since the abolition of slavery in the 1830s this continuum has been preserved, in that 'Standard English' has been taught in the education system. Jamaicans have been taught to see themselves as speakers of English, and their creole has been dismissed as dialectal, or at worst, inadequate. Thus, many Jamaicans have turned away from what they call their 'patois'. We can therefore describe the linguistic situation in contemporary Jamaica as a post-creole continuum, in which several varieties of local speech have emerged as speakers have oriented themselves towards the English of the schoolroom.

Arguments about the status of creole are similar to those we have encountered for Scots. Creole forms and structures are often felt to be too close to English to warrant a designation as a separate language; but unlike Scots, creoles have no traditions of literacy and standardisation. All the same, many educators have recently insisted that creoles should be regarded as separate languages, and their arguments are partly based on historical factors, partly on social ones, and partly on psychological grounds. Creoles should be seen as languages with their own histories, and their role as media for tales and proverbs recognised and if possible extended. Creoles have been standardised with written forms in different parts of the world; therefore, the argument goes, there is no reason why the same should not be done for those whose structure is ultimately based on English.

Jamaican speech shows its hybrid history: English dialect words, such as *maliflaking* (beating), borrowed from either convicts or servants; Hindi ones, like *roti* (bread), from contact with traders from the East Indies; words from African languages, like *jook* (pierce), and common English items with new meanings, such as *look for* (visit). In grammar, we find the kinds of morphological simplification we have described with respect to pidgins and creoles in chapter four. Plural inflexions are often absent, as are distinctive past tense forms; the latter because consonant clusters, such as /st/, are often reduced, so that *pass* and *passed* sound alike. Such features – which are also found in the Black speech of the United States – are often adopted by British-born children of West Indian background as they reach adolescence, as a means of identifying themselves with Caribbean culture. The fact that they are usually regarded as incorrect by their teachers raises a crucial issue in the teaching of English around the world. Are such deviations from taught English to be regarded as incorrect, or as instances of a local variety distinct from, but related to, English? We shall pose this question again, in a sharper form, when we come to consider the 'second-language Englishes' of Africa.

COLONIAL SETTLEMENT

The transplanting of English-speaking communities in different parts of the world was an intermittent process that lasted over 300 years. The motives for settlement were various, as political, social, and economic climates changed: the search for new lands to farm, or to grow a newly-discovered crop, tobacco; for new seas to fish, or for gold, which the Spanish had found in the Americas. Overseas possessions were also useful for getting rid of what was considered as surplus population, or for encouraging religious or political radicals to emigrate. Colonies were also established simply to stop other European nations from getting to certain areas first, or to furnish the English navy with depots. And as we have seen above, they were also handy dumping grounds for people convicted under English law to deportation.

The origins of the settlers were likewise diverse. Some of the first were gentry, as in the abortive attempts to colonise Virginia in the l580s. Later, they were sometimes bourgeois, like the religious dissenters of Massachusetts in the l620s; or lower class, like the convicts of the West Indies in the early seventeenth century, or of Australia after 1788. Others were just ordinary land-labourers, evicted during the Enclosures of various periods. And some were not English at all, but Irish displaced by the Plantations, or Scottish people emigrating to Canada as a result of the Clearances. These latter examples show the interconnection of events in the Celtic British Isles with those beyond Europe.

In many colonies the indigenous inhabitants were often treated in much the same way as the Caribs of the West Indies. Their languages were not widely learned by the white settlers, although the latter were not averse to borrowing individual words from them. Often these had references specific to the new locale, or to the practices of its inhabitants. In the course of three centuries of contact, Americans borrowed words like *raccoon* and *tapioca* from the pre-colonial peoples; more specific to Canada are *mocock* (a birch-bark container) and *kamik* (a seal-skin boot). In Australia, *dingo* and *budgerigar* were similarly adopted, and in New Zealand English, *pa* (fortified village) was borrowed from the Maoris. Although local conditions and circumstances varied in all these areas, the white settler populations eventually not only dominated the indigenous inhabitants, but came to greatly outnumber them.

In some colonies, however, speakers of English co-existed with those of other European languages. Some of the early Americans, for instance, were Dutch, French, and German: and some of their words, like *winklehawk* (right-hand tear in a garment, from Dutch) and *smear-*

case (cottage cheese, from German) are still used in some eastern states just as their languages in some instances have also been maintained. While early European linguistic minorities have generally been assimilated to the dominant English-speaking culture of the United States, their presence in other colonies has been the source of long-standing language conflicts. The early French settlements in Canada, for example, were taken over by the English in 1763, and parts of eastern Canada settled by speakers of English. The first of these were Americans who had stayed loyal to the English crown during the American War of Independence; after 1812 they were joined by emigrants from the British Isles. Ever since, the predominantly agrarian French-speaking community has felt beleaguered, and today Canada's population is still one-fifth monoglot French-speaking. Language activism eventually secured a policy of bilingualism in 1969, and speakers of French were given rights in the constitutional settlement of 1982 which made Canada fully independent of Britain. In South Africa likewise, an English-speaking community has co-existed with a larger one of Dutch origin, dating from 1652, and speaking Afrikaans. English settlement began in 1814, and until dominion status was granted in 1910 the English community and its language were dominant in South African society. By the 1930s, however, the newly urbanised Afrikaans community had developed a strong sense of its own identity, and its language had become a political issue. We shall see how the history of English in South Africa has been affected by the Afrikaans consciousness later in this chapter.

Contact with Dutch colonists had at least one interesting linguistic consequence. The process of settlement, as we saw in chapter one, is invariably accompanied by the adoption of new words, or the adaptation of old ones to denote the topographical features typical of a strange environment. It seems that wherever English-speaking colonists settled, their use of the term *bush*, a Scandinavian borrowing first recorded in the thirteenth century, was influenced by the meaning of the related Dutch word *bosch*. Already in England by the sixteenth century *bush* had developed extended meanings, to refer to nettles, heather, ferns, or clumps of shrubs; and this extension was carried further in the colonies. The words *wood* and *forest* were subsequently used less: by the end of the eighteenth century the word meant 'forest' in both the United States and Canada. But the forest was also the wilderness: so the term eventually denoted land that was uncleared or uncultivated and, by extension, anywhere that was beyond or opposed to the 'civilising' atmosphere and values of urban settlement. We find such meanings in Australia, where *bush* denotes the outback, in contrast to the town and city. In New Zealand and South Africa, however, the term usually refers to a *type* of landscape: dense forest in the former, grassland and scrub in the latter.

STANDARDISATION AND COLONIAL SETTLEMENT

It has often been said that an international standard of English exists in the medium of writing. It is used in the areas of colonial settlement we have described with hardly any modifications. Among the most well-known of these are American variations in spelling, such as *tire* for *tyre*, *honor* for *honour*. Differences in grammar and vocabulary are also minor, and again American examples will serve: the past participle form *gotten* (cf. *forgotten* in England) is used as well as *got* (in a slightly different way); and instead of *autumn, fall* is used, a word originating in English dialect and still used in some south-western counties. Some of these written forms are used beyond the USA, however: in Australia, and as we shall see in a later section, beyond the areas of colonial settlement.

Standardisation is actually a contested issue in most former colonies. Not surprisingly, it is most contentious when speech rather than writing is involved. And in respect of speech, divergence is most noticeable at the level of pronunciation. The United States, Canada, South Africa, Australia, and New Zealand are sometimes said to have their own national standards; and most people in the British Isles can probably recognise the accents of the United States and Australia, although many might have difficulty in distinguishing Canadians from Americans, New Zealanders from Australians, and either of the latter from South Africans. As we have seen, however, national standards in pronunciation are very difficult to define, as are the regional accents of England. It might be more accurate to say that each area has its own norms of pronunciation, at times formulated with an ear to the RP in England, at other times responding to local circumstances. Even then, there are sometimes considerable variations in pronunciation within these areas, as we shall see.

The sound-systems in each of these areas are closest to those of the south-east of England. This reflects the origins of the earliest settlers in East Anglia, London, and what are now known as the Home Counties. It was the early colonists who set the pattern, and although they came from many areas the south-eastern influence was dominant. Theirs was the voice of the new colony; and each second and subsequent generation of immigrants – drawn from the most diverse sources – tried to assimilate to the local voice. Thus, speakers of many different European languages learned to sound like Americans, while on the other side of the world large numbers of Irish people, and later immigrants from Germany and Italy, were to Australianise themselves in the course of the nineteenth century.

When people settle in a new area their children generally try to identify with the new-found norms of language and culture. This was as true of settlement in the colonies as it is of movement today between, say, the towns and cities of England. But when people emigrate, they also often cling tenaciously to some vestige of their past. For many early settlers from the British Isles, the Bible was a precious link with the past, its language an enduring point of reference. Minority languages, such as the German of Pennsylvania, have also been maintained for centuries; and we find therefore that conflicts of identity can often be traced in the histories of each colonial variety. They help to explain, for instance, the development of some variations and changes in the speech of the early American colonists. Their first settlements were on, or near, the ocean, which they or their ancestors crossed; and this meant that they could stay in touch with developments, linguistic or otherwise, that occurred in England. Thus, when '*r*-pronouncing' ceased to be prestigious in south-east England, cities like Boston, New York, Jamestown, and Charleston followed suit: 3,000 miles is no distance when a prestige feature is at stake. In England, however, the hundred-odd miles between Bristol and London have been enough to resist it.

The prevalence of south-eastern features in the speech of colonial settlers may account for the frequent assertions of English visitors that such speech was more 'correct' than could be generally heard among ordinary people in England. This was said of American English until the last quarter of the eighteenth century, and of Australian in the nineteenth. Observations like these, however, must be treated with caution. We generally do not know what the observers were used to hearing, and what their expectations were when they sailed, perhaps with some trepidation, to the new lands. If their experience was of the immense dialectal variety in England, and their expectation to find something wild or exotic, they may well have been agreeably surprised.

Another comment made by observers at this time was that colonial speech was more uniform than speech in England. And this is something that has been said ever since. It is important to remember, however, that such statements can only be relative: we must not see the new varieties of English as monolithic. What they lack is the extent of regional variation that is found in England. The reasons for this are clear. Colonial society has in most cases been mobile, especially since the introduction of railways in the nineteenth century. It was often

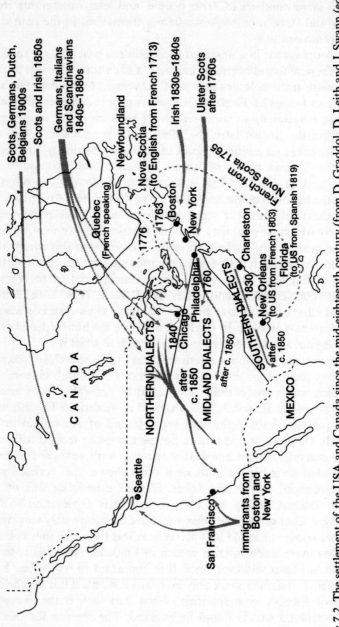
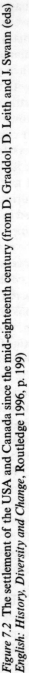

Figure 7.2 The settlement of the USA and Canada since the mid-eighteenth century (from D. Graddol, D. Leith and J. Swann (eds) *English: History, Diversity and Change*, Routledge 1996, p. 199)

Scots, Germans, Dutch, Belgians 1900s

Scots and Irish 1850s

Germans, Italians and Scandinavians 1840s–1880s

Irish 1830s–1840s

Ulster Scots after 1760s

Newfoundland

Nova Scotia (to English from French 1713)

Quebec (French speaking)

French from Nova Scotia 1765

Boston

New York

1763

1776

Charleston

New Orleans (to US from French 1803)

Florida (to US from Spanish 1819)

CANADA

1840

Chicago

Philadelphia

1760

after c. 1850

NORTHERN DIALECTS

MIDLAND DIALECTS

after c. 1850

SOUTHERN DIALECTS

1830

after c. 1850

MEXICO

Seattle

San Francisco

immigrants from Boston and New York

relatively urbanised, or semi-urbanised, from the start: we do not find the kind of village structure so characteristic of England. Education, furthermore, often took root early: we shall see the consequences of this below. Only in the eastern parts of the United States, where there was substantial early settlement, can we speak of regional dialects in the sense understood in Europe, but here, as in other former colonies, the English language has not had long enough in a stable environment for regional varieties to develop to the extent known in England. But as we shall see below, there is now ample evidence that regional and social differentiation is gathering force.

The absence of marked dialectal variation has meant that there were few of the social problems associated with the selection stage of standardisation that we have seen in England and other European societies. In a sense, processes of dialect levelling themselves created a kind of standard within each colony. This is not to say that the early colonial societies were egalitarian; but there was less social stratification, in general, among the settler populations, than in Europe, and at times they were strongly anti-elitist. It has been suggested that in early Australian society, for instance, the elite were actually the ex-convicts who had completed their sentence, and had subsequently become expert in sheep-shearing and cattle-herding. And in newly-independent America, some argued that questions of a standard in the language would be settled by the nature of American society – for instance its mobility – rather than any kind of academy of intellectuals: many Americans wanted to get away from the identification of correctness, or standardisation, with a wealthy, powerful elite. Instead, they concerned themselves with elaborating the functions of American English, by encouraging the writing of scientific and imaginative prose; and they also concentrated, to the point of obsession, on the process of codification.

Standardisation has inevitably been less of an issue in those areas which were to become Dominions in the course of the nineteenth and early twentieth centuries. In Canada, South Africa, Australia, and New Zealand linguistic usage was for a long time exonormative: speech as well as writing was orientated towards the metropolitan variety in England. In Australia today, however, there is a strong sense of a local norm in matters of vocabulary and pronunciation, a development hastened perhaps by the growing dominance of the USA and its variety of English. Such influence is not surprisingly felt most acutely in Canada, where usage reflects the conflicting models: *tap* is more common than the American *faucet*, but many features of pronunciation, such as that of *Mary* to sound identical to *merry*, are shared by most Canadians and many Americans, especially in the Mid-West. It remains to be seen whether Canadian usage will be increasingly Americanised. In South Africa, the development of a local prestige norm has corresponded, very roughly, with the gradual rise of Afrikaaner political power in the course of the twentieth century. Declared the only official language in 1822, English was widely learned by an often resentful Afrikaans-speaking community; and the RP norms of the Victorian middle class were reinforced when English entrepreneurs came to dominate economic life after the discovery of minerals in the 1870s led to industrialisation. The power of the English-speaking community in both political and economic life was subsequently challenged, and in 1925 Afrikaans was declared an official language alongside English. A variant of South African English, often showing traces of Afrikaans influence, has acquired the status of a local prestige norm of pronunciation.

It seems that the absence of rigid social stratification in the early English-speaking colonial communities has meant that a clear relationship between variants of pronunciation and social class has been relatively slow to emerge. An interesting feature of both Australian and South African pronunciation, for instance, is that neither has the stigmatised consonant pronunciations so common in the south-east of England, especially London. Initial /h/ is sounded, and neither the glottal plosive nor the Cockney substitution of /f/ for the initial sound in *thin*, and of /v/ for the medial consonant in words like *other*, is widely heard. There may be several explanations for this. First, we could seek an explanation in terms of what we know about the British sources of pronunciation in these colonies. The stigmatised pronunciations are most characteristic of Cockney today, but we do not know how common they were in London speech at the end of the eighteenth century when people were moving, or being taken, to these colonies. Although some of them were recorded by Walker (1836), they may have been relatively infrequent variants which have since spread in London; Australian and South African speech may therefore preserve an earlier set of patterns. Alternatively, non-Cockney variants in south-eastern pronunciation may have been dominant: elderly people in rural parts of East Anglia and Kent, at least until very recently, have been largely '*h*-pronouncing'.

An explanation in these terms, however, ignores the possibility that pronunciation within these former colonies has itself also changed within the last two hundred odd years. There is evidence, for instance, that Australian, New Zealand and South African Englishes were originally not entirely '*h*-pronouncing'. It is possible to argue that the desiderata of so-called educated pronunciation in the nineteenth century may have been easier to disseminate in the more fluid social conditions of the early colonies. More recently, however, it has been suggested that the substantial immigration from Ireland and Scotland to these territories may have generalised pronunciation of the initial *h*.

Other variations in the speech of south-eastern England can be traced in some of these areas. Both South African and Australian Englishes have 'Cockneyfied' diphthongs in words like *mate* (starting with a vowel more like that of *mat* than *met*) and *might* (starting with a vowel like that of *mock*). In Australia these diphthongs have often been modified by educated people in the direction of RP. The vowel in words like *dance*, *plant*, and *sample* also fluctuates according to the patterns we have described in chapter five. In South Africa and New Zealand the vowel in these words is a long back one, as it is in RP; but in Australian pronunciation a front vowel is common in these words, although a back one is used in *path*, *pass*, etc. These examples suggest that the back vowel was first introduced before voiceless fricatives, as in *path* and *pass*, in the south-east of England, and Australian pronunciation preserves this early stage. Later, the backing spread before nasals, as in *dance*, in time for it to be used by the later immigrants to New Zealand and South Africa. Most Americans, however, tend to use the long front vowel, which is also of course found in parts of south-east England, and which is the earlier pattern.

A recent study of pronunciation in Australian cities shows once again that it is not enough to assume that pronunciations in former colonies can be adequately explained on the basis of their British origins. Still less is it appropriate to use colonial speech-data merely as evidence for dating the stages of a sound-change in England. In certain Australian cities there is no evidence of a general substitution of the long vowel in words of this type; if anything, there is a tendency to favour the short vowel, perhaps because it is *not* the vowel used in RP and symbolic, therefore, of British hegemony.

A particularly good example of change within a colonial speech-community is afforded by pronunciation in New Zealand. In 1912 some educationalists were deploring the rise of what they called a 'colonial twang', manifested in the diphthongs of words like *house* and *no*, in which there is wide tongue-movement between a fronted initial element and a back vowel. In response to these so-called wide diphthongs, some New Zealanders affected a 'colonial-genteel' pronunciation reminiscent of certain aspects of the Edinburgh Morningside accent, in which words like *my* come to sound like *may*. Interestingly enough, this kind of pronunciation has attracted much the same level of opprobrium as the 'twang'.

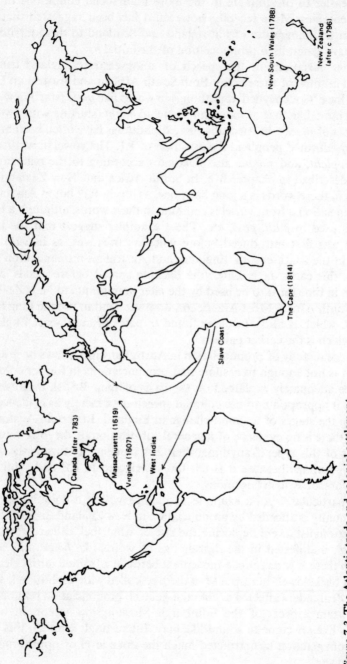

Figure 7.3 The Atlantic trade and colonial settlement

Labels within figure:

New South Wales (1788)

New Zealand (after c 1796)

The Cape (1814)

Slave Coast

Canada (after 1783)

Massachusetts (1619)

Virginia (1607)

West Indies

AMERICAN ENGLISH

Only in America, it seems, have there been attempts to elevate the status of the colonial variety to that of a language separate from the English of England. Not surprisingly it was during the early years of independence that the issue was raised. For Webster, the lexicographer, a national language was 'a national tie', and what country wanted it more than America? Many Americans thought that now they had won independence (in 1783) their usage would diverge increasingly from that of England; and that this would be a good thing. Webster himself contrived to make it different by changing spellings; and his famous *Dictionary* of 1806 was inspired by the feeling that differences between the two varieties would multiply, necessitating the writing of a separate dictionary.

Some Americans also wanted to establish an Academy to regulate their new variety. An American Academy would be one in the eye for the English, who had demonstrated their inferiority by failing to set up one of their own. The American Academy of Language and Belles Lettres was accordingly established in 1821. But there was a great deal of argument about what it should do. Some members championed the cause of linguistic separatism; others were more conscious of England's literary tradition, and felt that America's best interests would be served by keeping cultural links open. Gradually, interest in the Academy waned. Some had seen the dangers of elitism, and in 1828 Webster himself argued that dictionaries and grammars should guide Americans on matters of usage, rather than the usages of a particular clique, or the recommendations of an Academy. To a large extent his wish was granted.

Nationalist feelings during this period were often expressed through partisan statements about language. A great deal of the acrimony came from the English side of the Atlantic. All the previously rather commendatory remarks about the correctness and uniformity of American English were replaced by hostility to American addiction to 'innovation', 'new-fangled words', and bombast. A sole neologism was, enough for one observer in 1803 to condemn American English as 'wholly unintelligible', like a teacher with a child who utters a single stigmatised form. Not only did some Americans use new words, like *crass*, they also made free with morphemes like *-ise*, and wrote *utilise.* And they were even guilty, like Shakespeare, of functional shift: *spade* was used as a verb as well as a noun. The much-praised uniformity was now a stick to beat them with. The American intellectuals of the eastern cities had no business talking like the people in the backwoods: they should cultivate elegant and correct speech, to show their class.

To some extent the acrimony continues. It is not unusual to hear English spoken of as though it were a purely national commodity; neither is it rare to hear America blamed for every new word and every disliked usage heard on the British side of the Atlantic. Sometimes this has bizarre results: a long-standing feature of south-eastern English dialect, *ain't*, has often been attributed to the influence of American films. (In fact, it is a variant of both *aren't* and *haven't;* in the latter, a /vnt/ consonant-cluster has been simplified, and the preceding vowel lengthened, raised, and subsequently diphthongised.) Examples like this show the difficulty of drawing clear-cut distinctions between the English of America and that spoken in the British Isles. It is difficult to find 'Americanisms' that are not used by some people, in some context, on the British side of the ocean. Many Americans may say (but tend not to write) *mad* instead of *angry*, but this usage is also known in some English dialects. And sometimes the difference is more subtle. Americans see *hogs* in fields, but tend to *pig* their food; in England, the opposite pattern is more common.

It is not usual to hear people today insist that American English is a separate language. But like Scots, it is another example to expose the coarseness of our terminology: so American English might best be called a national variety of English, with its own norms. The closer we look, however, we find that those norms are partly regional – not surprisingly, in a country of such vast size – but are also, more importantly, social ones as well. Social variation in American English, which has been the subject of a vast amount of research, has a great deal to do with the presence of ethnic minorities, who together form a significant proportion of the population in the United States.

As we have seen, other language groups had settled in America from the earliest times. Some of the intellectuals who steered America to independence saw these languages as cultural assets: people would learn English if they felt they needed to, and it was not up to the government to tell them what to do. Bilingual schooling was quite common in parts of the country until the early twentieth century. But in many ways these liberal ideals were crushed in the entrepreneurial climate of the nineteenth century. As the frontier moved west, those Native Americans that remained were to be taught English, and Americanised, according to a statute of 1868. And speakers of Spanish in the south-west came in for similar treatment. Only about 30 per cent of the population of New Mexico could speak English in 1874 (most of these were bilingual), but a statute of 1891 demanded schooling in English, and eighty years later some Texan schools were discouraging the use of Spanish even in the playground.

In the course of the nineteenth century immigrants from Russia, Germany, Italy, Scandinavia, Ireland, and other European nations settled in the United States, many of them in the cities which mushroomed in the otherwise empty West. Unlike the early European colonists the later immigrants were often working class, and were keen to Americanise themselves in the hope of economic improvement. We can see the results of such adaptive behaviour in the speech of some New Yorkers of Italian descent. Immigration from Italy continued into the twentieth century, and second-generation speakers from this background tend to try to avoid the 'Italian' vowel in words like *bad*, and *bag*. This is a low vowel, not unlike the 'north country' vowel in England; but for these descent groups, it sounds too Italian. They therefore avoid it by adopting a raised vowel, but tend also to over-compensate, so *bad* sounds like *beard* (without the *r*). Such processes introduce new variants into city speech; they subsequently often acquire a social value, in turn promoting changes in the pronunciation of other social groups.

Other ethnic minorities have a more ambivalent attitude to the local variety of American English. Mexican-Americans in California and the south-west suffer discrimination in jobs, and are generally low-status. Accordingly, some are loyal to Spanish, while others, indifferent to language affiliation, speak a variety of Spanish heavily influenced by English: *birria* and *ganga* in Spanish mean 'a meat dish' and 'bargain' respectively, but in this group – known as *pachucos* – they often mean 'beer' and 'gang'. Rapid urbanisation since the Second World War seems to have prompted many Spanish speakers to Americanise themselves. Upwardly mobile bilingual speakers in San Antonio, Texas, tend to use two pronunciations of unavoidable Spanish words in the local vocabulary, such as *corral* and *plaza*: a Spanish one with other bilinguals, and an Americanised one with monoglot *Anglos*. And in California, they tend to avoid using *sofa* (beside *couch*, and the more regionally marked *chesterfield*) because it sounds like a word from Spanish. Despite these trends, the existence of a large Spanish-speaking minority in Southern California has recently been seen by some Americans as a threat to their own notion of American identity, and there have been demands for legislation to make English the defining component of American nationality.

Black speech in the United States has attracted a great deal of research since the 1960s. This variety – which nonetheless has variations within it – is spoken in many northern cities such as New York, Chicago, and Detroit, and has many of the features associated with creoles, which we have also seen in the discussion of Jamaican English. Thus, the consonant-cluster /st/ is simplified, even before vowels, so that *testing* sounds like *tessin';* and in common with many languages around the world, the verb *be* is often not expressed, so that we hear *he mad, she gone.* But one of the most important features of the Black English Vernacular, as this variety has been called, is that in many respects it is like that of whites in the Deep South – whence many Blacks migrated after the Civil War in the 1860s. The direction of linguistic influence – Black to white, or white to Black – has been the source of much speculation in recent years.

Southern speech, with its distinctive vowels – such as that of *die, dive,* etc., which sounds like a lengthened /æ/ – and forms, such as *you-all* as a plural of *you* – is an important reminder that there have been long-standing variations in the speech of the earliest colonies. The southern plantation economy, based on tobacco and cotton, led to a more stratified society than was to be found in the north-eastern colonies of, say, New England. It seems also to have been more receptive to new prestigious pronunciations emanating from England. Thus, southern speech is, broadly speaking, not 'r-pronouncing'; and this marks a significant divergence from usage in many other parts of the USA.

'R-pronouncing' is associated with the speech of the Mid-West of the United States. This variety tends to be the one that is broadcast; and since it is also spoken over a very large area (corresponding, very roughly, to that developed and settled during the last century) it has been termed General American. Most people outside the United States tend to think of this pronunciation as constituting some kind of spoken standard; it has never, however, enjoyed the prestige of RP in England. Since the Second World War many of its features have been spreading geographically, a notable example being the introduction of *r*-pronunciation in eastern cities like New York. Here, upper-middle-class speakers have generally adopted it, though many working-class speakers have not; while lower-middle-class people, anxious to identify with the prestige feature, register the highest incidence of all when they are conscious of how they are sounding. In many parts of the United States, therefore, *r* has almost become to Americans what *h* is to the English.

Different regions of the USA still preserve to a large extent their own norms of usage. In the Mid-West, for instance, especially among young people, there is a tendency to merge the vowel in words like *cot* and *caught.* Such variations have often become stereotypes, and evaluated negatively. In a recent survey of language attitudes people of southern Indiana rated the speech of certain eastern areas such as Washington, DC, Connecticut and Delaware, along with that of Washington state in the north-west, as most 'correct'. Least favoured was the speech of New York and of the South. Southern speech in, say, the Mid-West has often given rise to comment and even hilarity. Even educated Southerners, it seems, use the stigmatised 'ain't'. To the Southerner, however, the speech of the Northerner or Mid-Westerner might appear stiff or even pompous. For *ain't*, like most disapproved usages, is not merely a solecism: it can be used in the South for interactional effect as a means of putting a stranger at their ease. Throughout the USA it seems also that certain pronunciations and morphological items are widely stigmatised. The pronunciation of *pen* to sound like *pin*, the insertion of an *r* in *wash* (so that it sounds like *worsh*), and the past tense form *drownded* tend to be regarded as the marks of low social status. This has much to do with the fact that in the course of the last century dictionaries were vigorously promoted, even to the extent of supplying one to every frontier cabin that already possessed at least two books. Courtesy books listing stigmatised usages were also popular, and the bestseller of the nineteenth century was Webster's *Elementary Spelling Book*, which encouraged Americans to see written forms as the most important guide to correctness.

As we have already hinted, American English has influenced the development of local Englishes in many different parts of the world. This influence is usually attributed to the pervasiveness of American broadcast media, but it is clear that it reflects American economic power in the world today. English has increasingly been associated with cultural hegemony, and as Britain declines as a world power, a new wave of British antipathy to American English has arisen because it is seen to be competing for world dominance with the English of Britain. The latter is now often described in respect of its 'export' value of £500 million and of the need to maintain its 'market share'. In 1995 the Prince of Wales launched a British Council campaign on behalf of British English by describing American English as 'very corrupting', as though it were an inferior product in a marketing drive.

THE LANGUAGE OF IMPERIAL RULE

Despite the misgivings of many politicians, the activities of the trading companies intensified in the course of the nineteenth century. By 1900, Britain had come to control five times the area it possessed in 1860. The most spectacular gains were in Africa, the greater part of which was shared out among the European powers between 1880 and 1900. Increasing awareness of the role of colonies in the industrialising economies of Europe led to more and more government intervention in their administration. Exploitation by trading companies slowly gave way to exploitation by government. In this era of colonial expansion, which we shall call imperialism, Britain was the most successful among the nation-states of Europe.

Developments in India to some extent foreshadowed events else-where. In 1813 the trading monopoly of the East India Company was abolished; new territories were subsequently seized, railways were built, and local economic activity shaped to fit the needs of British capital. India became the keystone of the Empire, and the British took steps to protect their access to the sub-continent. The opening of the Suez canal brought British armies and influence to Egypt; and a British presence was established in Burma and in what is now Malaysia to protect its most prized possession against encroachment from the south-east. India came to be ruled by a white English-speaking administrative caste, imbued with a belief in European superiority. Unlike their predecessors of the East India Company, who had been happy to assimilate in many respects to Indian life and customs, the new ruling class sought to dis-tance itself from the local populations.

Colonial settlement was not a feature of the nineteenth-century Brit-ish imperial possessions. Although there was some white settlement in Africa (for example in Southern Rhodesia, now Zimbabwe, and Kenya), the newcomers, like the earlier colonists in South Africa, con-stituted only a small minority of the population. They tended not to exterminate the indigenous inhabitants, but to exploit their labour in farming the most fertile land. Power was therefore vested in a small, white, land-owning and employing caste, living by a code similar to that adopted by the imperial administration in India. Africans, like Indians, were felt to be backward and untrustworthy, and incapable of looking after their own lives.

In many areas, however, imperial rule necessitated the cultivation of local leaders or tribes to act as its agents. Conquered peoples fought in British armies in campaigns to secure new possessions and to consoli-date older ones. Often the British ruled indirectly through local puppet rulers; and certain sections of the population were increasingly edu-cated into the role of administrators, although they invariably consti-tuted only a lower stratum in the imperial hierarchy. It is to this process that we can trace the origins of new varieties of English among the native populations of areas ruled by Britain.

Like Latin during the Roman Empire, English was imposed over an enormous area as the language of law, administration, and commerce. English enjoyed the sanction of military superiority, but two other fac-tors helped it to spread. Like the territories ruled by Rome, the colonies seized by Britain were areas of striking social, cultural, and linguistic diversity. Territorial boundaries imposed by European powers cut across tribes, polities, empires, culture-areas, and language-groups. In Nigeria alone, it has been estimated that over 200 languages are spoken. English therefore has often been invaluable as a lingua franca (although there were local ones, too: Hausa in northern Nigeria, Swahili in much of East Africa, and Bazaar Malay in Malaysia). In addition, knowledge of English could lead to a prestigious job: there were clear economic advantages in learning it.

Many British administrators, however, did not view the spread of English as an end in itself. Provision of education was often on an *ad hoc* basis and in some areas such as northern Nigeria the spread of English may actually have been discouraged. It was more useful for Britain to deny access to a lingua franca in certain areas, since divided populations might be easier to rule: English opened up the possibility of unity among diverse peoples, and subsequently ideas about independence and nationalism. Also, some missionary societies favoured use of major vernaculars as vehicles of evangelism and of education. Thus, local languages were sometimes encouraged and even taught in some areas, reinforcing the distinction between ruling elites and subject populations. These practices contrast markedly with those of the French, which tended to promote the idea that to speak French implied citizenship of the French nation. The French language – specifically, its standard variety – was accordingly promoted in education, administration, and the army, as the Romans had promoted Latin; and the populations of French colonies were encouraged to think of themselves as French, and to place their ethnic or ancestral identities second.

It is as a second language, therefore, that we must trace the history of English in India, Malaysia and Singapore, and in many parts of Africa. But the term 'second language' tends to obscure its wide range of functions and the varying motives for learning it. Not only is English a major lingua franca, but it has functioned as the medium of independence movements and, more recently, of a considerable literature. And from the first, demands for the language have had a clear political significance, often reflecting the fact that we are not dealing here with the supposedly unified nation-states of the European imagination. In India, for instance, Bengal Hindus wanted to learn it in the first decades of the nineteenth century, not only because they thought it was the key to Western thought and science, but also because it was a means of checking the influence of Arabic, the language of Islam. In South Africa, denial of access to English education, and the promotion of African languages in education, are still associated by Black Africans with the newly-abandoned system of apartheid, which used to deprive them of any opportunity to participate in political life.

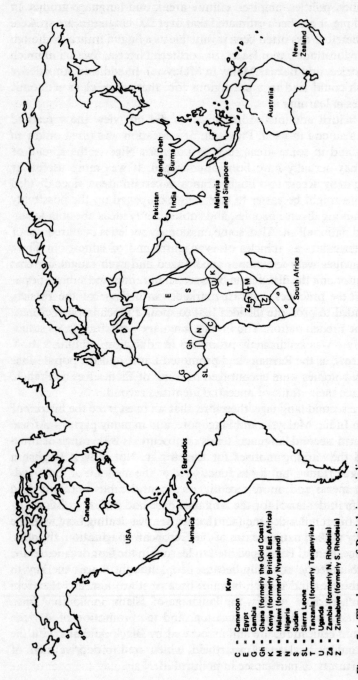

Key

C   = Cameroon
E   = Egypt
G   = Gambia
Gh = Ghana (formerly the Gold Coast)
K   = Kenya (formerly British East Africa)
M   = Malawi (formerly Nyasaland)
N   = Nigeria
S   = Sudan
SL = Sierra Leone
T   = Tanzania (formerly Tanganyika)
U   = Uganda
Za = Zambia (formerly N. Rhodesia)
Z   = Zimbabwe (formerly S. Rhodesia)

Figure 7.4 The legacy of British imperialism

English has also symbolised many different and even contradictory states and processes in the areas of imperial rule. As the language of the colonial era it symbolised dominance and exploitation and therefore collusion with the white master; it has often since become the dividing line between privileged and poor. But it also symbolises education and literacy, since in many areas these were virtually synonymous with English. It has also been an emblem of Christianity, of material and technological development, and of urbanisation and western capitalism; and since the Second World War in particular it has been seen as a key to nationhood, and the means of access to international diplomacy and commerce. Not surprisingly, different territories responded differently to this legacy of associations when they won their independence.

ENGLISH AND EDUCATION

The earliest educational institutions were the mission schools. In Sierra Leone, for instance, they were soon to follow the establishment of that West African colony in 1787, and others were founded in the colonies of Malaya in the first decades of the nineteenth century. In some places, such as South Africa, the mission schools at first appear to have done a competent job, and in southern Nigeria they have been accused of removing all African characteristics from their charges.

In general, the medium of education was English. Pupils were encouraged to use English as often as possible, and sometimes there were sanctions against speaking local languages in school. Above all, English was the language of literacy: in future years it was to become identified with education itself. But Protestant mission schools in some areas tended to use local languages in religious instruction, as befitted the ideals of the Reformation. Thus, Yoruba was developed in southern Nigeria as the language of Scripture.

As well as the mission schools there were other kinds of institutions such as the Free Schools of the Malayan colonies. But the existence of all these early schools depended on local initiatives, enthusiasm, and the availability of resources; we cannot yet speak of an educational policy. Something like this developed as British administration was extended and consolidated. But although local people began to acquire English as a means of employment in administration, education, and therefore English, reached only a very small proportion of the population. Since the expansion of state education, enrolment in African schools, for instance, has seldom reached half of the school-age population.

British educational policy can be seen in all its complexity in India. In 1835, the famous Minute associated with T.B. Macaulay, member of the

Supreme Council of India and later author of the *History of England*, called for the creation of a class of 'Indians in blood and colour, but English in taste, in opinions, in morals, and in intellect' who would be able to act as 'interpreters' between English-speaking rulers and the governed. They were to 'refine' the vernacular languages of India as vehicles for conveying the alleged benefits of Western civilisation to the indigenous 'masses'. An education in English, then, was for an elite only; education for the mass, as and when it might exist, could only take place in the vernaculars, and these were also used widely for administration at regional level. At the same time, English was used for many official purposes, and it was an important academic language in five universities that were founded in the course of the nineteenth century. After 1918 the establishment of more schools and colleges made English more widely available, and a survey of publications in 1928 found an influential amount of writing in the language.

In parts of tropical West Africa, the spread of English in education had been complicated by other factors. In 1807, the British slave trade was abolished; and one of its consequences was the re-settling of slaves, or potential slaves captured from slaving expeditions conducted by other powers, in the colony of Sierra Leone. A community of creole speakers receptive to English influence and education was established; and as early as 1827 Fourah Bay College had been set up as an institution of higher education, from which Africans preached Christianity and spread education in English in many parts of western Africa. It was here that the first Westernised, English-speaking Black intelligentsia emerged, and its influence spilled over into other British colonies of West Africa. During the latter half of the nineteenth century there was a vigorous tradition of political journalism in English, some of it openly critical of British colonialism.

It was after the Second World War that education expanded most dramatically in Africa. Again, this was more true of West Africa than the colonies in the south and east, where the racist attitudes of white settlers inhibited the development of schools for Africans. In Rhodesia in 1965, for instance, roughly the same amount of money was spent on education for Africans as for whites, although the latter were outnumbered by ten to one. As in other parts of Africa, such education was at the primary rather than secondary or tertiary level. The imperialist attitude remained what it had been in the previous century: the highest positions in all jobs and professions were to be open only to whites. Thus, although in the Gold Coast (now Ghana) in 1949 there were about 10,000 Africans employed in the elite professions, one-third of this number in the civil service, no African held a job at the top. This remained the case throughout Africa until independence was won in the late 1950s and early 1960s, even though by that time Africans had been able to study at universities in Britain and the United States.

THE EMERGENCE OF SECOND-LANGUAGE VARIETIES OF ENGLISH

Since we are dealing here with English primarily as the product of the educational system, we need to take account of levels of education, the origins, both ethnic and linguistic, of the teachers of English themselves, and their teaching strategies. We must bear in mind that these factors vary enormously and that access to education is extremely uneven: it is much more open in towns and cities, for instance, than in the country. Another factor is the language or languages also used by speakers of English as a second language: we need to allow for the possibility of those languages influencing the English of particular areas. We must also know how English functions in the communities where it is widely spoken. Is it a medium of everyday conversation, and what kinds of writing are undertaken? Finally, we must consider the status of these new varieties of English. To what extent should they be judged against the norms of the metropolitan variety in England? Should they be considered as varieties, even standards, in their own right? Do the attitudes of their speakers towards them differ from the attitudes of speakers of English as a first language? And are the new varieties felt to have different styles, and perhaps different levels of acceptability?

Several attempts have been made to describe varieties of English in former colonies by referring to the level of education of different groups of users. In Africa, for instance, it has been argued that changing social conditions brought about by urbanisation, availability of higher education, and opportunities of high status jobs in the professions, have enabled some Africans to develop a competence in English which exceeds that of their native or ancestral language. Thus, the terms first language and second language lose much of their value when the speech of this group is considered. An African language such as Twi or Wolof may be learned first in life, but English may be spoken in many more contexts, particularly within households where husband and wife speak mutually unintelligible languages. Among this small elite of Africans a local variety of English has emerged, and attachment to the African language(s) in an individual's repertoire will not be strong. A closely related variety of English is used, again in a wide range of contexts, as a second language by Africans who also have more occasion to use an African language to which they may express feelings of loyalty. This group will have been taught English at least as far as secondary school level. Finally, there is a variety of English imperfectly acquired, by those whose teaching in English has perhaps been limited to primary level, for whom English is a foreign rather than a second language. This variety must be distinguished from pidgins and creoles which evolved outside the education system and which, most importantly, Africans themselves do not consider to be English.

In most former colonies, English has rarely been taught by native speakers except in the early days of education in the colonial period itself. Latterly, although senior teaching positions may have been held by British-born speakers committed to the teaching of 'Standard English', the bulk of teachers have themselves usually been second-language speakers. Opportunities for contact with first-language speakers have therefore been limited; where this has occurred the effects are often obvious, as in the reported case of mission school pupils speaking with the Scottish accents of their expatriate teachers. Since speakers of many different languages may turn out to be teachers of English to pupils whose range of languages is also very wide, the possibilities of influence from those languages on the local variety of English are likely to be immense. Not only is this true of Africa; in Malaysia and Singapore, many teachers of English have actually been from India, the source of much indentured labour on rubber plantations since the early twentieth century.

Limited contact with first-language speakers of English, and insufficient attention paid to spoken English in the education system, help to account for the flavour of literariness that is often found by first-language English speakers in the English of both Africa and India. Most Indians, for example, would have encountered the written English of administration and learning more than any other variety: hence, it has been said that Indians are over-fond of polysyllabic vocabulary, and are likely to say *demise* rather than *death*. They are also said to be prone to empty verbosity in their use of phrases such as *each and every* and to favour formal variants such as the uncontracted *do not*, *cannot* rather than *don't* and *can't* in their speech. Similar tendencies have been found in African usage: the use of *witness* rather than *see* has been noted, as have some spelling pronunciations arising from unfamiliarity with native models. *Plumber*, for instance, has been heard with the /b/ pronounced.

Influence from African and Asian languages can be readily identified. Well-known examples include the phonetic realisations of certain phonemes, such as the Indian retroflex pronunciation of /t/ and /d/, made with the tongue curled back, as in the pronunciation of /r/ in the south-west of England. An African grammatical pattern underlies *he values his car than his wife*, where there is no word corresponding to *more*. Local vocabulary is also used: in the English of Malaysia and Singapore, the Malay word *(h)ulu* (upstream) has come to refer to a place where not much is going on, so that people speak of an *ulu area*.

Other tendencies, with greater structural consequences, are more widespread. Many Asian languages do not have the range of fricatives that are found in English, so we often find them substituted by plosives. This is particularly the case with the initial consonants of *thin* and *then*, replaced by /t/ and /d/ respectively (as they are in many non-standard urban varieties of England and the United States). Consonant-clusters similarly are reduced or re-structured. In Hindi, /sp/ does not occur in initial position, so Hindi speakers often insert a vowel before the cluster, giving *ispeak*. In Malaysia and Singapore, a vowel is sometimes inserted *between* the consonants, producing *setem* for stamp. In the same area, clusters in final position are often simplified: *recent* becomes *recen*.

Another general tendency concerns the system of tense and aspect. Many Indian speakers, like the Celtic language speakers of the British Isles, use continuous forms for habitual actions: *I am doing* for *I do*. Neither Malay nor Chinese, as spoken in Malaysia or Singapore, have tense systems of the kind associated with western European languages, although they have ways of marking aspect: thus, a perfect is often signalled with the use of an adverb, such as *already*. *My father already pass away* means 'my father has passed away'. In parts of West Africa *I am having a cold* is used instead of *I have (got) a cold*: this reflects the aspect system of the Kwa languages, where temporary states, such as having a cold, are distinguished in the grammar from permanent ones, such as having a body.

A significant point about many of the features listed is that they are found among speakers whose first languages do not themselves have the structures that have influenced the development of the feature in question. *I am having a cold* is also heard in East Africa, where the aspect distinction characteristic of Kwa is not made among local languages. It seems therefore that certain local variations in English have spread widely among speakers of many different first languages. It has recently been argued that both West and East African Englishes share many features, but that those features are also essentially African, rather than Caribbean, Black American, etc. Similarly, different varieties of English in India, Sri Lanka, Pakistan, Nepal, and Bangla Desh influence each other; and some of these in turn have influenced the English of Malaysia and Singapore through the teaching of English in the schools.

In each broad area under discussion, therefore, we can speak of a local variety of English, within which there is a range of variants. These variants are partly determined by geography, but more importantly perhaps by the level of education and social position of the speaker. There is a continuum, therefore, between the broader, most local usages of the less educated to the less markedly local varieties of educated elites. At first the usage of this latter group would have been orientated towards the English of England: usage was exonormative. Gradually, however, local norms have developed; even the most educated speakers are aware of these. Attempts to speak English with an RP accent are often greeted with ridicule in these areas. English-speaking Africans, for instance, want to sound like Africans. And while the broader local variants are stigmatised, many Africans resist changing their linguistic habits, either because they want to assert their ethnic identity, or because they sense that there is no immediate or automatic prospect of economic advancement if they do change them.

Some scholars have used the term standard to refer to these local varieties. A 'South Asian Standard' is said to exist in the area of the Indian sub-continent; similarly, people speak of a West Indian one, although there we need to take account of a different historical development. The English of Singapore and Malaysia is distinctive, as is the English of Africa, where it has been claimed that a West African and East African standard will in time emerge. The vital point about all these varieties is that they have their own norms. The fact that these are not the norms of people in England or America is of no consequence; nor does it matter that these varieties are in origin second language ones. They are increasingly used as media of communication among educated people; in addition, they are used in writing, for a number of purposes. They are legitimate Englishes in their own right: if not national standards, at least areal ones.

Since at least the early 1980s, however, there has also been a tendency to see standardisation in some of these territories as a *national* phenomenon. In the past it has been assumed that standard varieties cannot exist in them because the local Englishes are not 'native', and are therefore imperfect. These so-called imperfections have often been seen either as resulting from the effect of interference from other languages, or as deviations from 'native' usage. The latter assumes that local usage has tried, but in many cases failed, to attain the 'target' variety. Whatever the cause, it has been assumed that the local Englishes can only be improved through better teaching.

For the government in Singapore during the 1970s the answer lay in recruiting teachers who were so-called native speakers. In practice, these were white people from Britain and former dominions. But the teachers hired not only spoke different varieties of English but tended to be tolerant of linguistic diversity. Moreover, they did not consider it their job to insist on any particular pronunciation. As a consequence, there has since been an explicit emphasis on teachers who speak RP. This experience highlights many of the problems involved in defining a 'native speaker' of English. Does one have to come from a particular country or countries? Does being one entail also a use of 'Standard English', even an RP accent? For the government of Singapore, the concept of the native speaker seems to have been conflated with that of the RP-pronouncing speaker of 'Standard English'.

An irony in the case of Singapore is that today about half the population has learned English in the home, and a large proportion of those consider themselves to be native speakers. And as in the British Isles, the mystification surrounding the notions of 'Standard English' and RP are such that some Singaporean speakers of English imagine that postvocalic *r* is a feature of RP, and that the use of the perfective aspect as in *you've written* in the English English *this is the first time you've written in to the programme*, instead of the local *you're writing*, must be incorrect since it appears to imply a past action. It seems, therefore, that Singaporeans have developed their own normative judgements about the use of English.

Studies of English in Singapore have emphasised the role of local standardising agencies such as education and publishing in attempting to define a national 'standard'. In writing, the spellings *color*, *program* and *check* (cheque), the form *gotten* and vocabulary such as *garbage* and *faucet* (tap) show the influence of America (the source also of postvocalic *r* mentioned above). So, although many standardised written forms *are* international, there are pressures here, as elsewhere, to adopt forms from more than one source, and also to adapt to local usage. Not surprisingly, such usages are sometimes also disputed locally, and it is often newspapers that are instrumental in making decisions about them, for instance the *Straits Times* in Singapore. The spelling *kampung*, for instance, meaning village, has been preferred over the earlier form *kampong*, on the grounds that the first reflects the spelling of the word's Malay origins.

Given the influence from America, and the desire of the Singapore government to recruit 'native' speakers as teachers, it is possible to understand the attempt to maintain British influence in the sphere of language teaching, as mentioned in an earlier section. In Singapore itself, however, the notion of a native Singaporean English has been separated from that of a Singaporean 'standard' of English. First-language speakers of English tend to learn what has been called Singapore Colloquial English, which has many of the simplified features associated with creoles. By the age of about four, however, they have begun to learn that marking tense and number, for instance, is a feature of another kind of English which is considered more standardised within Singapore. It has been argued that standardisation of English in Singapore necessarily involves making a distinction between these varieties.

Many of these issues have also been aired in a study of standardisation in Nigerian English. But a further one has also been raised. Instead of labelling local features as products of interference and deviation, it has also been possible to see them as evidence of creativity. In Nigeria a new compound noun, *been-to*, has been coined from utterances such as *she has been to Britain* to refer to people who have travelled overseas. It has been argued that such coinages, if used by 'educated' speakers, can legitimately be seen as 'standard' Nigerian English. But as we saw in chapter two, there is always a problem about drawing the boundary between standard and non-standard, a problem clearly seen when imaginative literature is discussed.

For whatever reason, it is in the writing of fiction, plays and poetry that the status of local Englishes is widely felt to be crucial. Many novelists and poets from different parts of Anglophone Africa, southeast Asia and the Caribbean have tried to find a personal voice in the local variety of English. For such writers the question of audience is a vital consideration. To be taken seriously throughout the English-speaking world their English must not be too marked for localisms; but how else can local feelings, ideas, and identities be expressed? Indian writers have spoken about the difficulties involved in representing Eastern modes of address and greeting among characters in novels, and in referring to systems of kinship and authority in an alien language. For West Indian writers, the problem concerns the status of creole, the language of many central characters in their novels. In Africa, many Black writers have unashamedly appropriated the language of their colonial past, and found an African voice by drawing on images, metaphors, and allusions current in African languages. In this, the lead was given in West Africa in the 1950s; since then more and more writing has come out of Africa, including East Africa, where Nairobi has emerged as an important centre for the publication of African writing in English.

In Africa some academics have not been happy, however, about the linguistic creativity shown by certain writers. The Nigerian novelist Amos Tutuola, for instance, uses the phrase *born and die babies* to refer to an African belief in babies who die but return, usually to the same parents. For some tastes the coinage is aptly poetic; for others it is too reminiscent of either imperfectly-acquired, or pidgin, English. On this latter view, publishing it in a widely-read and admired work of imaginative fiction only serves to stigmatise African varieties of English in the eyes of the world.

Among many English speakers in the United Kingdom and America, however, attitudes to such overseas varieties are still often rooted in the colonial era when Indian English, for instance, was referred to derogatively as 'Babu' or 'Cheechee' English. The 'literariness' of Indian English is thought to be evidence of an inadequate grasp of levels of style; other aspects are dismissed as quaint, pompous, or the hallmarks of a deferential, even grovelling disposition. Empty verbosity, however, is by no means limited to South Asian speakers of English: and these attitudes also forget that there are many different users and uses of English. If a feature becomes general among a group of users of a language, then that feature may be described as characteristic of the local variety, whatever its origins. Thus, in parts of Africa where many children learn only a little English, it is in principle impossible to know where to draw the line between a 'mistake' and a usage that enjoys local currency. 'Standard English' is not the only norm in English today, just as the Classical Latin of Rome was not the norm in the Gaul of the fifth century.

INDEPENDENCE AND LANGUAGE PLANNING

Britain's colonies generally achieved independence after the Second World War: India in 1947, others in the 50s and early 60s. New governments had to come to terms with the multicultural and multilingual character of their territories, their borders arbitrarily defined, their economies unbalanced by European imperialism. The European ideology of the nation-state was thrust upon them, putting their leaders under pressure to find a single language supposedly capable of expressing the will of the population, the 'nation'. The processes associated with standardisation discussed in chapter two – selection, acceptance, elaboration, codification – had to be telescoped within a time-scale unknown elsewhere. In short, the new nation-states felt constrained to evolve a language-plan, with a degree of engineering far more conscious than that we have described in the context of England.

The language problems of the new nation-states are akin to those of many Central and Eastern European states of the nineteenth century, which had newly emerged within the empires of the Austro-Hungarians and the Turks. The choice of a so-called national language in all cases is partly governed by the desire to establish distinctiveness from neighbouring states, and partly by the need to promote cohesiveness among many different languages and cultures within a single territory. But the choice has often been extremely difficult. Internal rivalries, themselves often exacerbated by imperial practices; shortage of educational resources and the influence of super-power politics have complicated the issue. Today, many problems remain unsolved, and language-policies are often incoherent and riddled with contradictions.

In choosing a 'national' language, symbolism plays a large part. Many governments have wanted to choose a local one, as the emblem of an indigenous culture. One problem is, which one? Many local languages are not spoken by a majority of the population in a given area; nor do they have traditions of literacy and use within the specialised domains required by a modern state. Some governments have eschewed such a nationalistic, or *authenticist* course, and opted instead for a language which they feel answers to the needs of a modern nation-state. Efficiency, rather than symbolism, is the keyword of such a *modernist* course.

In many former colonies, especially in Africa, the language chosen has been English. Although in many African territories it had less than a century to take root, its usefulness as a lingua franca and as an international language of commerce has ensured its survival and continued use. While it may have been the language of the colonial master, it was also the language of nationalism, of independence movements; and it is also the language of America, the most powerful nation in the world. Conditions both internal and external have therefore favoured its retention, and it is worth noting that for many of the same reasons it is also in great demand among nation-states that were never part of the British or any other European empire.

Those nation-states which have chosen an indigenous tongue as the 'national' language have usually retained English as an official language. Thus, while the national language of India is Hindi, English is retained as a subsidiary language. A great deal of writing is undertaken in it, and it is also a lingua franca among peoples who have been estimated to use as many as 800 different languages. From the linguistic point of view Hindi is actually closer to English than to, say, the southern Indian language Telugu. India has a bilingual education policy: English is taught in schools, as are those languages which have been designated the official languages of different Indian states, so that some Indian children need to learn four languages: Hindi, English, the state language if it is not Hindi, and sometimes their own native language if it is not one of these.

The choice of language will inevitably affect the character of the local variety of English. Malaysia has developed Bahasa Malaysia as its 'national' language, although Singapore retains English: we can expect the latter to develop a more local variety of English than the former which also uses English in commerce and teaches it in schools. But now that Bahasa Malaysia is being developed in domains previously associated with English, the latter's functions will contract, and it will take on more of the features of a taught language rather than of a medium of inter-ethnic communication.

English is also used extensively in Africa. But although it is an official language for over 160 million Africans, it is almost always a second language only, and many have little knowledge of it. Many nation-states, such as Nigeria, Kenya, and Uganda, have adopted it as an official language, but bilingual education programmes are of necessity also quite common. In one former colony, Tanzania, the national language is the East African lingua franca, Swahili. This choice may be seen as an assertion of authenticist values: the decision was helped, however, by the fact that Swahili was the language of the nationalist movement there. English has also been retained in Tanzania as an official language; as in most African states it has had a head-start in the education system in a continent too poor to develop rapidly the necessary resources in the local languages. As a result, English is still dominant in secondary and tertiary education, and Swahili-medium education at these levels has yet to take root.

Recent debate about the status of English in a number of former colonies suggests a gap between official language policy and planning on the one hand, and, on the other, what actually happens on the ground. While some Indians, for instance, continue to see English as expressive of internationalism and even universalism, and as therefore capable of overcoming barriers of nation, religion and culture, others in India argue that this view is only held by a tiny elite with a professional interest in the spread of English. The numbers of English speakers in India, according to this latter view, have been over-estimated; English is now less widely used in law, civil administration and education than formerly, and is rarely used as a medium of inter-state communication by ordinary working people. A further issue suggested by this debate is the extent to which language-planning is, or should be, determined solely by those in power.

In South Africa, for instance, some non-governmental agencies and academics have argued against the uncritical acceptance of English as an official language now that apartheid has been dismantled. Of eleven recognised languages, English is spoken as a first language by about 8 per cent of the population. Zulu, on the other hand, is spoken by about one-fifth, and is widely used in addition as a lingua franca. In between is Afrikaans, first language of about 15 per cent. Zulu, however, tends to be associated with the opposition Inkatha Freedom Party; Afrikaans, though also spoken by a large number of Black people, with the legacy of apartheid. One aspect of the latter was a language policy which promoted African languages as media of primary education for Blacks in their respective 'Homelands', granting them only very limited access to Afrikaans or English, the languages of political participation.

A new language policy has recently granted official status to all eleven languages. But an innovative part of this policy was to consult all parents about the languages they preferred their children to be educated in at school. An additional principle was that no-one would be forced to accept an unwanted language as a medium of instruction. Given this experience of education under apartheid, and the fact that while English is widely seen as a way out of poverty it is spoken by less than sixty per cent of the population, it remains to be seen how language planning on this scale can meet the demands of the people, and what role English will play in the future.

Part IV

Evidence, interpretation and theory

8 A critical linguistic history of English texts

Published histories of English are usually illustrated with textual extracts drawn from different periods. It seems that there are two broad categories of text. Those of the first kind exemplify the linguistic features of central interest to the historian of language. The second kind embody particular *attitudes* to English. Linguistic historians have often interpreted the latter for the light they throw on the linguistic features exemplified in texts of the first kind.

In many cases, histories of English have made the same selection of textual extracts. In fact, there exists a *canon* of texts which allegedly 'shows' how modern English has developed from Anglo-Saxon (or Old English, as it is now more usually called). The impression is given that the history of English emerges, as it were, from close inspection of the texts. But does this put the cart before the horse? When the systematic study of the history of English began in the last century, there was a strong tendency to view that history as the story of standardisation. Accordingly, the appropriate texts were selected and interpreted so as to illustrate that story, as we shall see in discussing the *Oxford English Dictionary* below.

Both textual categories involve problems of interpretation. In the first, there is a tendency to concentrate on linguistic features, which, in varied ways, support the story mentioned above. In practice, texts have often been arranged in chronological order to show increasing intelligibility the more 'modern' they are, almost as if English developed in a purely linear fashion from one unified state to another. In the second textual category, statements embodying particular attitudes have often been taken at face value, almost as though they were the authoritative products of a purely disinterested observation. Editing texts for an anthology tends, moreover, to obscure their many different kinds of social functions, audiences and communicative effects. In the discussion that follows I have tried to highlight these issues of interpretation.

Any historian of English must decide which texts to select; and how to interpret them. Inevitably, this will reflect his or her idea of what the history of English actually is. But there is also the question of *audience*. Traditionally, histories of English address a readership familiar with the concerns of philology and modern linguistic theory. More recently, however, scholars from other disciplines – such as Literature, History and Cultural studies – have shown an interest in the field. They have other, important, questions to ask. So also do the many second-language users of English in different parts of the world: does, for instance, a textual history of English also include texts produced beyond England? These issues of selection and interpretation are therefore central to opening up the field.

Below I have included many of those texts I consider canonical, and have marked them with an *. I have also added some other kinds of texts in the hope that unusual juxtapositions may provoke new questions. These include scholarly works such as dictionaries, so that readers can see how a certain kind of historical inquiry has been undertaken, and can learn to apply it for themselves in the Exercises at the end of the book.

*1

When he   that   (on a) certain occasion did,   (that) he   left   the   house of the   feast
Þa he þaet þa sumre tide dyde, þaet he forlet þaet hus þaes gebeor-

and   out   was   going   to of cattle the shed   whose   care to him   was
scipes ond ut waes gongende to neata scipene, þara heord him waes

that   night   entrusted   when he   there   at   the appointed   time his   limbs   in
þaere neahte beboden, þa he ða ðaer in gelimplicre tide his leomu on

rest   laid down and   fell asleep   then   stood   him a certain man before in (a)   dream   and
reste gesette ond onslepte, þa stod him sum mon aet þurh swefn ond

him   hailed   and greeted and   him   by   his   name   called: ·Caedmon,
hine halette ond grette ond hine be his noman nemnde: 'Cedmon,

sing me ,   something'.   Then   answered   he   and   said: 'Not know I
sing me hwaethwugu'. Þa ondswarede he ond cwaeð: 'Ne con ic

not (how) to sing';   and   I because of this from   this   feast   out   went   and
noht singan; ond ic for þon of þeossum gebeorscipe ut eode, ond

here   came because   I nothing to sing not knew how'. Again he   said,   he who with
hider gewat, for þon ic naht singan ne cuðe'. Eft he cwaeð, se ðe mid

him   speaking   was: 'However   you   can for me   sing'.   Then said. he
hine sprecende waes: 'Hwaeðre pu meaht me singan.' Þa cwaeð he:

'What   shall   I   sing?'   Said   he;   'Sing to me (about the) Creation.'   Then he
'Hwaet sceal ic singan?' Cwaeð he: 'Sing me frumsceaft.' Þa he ða

this *answer* *received,* *then* *began* *he* *at once to sing* *in* *praise* *of God*
þas andsware onfeng, þa ongon he sona singan in herenesse Godes

the Creator *these lines* *and* *these words* *which he* *never* *(had) heard*
Scyppendes þa fers ond þa word þe he naefre gehyrde.

This is an extract from the West Saxon translation of Bede's *Ecclesi-astical History of the English People*, originally written in Latin in the early eighth century. It tells the story of Caedmon, customarily shy when it comes to feasting, who one night receives the gift of verse. I have added a modern English 'gloss' to the West Saxon.

The extract gives us evidence of what the dominant dialect in Anglo-Saxon times looked like. The language reflects that of the late ninth century, when King Alfred of Wessex was commissioning translations of learned works written in Latin. Translating Bede was politic: Alfred's monarchical ambitions needed the support of the Church, and Bede was widely revered. Furthermore, by translating him into West Saxon Alfred was also boosting the prestige of his own kingdom of Wessex. In fact, more West Saxon translations of the same text were made in the next two hundred years, all of them reflecting the process of 'West Saxonisation' of English texts, which was largely disrupted by the Norman Conquest in 1066.

Our view of the Anglo-Saxon period as a whole is heavily influenced by West Saxon perceptions. The history of English in this period is often portrayed as a progress towards a West Saxon 'standard' (associated at first with Alfred, but by more recent scholarship with the regularising practice of scribes at Winchester from later in the period). The relative paucity of texts written in other dialects makes it difficult to reconstruct the perspective of other kingdoms. Somewhat ironically, there is some linguistic evidence suggesting that the translation of Bede was originally done with the help of Mercians, whose once-powerful kingdom had been largely overrun by the Vikings at this time.

As its title states, Bede's *History* is a *church* history, reflecting the viewpoint of that institution. In fact, at this time almost all writing was associated with the Church; and Bede's 'Christianisation' of the Caedmon story shows the power of the Church to control the interpretation of events. Perhaps this should be borne in mind when we read Bede's famous account of the Anglo-Saxon invasions, which has often been seen as authoritative.

*2

truly
Ic willo uutetlice and ðissum hlaetmesto sealla swa and ðe; vel ne is rehtlic me þaet ic willo doa vel ego ðin wohgfull is forðon ic god am.

Extract 2 is another translation from a Latin original produced in early Northumbria, but this time in the Northumbrian dialect of the late tenth century. It is from the Lindisfarne Gospels, part of Matthew, Chapter 20 (the Parable of the Vineyard), where the owner seeks to justify paying the same wage to his labourers irrespective of the length of time worked. The same passage (verses 14–15) in the Authorised Version of the Bible (1611) runs thus:

I will give unto this last, even as unto thee. Is it not lawful for me to do what I will with mine own? Is thine eye evil, because I am good?

The Northumbrian translation can be compared with a late West Saxon one in a homily delivered by Aelfric, the famous abbot of Eynsham, Oxfordshire, written about 1000 AD.

truly
Ic wille soðlice syllan þisum latestan swa micel swa ðe. Hu ne mot ic don þaet ic wylle? Oððe ðin eage is yfel, for ðan ðe ic eom good?

Comparing the Old English extracts gives us evidence of dialect diversity in Anglo-Saxon times. The final unstressed vowel *o* in *ego* (eye) for instance, contrasts with the *e* in the late West Saxon *eage* (see *willo/ wylle*); and instead of the WS *ea* diphthong the Northumbrian text has *e* (a feature shared by the other 'Anglian' dialects of Mercia). But the late Northumbrian text can be seen as canonical largely because it shows evidence of the general *direction* of change in English. The infinitive forms *sealla* (give) and *doa* (do) lack the final *n* of the West Saxon *syllan* and *don*. This is an example of the inflectional breakdown that has been seen as a crucial point of difference between Old and Middle English. The late Northumbrian extract shows that the process may have begun in the north (assuming that the infinitive ending was general in Old English).

3

first   from   hawk's   mound   to   Windrush   to   the   willow   row   to   nut slope from
Aerest of hafoces hlewe on wenrisc on þa wiðig rewe on hnut clyf.of

the   slope   to the high clearing   then   to   Langley   way   along   way
þam clyf on hean leage. þ' on lungan leage weg. and lang weges.

then   to wood-chips clearing   along   way until it reaches
þonne on spon leage þonne on spon weg. andlang weges þ' hit sticað

to   the north part   of the king' tongue of land.   Thence   to marsh clearing   clearing
on norðe weardum kynges steorte. Þa non on sugarode and lang rode

huntsmen's   way   Wickham   always by
on huntena weg. andlang weges þ' hit sticað aet wic ham. ða non a be

the root   ?   acre   old   way
wyrt wale on ofling ecer. Þa non on ealdan weg andlang weges on

?   stone from the   stone   the   green   way
cycgan stan. of þam stane on þane grenan weg.

Extract 3 is from a text of a very different kind. It is part of a charter, dated 969, describing the northern half of the boundary of an Anglo-Saxon estate near modern Witney, in Oxfordshire. The charter, issued by King Edgar, awards the estate to a noble; it is thus a text which expresses monarchical, rather than ecclesiastical, authority. As in most other Anglo-Saxon charters, the part written in Old English – known as the *perambulation* – follows a section in Latin.

The perambulation names boundary features as one walks round the estate in a clockwise direction. Some of these, such as *ofling* and *cycgan*, are not identifiable and are hard to translate. Others, however, are still visible today: a burial mound (*hlewe*), a slope with (hazel) nut trees (*hnut clyf*), several tracks (denoted by *ealdan weg* or *grenan weg*) and streams (*wenrisc*). *Wyrt wale* here probably means the edge of a wood (still existing). By the date of the charter's issue that landscape may have been settled by the Anglo-Saxons for 300 years. These invaders came, perhaps, by way of the River Thames to the south, perhaps also by way of pre-Roman trackways (such as the *ealdan weg*?) and a local Roman road known as Akeman Street. It is probable that much of the area was settled by the Anglo-Saxon tribe known as the *Hwicce*, whose name survives in Wychwood, formerly a royal hunting forest marking the estate's northern boundary. The Hwicce were absorbed into Mercia; since the Thames marked the border between Wessex and Mercia this area may have been disputed between the kingdoms.

The charter is an example of an official, bureaucratic document. Such documents in Old English (about 2,000 remain, but there is no way of knowing how many have been lost; they are less likely than literary works to be preserved) are perhaps evidence of a higher level of literacy among the Anglo-Saxons than existed among the Norman invaders (who would not have used Norman French for these purposes).

*4

| therefore | my | beloved | sisters | above | all | things | be | diligent | | have (a) | pure |

Forþi, mine leoue sustren, ouer alle þing beoð bisie to habben schir

| heart | what | | | I | it | have | said | before | that is | that you |

heorte. Hwet is schir heorte? Ich hit habbe iseid ear: þet is, þet ʒe na

| nothing | | want | nor | love | except | God | alone | | very | things for (the |

þing ne wilnin ne ne luuien bute Godd ane, ant te ilke þinges, for

| sake of) | God that | you | | | | | | say | love | them |

Godd, þe helped ow toward him. For Godd, ich segge, luuien ham,

| not | | themselves |

ant nawt for hamseoluen.

Extract 4 is the first example of what scholars usually call 'Middle English'. It is an extract from a text known as *Ancrene Wisse*, written perhaps in a Herefordshire priory about 1230. Its language is so close to a number of others produced in the same area that scholars have assumed the existence of a scriptorium in this area exercising a form of written standardisation. The text aims to instruct a small group of wealthy women dedicated to a life of religious devotion.

The text invites the question: what criteria are to be used to distinguish Old from Middle English? For the language of *Ancrene Wisse* has usually been described as being much closer to Old English than other texts of the same period. In line 2, for instance, the initial *i* in *iseid* derives from the Old English form *ge-*, which marked a past participle. In line 3 *luuien* derives from Old English *lufian* which belonged to a class of 'weak' verbs with *i* in the infinitive form. In line 4, *ham* shows that the Old English *h-* forms of the personal pronouns have not yet been replaced by the Scandinavian *þ* forms. In line 2 the form *hwet* (instead of *hwaet*) derives from a sound-change in the Old English dialect of Mercia in which many instances of *ae* were raised to *e*. Finally, it is interesting to note the plural of *sustren* (sisters) with *-n*. In West Saxon *sweostor* (sister) had an uninflected plural form identical to the singular; *-n* was the plural ending of weak nouns only; here it has been added to what was historically a different class of noun. It has since become quite widespread for marking plurals in dialect, as in *housen* (houses).

*5

alas who shall these   blow
wel qwa sal thir hornes blau

holy   cross (on)   thy
haly   rod   thi day

now   dead   low
nou is he dede and lies law

(who)   blow   them   always
was wont to blaw thaim ay

Extract 5 is from later in the same century, a verse fragment from York, dated 1272. It is our first example of a *literary* text in the modern sense of imaginative (or fictional) writing. Histories of language, and especially the study of Middle English, have traditionally been over-dependent on such texts. It is also important to point out that until the last century 'literary' used to include devotional and historical writing such as that of Bede (see *1).

There are many more surviving texts from the Middle English period than from the Old English: in fact, the former have often been used as evidence for filling the gaps in our knowledge of the language in Anglo-Saxon times. In describing Middle English, historians of English have usually chosen texts to illustrate the extent of regional diversity during this period. Thus, unlike the *Ancrene Wisse*, the *York Fragment* (as Extract *5 has been called) has the *th-* forms in *thaim*, and the 3rd person singular *s* ending in *lies*: these we might expect from a text produced in what was once a Viking stronghold in Northumbria. Another feature, the *unrounded* vowel in *haly* (holy), deserves more comment. In all Old English dialects the equivalent form was *halig*, probably pronounced in much the same way. The process of rounding, which eventually produces the form *holy*, was well under way in the south of England by about 1200. But the older, unrounded, variant was retained throughout the Middle English period in manuscripts produced north of the rivers Aire and Ribble (where today stand, respectively, Leeds and Preston), and has been a feature of dialect speech there until the present day. It was also retained in part of the extreme west, as in the *Ancrene Wisse* (no example in extract).

The variability in texts of this period can also be seen at another, *internal* level in the *York Fragment*. 'Blow' is spelt both *blau* and *blaw*. Consistency in spelling was at that time not seen as so important as it is today. Both kinds of variability, however, have often been viewed pejoratively, as evidence of linguistic 'instability'. But this is to project

back onto the Middle English period the *standardising* preoccupations
of later periods.

6

shepherd   *Mary's*
Iohon Schep, som tyme Seynte Marie prest of ȝork, and now of

Nobody
Colchestre, greteth wel Iohan Nameles, and Iohan þe Mullere, and

beware   deceit   town
Iohon Cartere, and biddeþ hem þat þei bee war of gyle in borugh,

together
and stondeth togidre in Godes name, and biddeþ Peres Plouȝman go

Rob
to his werk, and chastise wel Hobbe þe Robbere, and takeþ wiþ ȝow

look   to prepare
Iohan Trewman, and alle hiis fellawes, and no mo, and loke schappe

yourselves for one head (=unity)   *more*
ȝou to on heued, and no mo.

Iohan þe Mullere haþ ygrounde smal, smal, smal;
Þe Kynges sone of heuene schal paye for al.

wary   woeful
Be war or ye be wo;
Knoweþ ȝour freend fro ȝour foo;

flee   sin
And do wel and bettre, and fleth synne.

peace
And sekeþ pees, and hold ȝou þerinne;

and so biddeþ Iohan Trewman and alle his felawes.

This is the complete text of a letter reputedly addressed to the Essex
members of the Great Society of Peasants by the radical preacher John
Ball in 1381, on the eve of the Peasants' Revolt. The Great Society,
which was particularly strong in the south-east, was formed from
numerous local unions of land-labourers in their demands for higher
wages from the landowners, both secular and ecclesiastical. The actual
armed insurrection of 1381 was prompted by the imposition of a poll
tax, which hit the peasants hard. Their cause was supported by many of
the poorer clergy, whose belief (to quote from the contemporary poem
Piers Plowman) 'That alle thynges under heuene ouhte to be in com-
mune' was inspired by the idea that all men, being descendants of

Adam, were equal. One such priest was John Ball, who was later executed for his part in the Revolt.

Historians of English have usually seen the fourteenth century as witnessing a rise in the status of English, which since 1066 had been a minority written language within England. The reason usually advanced is that the English were experiencing a sense of national identity. But while anti-French *patriotism* was certainly widespread, there were also sharp conflicts internal to England, as the Peasants' Revolt shows. These conflicts were not confined to labour-relations: the peasants' cause was supported by many clergy because the Church itself was widely seen as corrupt. There was a large amount of theological argument and exhortation in English, to appeal to a popular audience, which, as Ball's letter also implies, was by no means entirely illiterate.

The letter also shows how certain literary works in English could permeate the thought and language of a priest such as Ball, and could appeal to ordinary people. *Piers Plowman*, mentioned above, may have inspired the references to 'Hobbe the Robbere' and 'do wel and bettre' (Dowel, Dobet, Dobest are names in the poem).

7

And þis corrupcioun of Englysshe men yn þer modre-tounge,
<small>their</small> <small>mother-tongue</small>

begunne as I seyde with famylyar commixtion of Danys firste and of
<small>said</small> <small>mixing</small> <small>Danes</small>

Normannys aftir, toke grete augmentacioun and encrees aftir þe
<small>Normans</small> <small>took great</small> <small>augmentation</small> <small>increase after</small>

commyng of William conquerour by two thyngis. The firste was: by
<small>coming</small> <small>things</small>

decre and ordynaunce of þe seide William conqueror children in
<small>decree</small> <small>order</small> <small>said</small>

gramer-scolis ageyns þe consuetude and þe custom of all oþer
<small>grammar schools</small> <small>against</small> <small>practice</small>

nacyons, here owne modre-tonge lafte and forsakyn, lernyd here
<small>nations</small> <small>their</small> <small>left</small>

Donet on Frenssh and to construyn yn Frenssh and to maken here
<small>Donatus in</small> <small>interpret</small> <small>do</small>

Latyns on þe same wyse. The secounde cause was þat by the same
<small>Latin</small> <small>way</small>

decre lordis sonys and all nobyll and worthy mennys children were
<small>lords' sons</small> <small>noble</small>

     learn   *before*   *could*
fyrste set to lyrnyn and speken Frensshe, or þan þey cowde spekyn

  English   *writings*   *contracts*   *kinds of* *pleas*
Ynglyssh and þat all wrytyngis and endentyngis and all maner plees

    disputes   *reckonings*
and contrauercyes in courtis of the lawe, and all maner reknyngis

  accounts   *household*   *should*   *done*
and countis yn howsoolde schulle be doon yn the same. And þis

  seeing   *country people* *so that*   *seem*   *estimable*
seeyinge, þe rurales, þat þey myghte semyn þe more worschipfull and

          more easily   *acquaintance*
honorable and þe redyliere comyn to þe famyliarite of þe worthy and

                  strove   *learn*
þe grete, leftyn hure modre tounge and labouryd to kunne spekyn

                  mangled
Frenssh; and thus by processe of tyme barbarizid thei in bothyn and

    neither
spokyn neythyr good Frenssh nor good Englyssh.

This extract is from the friar Osbern Bokenham's *Mappula Angliae*, a fifteenth-century translation of Higden's *Polychronicon*. An earlier translation by John Trevisa, mentioned in chapter two above, has become a canonical text for historians of English. It suggests that by the fourteenth century, perhaps for the first time in its history, English had become a language to be commented on. Most of the comment at this time concerned its relations with French, a theme developed here by Bokenham in the following century.

  A significant aspect of the original Latin *Polychronicon* was a sense of linguistic history. English was characterised, in Bokenham's translation, by 'commixtion' with the languages of Danes and then of Normans. This mixing led to degeneration. What we have here is a very early application to English of classical ideas about linguistic purity, and the harm allegedly brought about by language contact. The focus on French was greatly fuelled by political considerations: by Bokenham's time England had been at war with France for over a century, and Bokenham himself adds to his translation the reference to William the Conqueror's 'decre and ordynaunce' which was in fact a fourteenth-century forgery.

  Like that of Trevisa, Bokenham's translation includes interesting material on the status of English and French and the use of French and Latin in the grammar schools. In particular, he refers to the fact that schoolchildren would learn Latin through the medium of French rather than English, from a grammar written by the Roman grammarian Donatus (*Donet*). This is revealing: Donatus had written one thousand years before Bokenham lived, and this grammar was in turn largely based on the approach taken by the Greek grammarian Thrax in about 100 BC, which identified eight 'parts of speech'. It was not until the latter half of the sixteenth century that anyone attempted to write a grammar of *English* based on these principles.

A further point to make about this extract concerns the large number of words derived from Latin, such as *augmentacioun, ordynaunce* and *consuetude*. This is what we might expect in a text of this kind at this date, but it might prompt the questions: is Bokenham's own discourse (based on the Suffolk variety of the south-East Midland dialect) 'good Englyssh'? Are adoptions from other languages a sign of corruption in speech but, when written, of learning?

Finally, it is worth pointing out that at least one of Bokenham's notions persists in the present century. His idea that bilingualism may result in two languages being 'barbarizid' is by no means unknown in the present century, when it has been described as *semi-lingualism*.

8

The rewarde for howndys [hounds]

When yowre houndes by strencith [force] hath done her to dede, [death]
The hunter shall rewarde hem then with the hede,

With the shulderis and the sides [flanks] and with the bowellis all

And all thyngis within the the wombe [stomach] save onli the gall

The paunche also, [internal organs]

Yeve [Give] hem [them] noon [none] of thoo. [that]

Wich rewarde when oon [on] the erth it is dalt [shared out]

With all goode hunteris the 'halow' [hallow] it is calt. [called]

Then the loynes [loins] of the hare loke ye not forgete, [take care]

Bot [but] bryng hem to the kechyn [kitchen] for the lordis meete. [food]

And of this ilke hare ^{self-same}

Speke we no mare ^{more}

A great deal of Middle English writing is anonymous. By the end of the fifteenth century, however, especially after the introduction of printing, it became customary actually to name authors (Caxton, for instance, printed *The Canterbury Tales* by Chaucer). Extract 8 is from *The Book of Saint Albans*, published by another printer in 1486. Part of this book, called *The Book of Hunting*, which contains this piece about the hare, is credited to a woman, a prioress known as Juliana Berners. If the text is indeed hers, it suggests that medieval women were involved in a wider range of affairs than today we might have expected. It also poses the question: how many of the anonymous writers of Middle English were actually women? The text further shows that verse was used to deal with topics which strike us today as 'non-literary'.

9

The kyng by þadvise and assent of the lordes spirituell and temporell beying in this present parlement woll and grantith þat þe said Sir Iohn Talbot haue and occupie the saide office of Chauncellor of Irelond by hym self or by his sufficient depute there after the fourme of the kynges lettres patentes to hym made þerof. The which letters patentes ben thought gode and effectuell and to be approved after the tenure of the same Also þat þe grete seal of þe saide lond belong-yng to þe saide office. which þe said Thomas hath geton vn to hym be delyuered to þe said Sir Iohn Talbot or his sufficiente depute hauing power of hym to resceiue hit

This fifteenth-century official document entrusting Sir John Talbot with the post of Chancellor of Ireland was produced by scribes working in the part of the royal administration known as Chancery. As such, it can be seen as an example of London English. Historians of English have taken a special interest in London as the economic and adminis-trative centre – and, therefore, as the *linguistic* centre – of England. In fact, London English from the fourteenth century has often been described as the embryonic standard. By that time the most influential usage was based on the East Midland dialect rather than the East Saxon of earlier times (as seen, for instance, in a royal proclamation of 1258). But the term *standard* is problematic here, since it has been used to include the related but rather different literary usage of Chaucer who, according to some scholars in the past, was the 'father' of modern (i.e., standard) English. In fact, the East Midland usage of London in the fourteenth and fifteenth centuries had a number of sub-varieties; *sich*, *swic* and *such* were all forms of 'such', for instance. Chancery English was a variety of formal written English for which scribes made a selection of usages, which were then regularised. The particular selection they made seems to have reflected, and partly crystallised, the dominant usage.

*10

(as it is)   *far (=a great deal)*

And certaynly our langage now vsed varyeth ferre from that whiche

are

was vsed and spoken whan I was borne. For we Englysshe men ben

moon

borne vnder the domynacyon of the mone, whiche is neuer stedfaste

always   changing   waxing

but euer wauerynge, wexing one season, and waneth and dyscreaseth

common (=colloquial)

another season. And that comyn Englysshe that is spoken in one shyre varyeth from a nother. In so muche that in my dayes happened

merchants   *on (the) Thames*

that certayn marchauntes were in a shippe in Tamyse, for to haue

Zeeland (=Holland)   *stayed*

sayled ouer the see into Zeland, and for lacke of wynde thei taryed

Foreland   *themselves*

atte Forlond, and wente to lande for to refreshe them; And one of

them   *Sheffield   merchant*   *house   asked*

theym named Sheffelde, a mercer, cam in-to an hows and axed for

food

mete; and specyally he axyd after eggys; And the goode wyf answerde, that she coude not speke no Frenshe. And the marchaunt was angry, for he also coude speke no Frenshe, but wolde haue hadde egges, and she vnderstode hym not. And thenne at laste a nother

eggs

sayd that he wolde haue eyren: then the good wyf sayd that she

Lo   *these*

vnderstod hym wel. Loo, what sholde a man in thyse dayes now wryte, egges or eyren. Certaynly it is harde to playse eueryman by cause of dyuersite and chaunge of langage.

Caxton's story about the north-country merchant trying to buy eggs near London and failing to make himself understood is in the Preface to his translation of the Roman author Virgil's *Aeneid*. The sentiments he expresses, that English has changed so much since his youth, and varies so much that its speakers cannot even agree on how to refer to eggs, have usually been taken at face-value by historians of English. They are used as incontrovertible evidence that even as late as 1490 English was still unstable and in need of the kind of attention and cultivation that is associated with standardisation.

It is important to remember, however, that Caxton is here writing a preface to a work he is trying to publish. The readership for his printed books was a newly-created one, so his portrayal of the English as a people as variable as the moon can be seen as a rather crude patriotic gesture. It was also a mainly middle-class readership, who might be expected to identify with the merchant in the story and his sense of linguistic putdown.

Caxton's fuss about the *eggs/eyren* example (the former derives from Old Norse, the language of the Vikings) can also be seen as trying to draw attention to the problems faced by a printer. This interpretation might be safer than the canonical one, which has tended to see him as a disinterested observer of linguistic variability. As an entrepreneur, Caxton stood to gain from not alienating too many of his potential readers by his choice of forms to print.

Perhaps what writers say in prefaces always needs careful interpretation. It was by no means uncommon throughout the sixteenth century, for instance, to complain about the state of English, to apologise for one's incompetence as a writer or translator, and also to claim that to write in English was to love one's country. Were such commonplaces a matter of convention rather than conviction?

*11

This part [i.e., language] in our maker or Poet must be heedyly [*carefully*] looked vnto, that it be naturall, pure, and the most vsuall of all his countrey; and for the same purpose rather that which is spoken in the kings Court, or in the good townes and Cities within the land, then [*than*] in the marches and frontiers, or in port townes, where straungers haunt for traffike sake, or yet in Vniuersities where Schollers vse much peeuish affectation of words out of the primatiue languages, or finally, in any vplandish village or corner of a Realme, where is no

uncivil

resort but of poore rusticall or vnciuill people: neither shall he follow
the speach of a craftes man or carter, or other of the inferiour sort,
thought he be inhabitant or bred in the best towne and Citie in this
Realme, for such persons doe abuse good speaches by strange
accents or ill shapen soundes, and false ortographie. But he shall
follow generally the better brought vp sort, such as the Greekes
call (*charientes*) men ciuill and graciously behauoured and bred.

poet

Our maker therfore at these dayes shall not . . . take the termes of
Northern-men, such as they vse in dayly talke, whether they be noble
men or gentlemen, or of their best clarkes all is a matter: nor in effect
any speach vsed beyond the riuer of Trent, though no man can deny
but that theirs is the purer English Saxon at this day, yet it is not so
Courtly nor so currant as our Southerne English is, no more is the
far Westerne ma(n')s speach: ye shall therfore take the vsuall speach
of the Court, and that of London and the shires lying about London
within lx. myles, and not much aboue. I say not this but that in euery
shyre of England there be gentlemen and others that speake but
spccially write as good Southerne as we of Middlesex or Surrey do,
but not the common people of euery shire, to whom the gentlemen,
and also their learned clarkes do for the most part condescend . . . we
finde in our English writers many wordes and speaches amendable,
and ye shall see in some many inkhorne termes so ill affected brought
in by men of learning as preachers and schoolemasters: and many

merchants

straunge termes of other languages by Secretaries and Marchaunts

travellers

and trauailours, and many darke wordes and not vsuall nor well
sounding, though they be dayly spoken in Court. Wherefore greet
heed must be taken by our maker in this point that his choise be
good.

This extract from *The Arte of English Poesie*, published in 1589 (when
Shakespeare was twenty-five) and attributed to the poet George
Puttenham, is famous for the association it makes between dialect and
social status. In particular, by narrowing its attention to the usage of
London and the Home Counties, it starts a trend which has been followed by language scholars ever since. The focus, moreover, is on the
usage of the 'better brought vp sort' of this area, rather than that of the
'inferiour sort' or, interestingly enough, that of 'Schollers'. This discourse of 'sorts' is discussed in chapter three above.

Puttenham seems to have had a hierarchical conception of usage, in which 'language' meant a kind of superordinate variety, much as the term 'standard' is often used today. But it is important to remember his interest in writing this passage. Puttenham was in effect recommending himself, as a literary man, to the royal court; so do his comments merely reflect late sixteenth-century courtly *prejudice* about English usage? Or can they be taken as evidence of the existence of a standard at this time? Many historians of English have thought the latter, and have been happy to limit their attention to the upper-class usage of London as though that were the only kind of English that mattered.

12

My deare Ned – I longe to see you, but would not haue you come downe, for I cannot thinke this cuntry very safe; by the papers I haue sent to your father, you will knowe the temper of it. I hope your father will giue me full derections how I may beest haue my howes

guarded
gareded, if need be; if he will giue the derections, I hope, I shall fooloow it.

My deare Ned, I thanke God I am not afraide. It is the Lords caus that we haue stood for, and I trust, though our iniquitys testify aganst vs, yet the Lord will worke for His owne name sake, and that He will now sheawe the men of the world that it is hard fighting against heauen. And for our comforts, I thinke neuer any laide plots to route out all Gods chillderen at once, but that the Lord did sheawe Himselfe mighty in saueing His saruants and confounding His enimyes, He did Pharowe, when he thought to haue destroyed all Israell, and so Haman. Nowe, the intention is, to route out all that feare God, and surely the Lord will arise to healpe vs; and in your God let your confidence be, and I am assured it is so. One meet Samuell and not knoweing wheare he dwelt, Samuell toold him he was a Darbesheare

entered into conversation
man, and that he came lately from thence, and so he did in discours;

Papist
the papis toold him, that theare was but a feawe puretaines in this cuntry, and 40 men would cut them all off.

This extract is the opening of a letter from Lady Brilliana Harley to her son Edward, an officer in the Parliamentary army, in 1643 (Ned is a familiar form of Edward). Married to Sir Robert Harley, politician and opponent of Charles I, Lady Brilliana was left in charge of their home,

Brompton Castle, in Shropshire near the Welsh border. As she was writing, the castle was about to be besieged by Royalist forces.

Historians of English have usually studied private correspondence of this kind for the possible light it throws on contemporary informal usage, especially pronunciation. It has been assumed that without the regulatory pressures of the scriptorium, printing press or publishing house, letter-writers have been relatively free to spell phonetically. An example of such 'occasional' spellings, as these are called, is *gareded*. The intrusive *e* after the *r* can be seen as evidence that at this date postvocalic *r* was still pronounced. In another letter Lady Harley has *ryteing* (writing), which perhaps shows that /w/ was no longer pronounced before /r/, and *enoufg* (enough) which could be a blend of the printed norm *enough* and the pronunciation of the final sound as /f/, the usual one today. The doubling of *e* as in *beest* (line 5, *best*) and *meet* (line 20, *met*) are harder to interpret, however; perhaps they indicate a lengthened vowel.

The letter is also interesting for the way it illustrates the cultural climate (or *temper*, line 3) of the 1640s. Despite her protestation to the contrary, Lady Harley had good reason to be afraid; not only because her life and home were in danger but because her husband and son were in arms against the king. Only a very strong religious and political creed could justify this, and the second half of her letter calls on the full discourse of Puritanism, with its reference to *all Gods chillderen* (note the absence of the apostrophe in *Gods*) and the Biblical allusions to Pharaoh and Haman, a Persian enemy of the Iraelites, God's chosen people. Many seventeenth-century Puritans saw themselves in the latter role, even wanting to include *all* the English, a view which some later historians have seen as an early form of nationalism.

13

I took a black oblong stiff Paper terminated by Parallel Sides, and with a Perpendicular right Line drawn cross from one side to the other, distinguished it into two equal Parts. One of these parts I painted with a red colour and the other with a blue. The Paper was very black, and the colours intense and thickly laid on, that the Phaenomenon might be more conspicuous. This Paper I view'd through a Prism of solid Glass, whose two Sides through which the Light passed to the Eye were plane and well-polished, and contained an Angle of about sixty degrees; which Angle I call the refracting Angle of the Prism.

This extract is from Experiment I in *Optics* by Sir Isaac Newton, the celebrated physicist and mathematician. This book, published in 1704, can be seen as exhibiting a new variety of English, 'scientific English', with its own ideals and developing conventions. These were largely based on discussions held by members of the Royal Society, and can be summed up by Sprat's statement in his history of that Society published in 1667 (when Newton, soon to become a Professor at Cambridge, was twenty-five). According to Sprat, members demanded a 'close, naked, natural way of speaking'.

Scientific English aspired to a 'primitive purity' of language. In finding this, the usage of '(a)rtizans, Countreymen and Merchants' was preferable to that of 'Wits and Scholars'. This view of language had by the seventeenth century become strongly associated with Puritans. It meant avoiding the importations from classical rhetoric so clearly displayed (and probably enjoyed) in the literary writing of the later sixteenth century, even by Puritans such as the soldier and poet Sir Philip Sidney in *Arcadia*:

> In the countrey of *Thessalia* (alas why name I that accursed Countrey, which brings forth nothing but matter for tragedies? but name it I must) in *Thessalia* I say there was (well I may say there was) a Prince: no, no Prince, whom bondage wholly possessed, but yet accompted a Prince and named *Musidorus*.
>
> (Partridge 1969: 213)

Here Sidney employs a rhetorical device known as *Epanorthesis* – the recalling of a word in order to suggest a more precise or appropriate expression. According to Sprat, scientific language should aim to be more concise: one word for every 'thing' referred to was the ideal.

For some Puritans such rhetorical devices were to be avoided because their immediate source was usually Latin, a language they associated with the Catholic Church. But for serious academic writing Latin still could not be avoided altogether and many scientific terms, for instance, had a Latin origin. In Extract 13, *plane* has been consciously re-spelt to evoke Latin *planus* (flat). The more usual spelling, *plain*, had come to be used in a wider variety of senses, looser than the meaning of 'perfectly flat' (as in the noun *plane* used in geometry today). Here we see an instance of the conscious cultivation of scientific terminology that began in the seventeenth century.

14

(a)

Lucy. Well really, mamma, you do not expect that I can understand the *subjunctive mood,* for I know nothing about the *conjunctions.*

Mamma. The conjunctions that are used before verbs of the subjunctive mood are *if, though, unless, except, whether.* And when you find any of these before a verb, you are to *expect* that the verb is of the *subjunctive mood.*

Lucy. But, mamma, am I only to *expect* that a verb which follows one of those conjunctions is of the subjunctive mood; shall I not be sure of it?

Mamma. No, Lucy, you will not always be *sure* of it, because a *conjunction* does not always imply that the circumstance is uncertain or doubtful, as you will see in the following example:

'Though she works hard she earns very little.' In this sententence there is no doubt expressed . . . and therefore the verb is of the *indicative mood,* though it has a *conjunction before* it.

Lucy. Mamma, in the following sentence is the verb 'work' of the subjunctive mood?

'If she *work* hard she will earn very little.'

Mamma. Certainly it is, Lucy, *for the working is uncertain*; she may work, or she may not work.

(b)

A verb is called active when it expresses an *action*, which is produced by the nominative of the sentence: as 'Sidmouth *imprisoned* Benbow'. It is passive, when it expresses an action, which is received, or endured, by the person or thing which is the nominative of the sentence, as, 'Benbow is *imprisoned*'. It is neuter, when it expresses simply the state of being, or of existence, of a person or thing: as 'Benbow *lies* in irons'.

Extract 14(a) is from Helen Wood's *A Grammatical Reading Class Book* (3rd edn 1828). Lesson XVI concerns number, person, mood and tense. Mamma has named five moods: 'the *Infinitive*, the *Indicative*, the *Subjunctive*, the *Potential*, and the *Imperative*' (p. 87). Lucy protests about the difficulty of these terms: her mother's rejoinder is that Lucy 'will never be clever without learning the meaning of long difficult words'.

Wood's *Grammar* is one of several hundred published in the aftermath of Lowth's *Grammar* of 1762. Conceived as a series of 'entertaining conversations' between a mother and her daughters, it adopts many of Lowth's precepts and concerns. On the subjunctive itself, Lowth's terminology is more clearly Latinate: 'Hypothetical, Conditional, Concessive and Exceptive Conjunctions seem to require properly the Subjunctive Mode after them.'

Lowth's *Grammar* is usually contrasted with the less prescriptive approach of his contemporary, the scientist Joseph Priestley. Priestley's promotion of 'usage' as the arbiter of acceptability has been lauded by modern linguists, who pride themselves on their 'descriptive' instincts, but also because Lowth seems to them to be too determined to fit the grammar of English into that of Latin. But the argument between 'propriety' (Lowth's term) and usage was not the only issue to surface at this time. Lowth's social position as a bishop, and the political climate of the late eighteenth century inspired the writing of other grammars based on quite different principles.

One of these is exemplified in Extract 14(b), which was written by the Radical, William Cobbett. Like Lucy, Cobbett was mystified by the 'long and difficult' terms for grammatical items and processes to be found in Lowth. He claims Lowth's Latinate definition of the verb, 'to be, to do or to suffer' made him think that words like *toothache, fever* and *rheumatism* were all verbs, since they were associated with suffering! Cobbett's own *Grammar* of 1819 took the form of letters to his son, and was addressed to 'soldiers, sailors, apprentices and ploughboys'. Much of it is devoted to exposing errors in passages written by men of letters, to show that 'a knowledge of the Greek and Latin is not sufficient to prevent men from writing bad English'. In this he was challenging the association between *acceptability*, both social and intellectual, and 'refinement' (or 'propriety') of language.

Cobbett wrote at a time when there was widespread popular demand for social reform, including the vote. The government, alarmed by the French Revolution of 1789, regarded such agitation as seditious, and tried hard to suppress it. One instrument of suppression was language: petitions to parliament were regularly turned down on the grounds that their language was unacceptable. Linguistic refinement was held to be part of the political order, which in turn was sanctioned by official religion. For Cobbett and other Radicals, oppression was served by grammatical obscurity: the means of fighting it was clarity of language.

Cobbett's own examples are sometimes designed to show the relevance of grammatical terminology to the workings of the political order. The action or state depicted in the example in the extract actually happened; Benbow was a Radical imprisoned by the government minister Sidmouth.

15

*(a)

So far have I been from any care to grace my pages with modern decorations, that I have studiously endeavoured to collect examples and authorities from the writers before the restoration, whose works I regard as *the wells of English undefiled*, as the pure sources of genuine diction. Our language, for almost a century, has, by the concurrence of many causes, been gradually departing from its original *Teutonick* character, and deviating towards a *Gallick* structure and phraseology, from which it ought to be our endeavour to recal it, by making our ancient volumes the groundwork of stile, admitting among the additions of later times, only such as may supply real deficiencies, such as are readily adopted by the genius of our tongue, and incorporate easily with our native idioms.

But as every language has a time of rudeness antecedent to perfection, as well as of false refinement and declension, I have been cautious lest my zeal for antiquity drive me into times too remote, and croud my book with words now no longer understood. I have fixed *Sidney*'s work for the boundary, beyond which I make few excursions. From the authours which rose in the time of *Elizabeth*, a speech might be formed adequate to all the purposes of use and elegance. If the language of theology were extracted from *Hooker* and the translation of the Bible; the terms of natural knowledge from *Bacon*; the phrases of policy, war, and navigation from *Raleigh*; the dialect of poetry and fiction from *Spenser* and *Sidney*; and the diction of common life from *Shakespeare*, few ideas would be lost to mankind, for want of *English* words, in which they might be expressed.

If the history of English is seen as the story of standardisation, then Johnson's *Dictionary* of 1755 will be seen as a landmark in that story, enabling England to compete, in a cultural sense, with France and Italy. It has also been widely seen as a monument to the heroic endeavours of a great scholar, which brought him acclaim in his own lifetime and whose influence lasted well over a century. Since it is useful to compare the approaches of later dictionary-makers with Johnson, I have placed this extract from his *Dictionary* **after** the grammars in 14.

One aspect of Johnson's *Dictionary* was its attempt at comprehensiveness (although it was not actually the first of this kind in English). This immediately raises the issue of what to include and what to exclude. Not surprisingly for this period, Johnson focuses on written rather than spoken usage (he equates writing with civilisation), but also consciously tries to exclude the usage of what he calls the 'laborious' (labouring) and 'mercantile' classes. In so doing he contributed to the culture of linguistic 'refinement' that played such a key role in late eighteenth-century society.

As in the case of grammar, the writing of a comprehensive dictionary has a patriotic dimension. In his Preface Dr Johnson is concerned to limit his attention to English as a 'native' tongue, ruling out that part of it (technical, artistic) which is shared by other European languages. Patriotism at this time was generated largely by hostility to France, which of course had its own linguistic Academy. Johnson's antipathy to academies was probably inspired by his anti-French feeling; from the extract note how he sees English as 'deviating towards a Gallic [i.e., French] structure', which for him means decay. This feeling was justified by appealing to the idea that 'love of liberty' was an innate 'English' characteristic. Liberty was central to the political settlement of 1688 which defined the English state as a 'Constitutional Monarchy', and for Johnson that settlement was always in need of defending, otherwise it would 'degenerate'. The English language was seen by Johnson as part of that settlement, and one of his intentions in writing his *Dictionary* was similarly to safeguard the language, so that 'the pronunciation . . . may be fixed, . . . its purity may be preserved, its use ascertained [fixed], and its duration lengthened', as stated in his Plan. In the course of compiling his dictionary Johnson came to see his antipathy to linguistic change as a lost cause, and in this he has been praised by some modern linguists.

Another aspect of Johnson's patriotism was literary. '[t]he chief glory of every people', he writes in p. xiii of his Preface, 'arises from its authors'. In the extract Johnson appeals to the literature (in the sense of serious writing) of Elizabeth I's reign as a 'Golden Age'. (The 'restoration' referred to took place in 1660; the 'wells of English undefiled' is a quotation, originally used by Spenser of Chaucer.) This emphasis, like his appeal to 'liberty', reflects the tone of a great many later works on literary and linguistic history. Just as Chaucer used to be seen as the 'founder' of standard English, Shakespeare is still cited as a touchstone of what Johnson calls 'the genius of our tongue'.

Johnson's emphasis on the specifically literary usage of a bygone age can be seen in the individual entries of the *Dictionary*. Spenser, Shakespeare and Milton are often the source of quotations demonstrating the different senses of a word. Johnson also cites the *etymology*, or earliest form, of a word where he knows it. For instance, he distinguishes three senses for the verb refund (from Latin *refundo*; see Figure 8.1):

To REFU ND. *v. n.* [*refundo*, Lat.]
1. To pour back.
   Were the humours of the eye tinctured with any colour, they would *refund* that colour upon the object, and so it would not be reprefented as in itfelf it is.   *Ray.*
2. To repay what is received; to reftore.
   A governor, that had pillaged the people, was, for receiving of bribes, fentenced to *refund* what he had wrongfully taken.
                                                                    L'Eftrange.
   Such wife men as himfelf account all that is paft, to be alfo gone; and know, that there can be no gain in *refunding*, nor any profit in paying debts.   *South.*
   How to Icarius, in the bridal hour,
   Shall I, by wafte undone, *refund* the dow'r.   *Pope.*
3. *Swift* has fomewhere the abfurd phrafe, *to* refund *himfelf*, for to *reimburfe*.

Figure 8.1 The verb *refund* from Samuel Johnson's *A Dictionary of the English Language*

(b)

It is not only important, but, in a degree necessary, that the people of this country, should have an *American Dictionary* of the English language; for, although the body of the language is the same as in England, and it is desirable to perpetuate that sameness, yet some differences must exist. Language is the expression of ideas; and if the people of our country cannot preserve an identity of ideas, they cannot retain an identity of language. Now an identity of ideas depends materially upon a sameness of things and objects with which the people of the two countries are conversant. But in no two portions of the earth, remote from each other, can such identity be found. Even physical objects must be different. But the principal differences between the people of this country and all others, arise from different forms of government, different laws, institutions and customs . . . the institutions in this country which are new and peculiar, give rise to new terms, unknown to the people of England. . . . No person in this country will be satisfied with the English definitions of the words *congress*, *senate* and *assembly*, *court*, &c. for although these are words used in England, yet they are applied in this country to express ideas which they do not express in that country.

Not only is this the first of our textual extracts to be produced outside England, it was actually written to *oppose* the English of England. Written forty-five years after America won its independence from England, Webster's Preface to what became America's counterpart to Johnson's *Dictionary* clearly had a commercial dimension. But Webster's claim that it was 'necessary' for Americans to have their own dictionary went beyond this, and depended on arguments that he had worked out in his *Dissertations on the English Language*. This was published in 1789, the year of the French Revolution.

In the extract it is the meanings of words like *congress*, *assembly* and *court* that Webster singles out for comment. In *Dissertations*, however, the focus is on spelling. Like many of his predecessors, Webster wanted to rectify the discrepancies between spelling and pronunciation that seemed so characteristic of English. One cause of this was that words adopted from other languages 'generally retained the orthography [=spelling] of the original', and Webster recommends that *fatigue*, from the French, and *character*, ultimately from Greek, should be re-spelt *fateeg* and *karacter*.

For Webster, such changes would be more 'democratic' than the old spellings, which were hard unless you knew the languages from which they came. Only the highly educated, like Johnson, did so. The latter, whose dictionary seems to have had a powerful influence on spelling, was committed to the older spellings; he was therefore an elitist in Webster's view. Webster shared Johnson's view of the 'Teutonic' character of English, but seems to have taken it more seriously. His ideas built on the Puritan celebration of the Anglo-Saxon elements of English and the association of 'foreign' usages with tyranny. For Webster, Johnson represented the English 'tyranny' from whom Americans needed to liberate themselves: he opposed American independence, and his long, complex sentences were an image of the 'refined' style associated with the English ruling class.

Webster made strong claims for his spelling reforms. In *Dissertations* he says they 'would make a difference between the English orthography and the American' and 'would encourage the publication of books in our own country'. The English 'would never copy our orthography for their own use'. He goes on to argue that

a *national language* is a band of *national union*. Every engine should be employed to make the people of this country *national*, to call their attachments home to their own country; and to inspire them with the pride of national character.

Webster bases his argument about spelling on the assumption that distinct nations need distinctive languages. America had been a colony, but was not yet a nation; and nations need to be *made*. National consciousness could be stimulated by cultivating a different *look* to the language. Although many of Webster's spelling reforms were not finally adopted into American English, the few that remain are a well-known sign of linguistic distinctiveness.

The nationalism espoused by Webster was, in his time, quite recent. Central to his idea of national identity were the 'common people' and political self-determination. It was becoming increasingly fashionable to argue that particular languages expressed the 'soul' of the people who spoke them (recall Johnson's phrase 'the genius of our tongue'). These ideas became dominant in the course of the nineteenth century, as we shall now see.

(c)

Subject to the conditions which thus encompass every attempt to construct a complete English Dictionary, the present work aims at exhibiting the history and signification of the English words now in use, or known to have been in use since the middle of the twelfth century. This date has been adopted as the only natural halting-place, short of going back to the beginning, so as to include the entire Old English or 'Anglo-Saxon' Vocabulary. To do this would have involved the inclusion of an immense number of words, not merely long obsolete but also having obsolete inflexions, and thus requiring, if dealt with at all, a treatment different from that adapted to the words which survived the twelfth century. For not only was the stream of English literature then reduced to the tiniest thread (the slender annals of the Old English or Anglo-Saxon Chronicle being for nearly a century its sole representative), but the vast majority of the ancient words that were destined not to live into modern English, comprising the entire scientific, philosophical, and poetical vocabulary of Old English, had already disappeared, and the old inflexional and grammatical system had been levelled to one so essentially modern as to require no special treatment in the Dictionary. Hence we exclude all words that had become obsolete by 1150. But to words actually included this date has no application: their history is exhibited from their first appearance, however early. . . .

Down to the Fifteenth Century the language existed only in dialects, all of which had a literary standing: during this period, therefore, words and forms of all dialects are admitted on an equal footing into the Dictionary. Dialectal words and forms which occur since 1500 are not admitted, except when they continue the history of a word or sense once in general use, illustrate the history of a literary word, or have themselves a certain literary currency, as is the case with many Scottish words. It is true that the dialectal words are mostly genuine English, and that they are an essential part of a *Lexicon totius Anglicitatis*; but the work of collecting them has not yet been completed; and, even when they shall have been collected, the phonetic variety in which they exist in different localities, and the want of any fixed written forms round which to group the variations, will require a method of treatment different from that applicable to the words of the literary language, which have an accepted uniform spelling and an approximately uniform pronunciation.

The General Explanation to what was then known as the *New English Dictionary*, from which these paragraphs were taken, was published in 1884. After 1895 it was called the *Oxford English Dictionary*; the first edition was not complete until 1933. Like Johnson, the author of this extract discusses at some length the problems of what to include in a 'complete' dictionary. But it should be clear from the first paragraph of the extract that the *OED* casts its net far wider than Johnson in relation to time. It includes words that have been known since the earliest records of English, illustrated with quotations from over one thousand years of history.

The justification for this is given in the *Proposal* to the Dictionary published in 1857. It was 'to trace the development of the senses of the word and the history of its use in the language'. So the *OED* was to be primarily a *historical dictionary*, and this meant in practice tracing a word back to its etymon, or earliest known (perhaps even the original) form. This emphasis reflected the nineteenth-century preoccupation with history and evolution in matters of language. This in turn had been inspired by the discovery that the different European languages could be grouped into 'families' descended from a common 'parent' language (Indo-European) perhaps once spoken on the Indian subcontinent. An important aspect of the study of a word's origins – *etymology* – was determining its relationships with words in *cognate* languages (those of the same family).

Nineteenth-century philologists regarded this project as scientific, much like the tracing of species in biology. But the Proposal also makes clear that it had a nationalist dimension. In the words of the Proposal of 1858 the dictionary project was the 'history of a nation from one point of view'. In other words, the English language was intimately bound up with the notion of English national identity, and that identity could be demonstrated by appealing to a sense of *continuity* from the earliest times. And since, as the extract makes clear, the English language up to about 1500 'existed only in dialects', it followed that dialect – the language of the common people – was an essential part of that history, and of the contents of a *Lexicon totius Anglicitatis* (the vocabulary of the whole of English).

However, as the final paragraph of the extract puts it, much dialect from 1500 onwards was excluded from the dictionary. In fact, the collection of dialect vocabulary was conceived as a separate project (see Figures 8.2 and 8.3 below). This exclusion was justified in the Proposal partly on the grounds that from about 1500 a 'standard English' existed, and 'the lexicographer is bound to deal with that alone'. It seems to have been assumed that 'standard English' was the medium of literature, and that the most persuasive way of demonstrating continuity between the present and the far past was through the study of literature.

The final paragraph shows further that dialect was also excluded on methodological grounds. In comparison with 'standard English' (this, significantly, seems to be the first recorded use of this term) dialect forms are characterised as fluid: great phonetic variety, no fixed written forms. So dialect, once it has been collected, will need a different treatment. We shall see an example of this below.

To see the *OED* as an example of nineteenth-century philological practice it is best to study how it treats a particular word. Figure 8.2 shows the entry for *hag*. But it should be immediately pointed out that the *OED* also lists six other words with the same form that can be used as nouns (*OED* uses the term *substantives*): *hag* can also mean an enclosure; a cutting; a piece of soft ground, or a firm piece of ground in a bog; in dialect, a task; and finally, a kind of boat. These entries have not been reproduced here for reasons of space.

These semantic subdivisions are justified partly on etymological grounds. The meanings just cited, except for the last, seem to be related to an Old Norse word denoting a blow, stroke or cut. But in the sense of 'witch', *hag* is perhaps derived from an Old English word with a similar meaning.

Immediately after the head word are listed the various spellings of the word in different centuries (3 = 13th, 4 = 14th century etc.). Then are listed its cognates in other Germanic languages: O, M = Old, Middle, H, L = High, Low, Ger, Du = German, Dutch. Then is posited a

hag (hæg), *sb.*[1] Forms: α. 3-7 hegge, 6-7 heg. β. 4-7 hagge, 6-8 hagg, 6- hag. [The form *hegge* is found once early in 13th c.; *hagge* once in 14th; otherwise the word is not known till the 16th c. Usually conjectured to be a shortened form of OE. *hægtesse, hæhtisse, hægtes, -tis, hegtes* 'fury, witch, hag' = OHG. *hagazissa, hagazussa, hagzus*, MHG. *hecse*, Ger. *hexe*, OLG. *hagatussa, MDu. *haghetisse*, Du. *hecse* (:—OTeut. **hagatusjön-*).

This derivation suits the sense, but the form-history is not clear, though an OE. *hægge might perh. be analogous to OE. abbreviated names, such as *Ceadda, Ælla, Æbbe*, etc. (The ulterior etymology of OTeut. **hagatusjön-* is itself unknown.) The order of the senses is uncertain; senses 4 and 5 may not belong to this word.]

1. a. An evil spirit, dæmon, or infernal being, in female form: applied in early use to the Furies, Harpies, etc. of Græco-Latin mythology; also to malicious female sprites or 'fairies' of Teutonic mythology. *Obs.* or *arch.*

1552 HULOET, Hegges or nyght furyes, or wytches like unto old women.. which do sucke the bloude of children in the nyght, *striges.* **1573** TWYNE *Æneid.* xii. (R), Your filthy foules, and hegges of Limbo low. **1573-80** BARET *Alv.* H 339 A Heg, or fairie, a witch that changeth the fauour of children, *strix.* **1581** J. STUDLEY tr. *Seneca's Hercules (Etæus* 204 b, After ruin made Of goblin hegge, or elfe. **1649** G. DANIEL *Trinarch., Hen. IV*, ccliv, The Grisly Hagge, With knotted Scorpions. **1810** SCOTT *Lady of L.* iii. vii, Noontide hag, or goblin grim.

† b. Applied to *manes* or shades of the departed, ghosts, hobgoblins, and other terrors of the night.

1538 ELYOT *Dict., Larua*, a spyrite whiche apperethe in the nyght tyme. Some do call it a hegge, some a goblyn. *a* **1557** MRS. M. BASSET tr. *More's Treat. Passion Wks.* 1307 2 Lyke shrycke owles and hegges, lyke backes, howlettes.. byrdes of the hellye lake. **1563** B. GOOGE *Egloges* iv. (Arb) 44 What soeuer thou art.. Ghoost, Hagge, a Fende of Hell. **1566** ADLINGTON *Apuleius* 3 Doest thou liue here (O Socrates) as a ghost or hegge to our great shame and ignomie? **1567** DRANT *Horace, Epist.* ii. i. (R.), The goddes above are calm'd with verse, with verse the hagges of hell [*carmine manes*]. **1634** MILTON *Comus* 434 Blue meagre hag, or stubborn unlaid ghost.

† c. The nightmare. *Obs.*

1632 tr. *Bruel's Praxis Med.* 50 In the Hag or Mare.. is no con[v]ulsion, as is in the falling sicknesse. **1696** AUBREY *Misc.* (1721) 147 It is to prevent the Night-Mare (viz.) the Hag from riding their Horses.

† d. *fig.* An object of terror, a 'bogey'. *Obs.*

1611 SPEED *Hist. Gt. Brit.* ix. viii. §50 That the Popes Curse was no such deadly and dreadfull Hagge, as in former times they deemed it.

2. A woman supposed to have dealings with Satan and the infernal world; a witch; sometimes, an infernally wicked woman. Now associated with 3.

1587 MIRR. *Mag., Forrex* iii, That hatefull hellish hagge of ugly hue. **1590** SPENSER *F.Q.* i. viii. 46 A loathly, wrinckled hag, ill favoured, old. **1591** SHAKS. *1 Hen. VI*, iii. ii. 52 Foule Fiend of France, and Hag of all despight. **1605** — *Macb.* IV. i. 48 How now you secret, black, and mid-night Hags? **1654** WHITLOCK *Zootomia* 437 The Poets.. made the Hag Circes Sister to Æsculapius. **1712** STEELE *Spect.* No. 266 ⁋2 One of those Hags of Hell whom we call Bawds. **1728** YOUNG *Love Fame* iii. (1757) 101 As hunted hags, who, while the dogs pursue, Renounce their four legs, and start up on two. **1816** SCOTT *Bl. Dwarf* ii, On this moor she used to hold her revels with her sister hags. **1833** HT. MARTINEAU *Cinnamon & P.* iv. 66 The dull roar of the distant sea spoke of hags riding the blast.

3. a. An ugly, repulsive old woman: often with implication of viciousness or maliciousness.

(The place of the first two quots. is doubtful.)

1377 LANGL. *P. Pl.* B. v. 191 With two blered eyghen as a biynde hagge. **1611** SHAKS. *Wint. T.* ii. iii. 108 A grosse Hagge: And Lozell, thou art worthy to be hang'd, That wilt not stay her Tongue. *a* **1711** KEN *Urania* Poet. Wks. 1721 IV. 481 The Hagg, who by Cosmeticks smear'd, Fair at first sight appear'd. **1713** STEELE *Englishm.* No. 40. 261 Oppression.. makes handsome Women Hags *ante diem.* **1791** COWPER *Odyss.* XVIII. 33 Like an old hag Collied with chimney-smutch! **1834** LYTTON *Pompeii* iii. ix, Perhaps in no country are there seen so many hags as in Italy. **1866** GEO. ELIOT *F. Holt* (1868) 19, 'I am a hag', she said.. 'an ugly old woman who happens to be his mother'.

b. *fig.* Applied to personifications of evil or of vice. (The place of the first quot. is uncertain.)

a **1225** *Ancr. R.* 216 þe seoue moder sunnen.. and of hwuche mesteres þeo ilke men serueð.. þet habbeð iwiued o þeos scouen heggen. **1577** tr. *Bullinger's Decades* (1592) 165 Ill fauoured enuie, vgly hagge. **1830** TENNYSON *Poems* 124 Shall the hag Evil die with child of Good?

† c. *transf.* Applied opprobriously to a man. (Skelton's use is uncertain.) *Obs.*

a **1529** SKELTON *Dk. Albany* 295 For thou can not but brag, Lyke a Scottyshe hag: Adue nowe, sir Wrig wrag. *a* **1529** — *Col. Clout* 51 My name ys Colyn Clowte, And [I] purpose to shake owte All my Connyng Bagge, Lyke A clarkely hagge. **1565** GOLDING *Ovid's Met.* iv. (1593) 80 That old hag [Silenus] that with a staffe his staggering limmes doth stay. **1587** — *De Mornay* xiv. 221 Giue to the oldest Hag that is the same eies that he had when he was young. **1676** W. Row *Contn. Blair's Autobiog.* xii. (1848) 492 Me who am an old hag that must shortly die.

Here perhaps belongs the following:

1553 BALE *Vocacyon* in *Harl. Misc.* (Malh.) I. 357 Than was all the rable of the shippe, hag, tag, and rag called to the reckeninge.

4. † a. A kind of light said to appear at night on horses' manes and men's hair. *Obs.* **b.** *dial.* A white mist usually accompanying frost.

1530 PALSGR. 228/2 Hagge, a flame of fyre that shyneth by night, *furolle.* **1656** T. WHITE *Peripat. Inst.* 149 *Flammæ lambentes* (or those we call *Haggs*) are made of Sweat or some other Vapour issuing out of the Head. **1825** BROCKETT *N.C. Gloss., Hag,* .. a white mist, similar to dag. **1855** ROBINSON *Whitby Gloss., Hag,* mist. 'Frost hag', frost haze.

5. A cyclostomous fish (*Myxine glutinosa*) allied to the lamprey, having an eel-like form, and living parasitically upon other fishes. Also HAGFISH.

1823 CRABB *Technol. Dict., Hag,* a particular sort of fish, of an eel-shape.. It is of so gelatinous a nature, that when placed in a vessel of sea-water it soon turns it to glue. **1835** KIRBY *Hab. & Inst. Anim.* II. xxi. 373 Those extraordinary animals, the hag and the lamprey. **1881** *Cassell's Nat. Hist.* V. 146 This destruction [of a Haddock] is sometimes accomplished by a single Hag, but as many as twenty have been found in the body of a single fish.

6. *attrib.* and *Comb.*, (chiefly from 2) as **hag-advocate, -finder, -seed, -witch; hag-born, -steered** adjs.; **hag-like** adv. and adj.; **hag-stone, hag's teeth** (see quots.); **hag-track** = FAIRY-RING.

1718 BP. HUTCHINSON *Witchcraft* Ded. (1720) 17 The odious Names of *Hag-Advocates. **1610** SHAKS. *Temp.* I. ii. 283 The Son, that she did littour heere, A frekelld whelpe, *hag-borne. **1637** B. JONSON *Sad Sheph.* ii. ii, That do I promise, or I am no good *hag-finder. **1634** RANDOLPH *Muses' Looking-Glass* i. iii, Her unkemb'd hair, Dress'd up with cobwebs, made her *haglike stare. **1824** J. MORIER *Adv. Hajji Baba* I. xiii. 148 There was also.. an old woman of a hag-like and decrepit appearance. **1610** SHAKS. *Temp.* i. ii. 365 *Hag-seed, hence. **1787** GROSE *Provinc. Gloss.* Superstitions 57 A stone with a hole in it, hung at the bed's head, will prevent the night-mare; it is therefore called a *hag-stone. **1867** SMYTH *Sailor's Word-bk.,* *Hag's teeth, those parts of a matting or pointing interwoven with the rest in an irregular manner, so as to spoil the uniformity. **1858** *Murray's Hand-bk. Kent* Introd. 32 'Fairy rings', sometimes called *hag-tracks. *a* **1658** CLEVELAND *Agst. Ale* v, May some old *Hag-witch get astride Thy Bung, as if she meant to ride.

Figure 8.2 Definition of *hag* from the *Oxford English Dictionary* second edition, 1989. Reproduced by permission of Oxford University Press

HAG, *sb.*[2] n.Cy. Yks. Lan. Chs. Der. Brks. Bck. Hrt. Ken. Sus. Hmp. I.W. Som. Dev. Also in forms aag w.Yks.; ag· Brks.[1] Sus.[1]; aga Ken. Hmp. Wil.; agg Bck.; aght Dev.; ague Chs.[3]; aig, haag w.Yks.; haeg w.Yks. Chs.; haga I.W.; hagga Brks.[1]; haghe n.Cy. w.Yks.[3] Der.[1] nw.Der.[1]; hague w.Yks.[1] Lan.[1] ne.Lan.[1] Chs.[1]; haig w.Yks.[4 5] Lan.[1] e.Lan.[1] Chs.[1]; haigh w.Yks.[2 3]; hoeg Chs.[3] [ēg, eəg, æg.] **1.** A haw, the fruit of the hawthorn, *Crataegus Oxyacantha*; *gen.* in *pl.* Also in *comp.* **Hag-berry.**

n.Cy. BAILEY (1721). w.Yks. Us lads kept blawin' aags at one another, *Leeds Merc. Suppl.* (Apr. 4, 1891); Getting stuff to eat —haegs and epps, SNOWDEN *Web of Weaver* (1896) 6; w.Yks.[1 2 3 4 5], Lan. (S.W.), Lan.[1], ne.Lan.[1], e.Lan.[1] Chs. *Science Gossip* (1865) 198; Chs.[1 3], Der.[1], nw.Der.[1] Brks. *Gl.* (1852); Brks.[1], Ken. (W.H.E.), Hmp. (J.R.W.), (W.H.E.), Hmp.[1], Wil. (W.H.E.), I.W. (B. & H.) Dev. GROSE (1790) *MS. add.* (C.) [RAY (1691).]

Hence (1) **Agarves** (? Hag-haws), (2) **Agasses** or **Hagasses,** (3) **Agogs,** *sb. pl.* haws, the fruit of the hawthorn; (4) **Haggises,** *sb. pl.* hips, the fruit of the dog-rose, *Rosa canina.*

(1) Sus.[1] (2) Sus. (R.P.C.), Hmp. (J.R.W.) (3) Brks.[1] (4) Hmp.[1]

2. The hawthorn, *Crataegus Oxyacantha.* Lan.[1]

3. *Comp.* (1) **Hag-blossom,** the blossom of the hawthorn; (2) **-bush,** the hawthorn; (3) **-leaf,** (4) **-paper,** the great mullein, *Verbascum Thapsus*; (5) **-rope(s,** the wild clematis, *Clematis Vitalba*; (6) **-taper,** see (4); (7) **-thorn,** (8) **-tree,** see (2).

(1) w.Yks. (D.L.) Lan. Wilt ha' this bit o' hague-blossom? BRIERLEY *Irkdale* (1865) iv. (2) w.Yks. (S.P.U.) (3, 4) Bck. *Science Gossip* (1869) 26. (5) Som. *N. & Q.* (1877) 5th S. viii. 358; W. & J. *Gl.* 1873. w.Som.[1] (6) Hrt. ELLIS *New Experiments* (1750) 22. (7) w.Som.[1], Dev.[4] (8) w.Yks. (S.P.U.)

[1. A form of lit. E. *haw,* OE. *haga,* the fruit of the hawthorn; cp. LG. *hagdoorn,* 'Crataegus oxyacantha' (BERGHAUS).]

HAG, *sb.*[3] n.Cy. Nhb. Yks. Also Cor. [h)ag, æg.] A thick white mist or fog.

N.Cy.[1] Nhb. *Gent. Mag.* (1794), ed. Gomme; Nhb.[1], Wm. (J.H.) n.Yks. A frost hag (T.S.); n.Yks.[1] Such as sometimes occurs coincidently with frost: whence frost-hag; n.Yks.[2 4], m.Yks.[1], Cor.[2]

Hence **Haggy,** *adj.* misty from the frost. n.Yks.[2]

HAG, *sb.*[4] n.Cy. Nhb. Lan. [h)ag.] The paunch, belly. See **Haggis, 3.**

n.Cy. GROSE (1790). Nhb.[1] Lan. GROSE (1790) *MS. add.* (C.); Lan.[1]

HAG, *sb.*[5] ? *Obs.* Bdf. Som. Idle disorder.

Bdf. You have got the hag, BATCHELOR *Anal. Eng. Lang.* (1809) 136. Som. (HALL.)

Figure 8.3 Definition of *hag* from the *English Dialect Dictionary*, ed. J. Wright, Oxford 1898. Reproduced by permission of Oxford University Press

reconstructed (hence the asterisk) 'ancestor' form from 'OTeut' (Old Teutonic = Germanic).

Next, the different senses are listed. According to the Preface of the second edition, 'that sense is placed first which was actually the earliest in the language: the others follow in the order in which they appear to have arisen' (p. xxix). The *OED* has a sophisticated system for indicating sense development. The numbers 1, 2, 3 etc. indicate the main senses; different 'branches' in the sense are marked I, II, III etc. A, B, C etc. mark different *grammatical* uses. It is this that gives the *OED* its aura of painstaking, classificatory science.

(d)

> The Dictionary includes, so far as is possible, the complete vocabulary of all English dialect words which are still in use or are known to have been in use at any time during the last two hundred years in England, Ireland, Scotland and Wales. All words occurring both in the literary language and in the dialects, but with some local peculiarity of *meaning* in the latter, are also included. On the other hand, words which merely differ from the literary language in pronunciation, but *not* in meaning, are generally excluded, as belonging properly to the province of grammar and not to that of lexicography. It also contains (1) the exact geographical area over which each dialect word extends, together with quotations and references to the sources from which the word has been obtained; (2) the exact pronunciation in each case according to a simple phonetic scheme, specially formulated for the purpose; (3) the etymology so far as it relates to the immediate source of each word. . . .
>
> It is quite evident from the letters daily received at the 'Workshop' that pure dialect speech is rapidly disappearing from our midst, and that in a few years it will be almost impossible to get accurate information about difficult points. Even now it is sometimes found extremely difficult to ascertain the exact pronunciation and the various shades of meanings, especially of words which occur both in the literary language and in the dialects. And in this case it is not always easy to decide what is dialect and what is literary English: there is no sharp line of demarcation; the one overlaps the other. In words of this kind I have carefully considered each case separately, and if I have erred at all, it has been on the side of inclusion.

The *English Dialect Dictionary*, published between 1898 and 1905, grew out of the work of the English Dialect Society, which was set up in 1873. The Society published a number of regional glossaries, which, together with information collected from a great many correspondents, formed the basis of the dictionary. The Society was wound up once the dictionary was published, but regional dialect societies have since been formed; one, the Yorkshire Dialect Society, has been in existence for a century.

In the extract the dictionary's editor, Joseph Wright, identifies two problems in its compilation: 'pure' dialect is rapidly disappearing, and it is not easy to decide on the boundary between dialect and what he calls 'the literary language'. The formulation of these problems is itself a problem, which in turn generates other problems. Notice how the notion of purity, familiar since Bokenham's time, is now applied, with all its associated difficulties, to dialect. It seems to assume the existence of a fixed system of linguistic forms and patterns which, if it is to change, can only change in the direction of the 'literary language'. Furthermore, how are we to categorise those words and structures that 'occur both in the literary language and the dialects' – as 'standard' or 'dialect'? Or is there a word which includes both? And are they any the less 'pure' if they are shared?

For Wright, the obsolescence of dialect seems to create a further problem: 'accurate information' about it is increasingly hard to get. But there may be a different reason for this. Many of Wright's correspondents were vicars and schoolmasters: not so much *users* as observers of dialect, for whom it is something exotic. And it is also worth pointing out that the disappearance of dialect has been regularly lamented during the last century, only to be proved wrong every time some systematic research is undertaken.

Dialect study in the nineteenth century was caught between two opposing forces. Those associated with 'modernisation' (among them the State with its compulsory education system, industrialisation, rail transport) favoured the imposition of 'standard English'. Against this some philologists, such as Professor Max Müller at Oxford, argued that 'the real and natural life of language is in its dialects'. Moreover, dialects were a vital source of information about the linguistic past. Perhaps the safest position was to argue that dialects were disappearing, but were eminently worthy of academic study. It is significant that the English Dialect Society disbanded itself on the grounds that once this study, in the form of the *EDD*, had been undertaken there was no longer anything for it to do.

The association of dialect with history did not originate in the nineteenth century. Around 1565 the churchman Lawrence Nowell published his *Vocabularium Saxonicum* in which he listed some 200 dialect words whose Anglo-Saxon etymons he could trace. An antiquarian like many of his intellectual contemporaries, Nowell helped pioneer the study of Old English by transcribing manuscripts. The Tudor monarchy found this useful since it helped establish the notion that England had a distinctive history: this served to justify the break with the Catholic Church.

Nowell's list also illustrates another important reason for interest in dialect. One hundred and seventy-three of his dialect words are labelled as from Lancashire, his county of origin. The issue of local speech often arises whenever geographical or social mobility occurs. Nowell may have become aware of the provenance of these words when, in the course of his work in the south-east, he found they were not universally used (for an example see below). Perhaps, as so often happens, he also associated them with a *personal* past, his own childhood. It is usual in such cases to claim that a particular word or pattern 'belongs' to one's own dialect. So an interest in dialect is also motivated by a kind of local 'patriotism'. Perhaps the best example of this belongs to the industrialised north of England in the nineteenth century, when poems and stories, usually written by self-educated working men, were published in the local dialect.

One of the 'Lancashire' forms listed by Nowell runs thus:

> Hazan. Hawes. The frute of the white thorne or hawthorne. Lanc., hagges.

Figure 8.3 (p. 245) is an extract from the entry for the same word, given under HAG, from the *English Dialect Dictionary*. As in the case of the *OED*, different substantive uses of the form HAG are numbered. HAG[1] is the same as that of *OED*; its inclusion in *EDD* perhaps owes to the distinctive compounds like *hag-begagged* (bewitched). HAG[2], however, is more clearly dialectal, a form of the 'literary English' *haw*, as in *hawthorn*.

Notice that the first kind of information *EDD* gives is *geographical*: it tells us where the form has been noted (the abbreviations are those of counties). The spread is quite wide: the north, part of the midlands and Home Counties, parts of the south and south-west. It then gives its pronunciations (in square brackets) and then its meanings, including those where it occurs in compounds (see under 3).

OED tentatively derives *haw* (the fruit of the hawthorn) from Old English *haȝa*, which seems originally to have meant 'hedge' and consequently a piece of hedged or enclosed ground (as in the cognate Dutch place-name The Hague). Hedges have often used hawthorns, so the two terms may have been synonymous. Old English ȝ usually became w (as in *boȝa*, bow) but this does not seem to have happened with dialectal *hag*. Either a different sound-change has occurred or perhaps there existed in Old English another related form (or doublet), **hagga*.

Nowell's linking of *hagges* with Lancashire raises a further problem in the study of dialect. There is a tendency to think of dialects, like languages, as having fixed geographical boundaries. Often this is related to county boundaries. From this it is easy to imagine, in a spirit of local patriotism, that a particular feature is *exclusively* linked to a given area. Modern dialect research however has confirmed the picture suggested by *EDD*, in that only a relatively few features have a clearly limited spread. So what characterises, say, the dialect of Lancashire is not so much a particular feature or features as the *co-occurrence* of a great number of lexical, phonological and grammatical forms which are also shared in differing combinations with other areas.

16

When I was a young man, I used to go here, there and everywhere doing almost everything and I used to work on a lot o fairms. I happened to land away up in the north o Scotland on this fairm sittin away up on the hillside and I asked the man for a job. 'Well', he says, 'ye're a big, strong-lookin laddie an I think ye could dae a good day's work, so I'll try ye out.'

'Very good', I says, 'I'll be willin tae dae the best I can.'

It was the beginning of the year when I come there, and I did a whole summer's work right through tae the hairvest time. I managed to build stacks an everything like that and we got in wur hairvest. When the hairvest was finished, they held a ceilidh an everyone was tellin stories or singin sangs or playin pipes an fiddles, but I couldnae dae onythin like that. But I sat in the corner enjoyin it aa. After everyone had done something, a song or a story or a tune, the fairmer says tae me, 'Look Willie, dae ye not think it's time ye were daein a wee bit turn?'

'I canny tell stories', I says, 'an I canny sing sangs. I canny play pipes. I can dae naethin like that. I'm useless.'

'Well, in that case', he says, 'dae ye mind daein a wee forfeit?'

'Oh no', I says, 'I dinny mind'.

'Well', he says, 'ye ken where the old boat is down on the shore?'

'Aye', I says.

'Ye know the bailer for bailin oot the water oot o the boat?'

'Yes, I know it well.'

'Well, I want that bailer tae use tae measure oot the feed for the cattle, the morn', says the fairmer. 'Just you go doon there an get it an bring it back up here.'

'Aw', I says, 'that's an easy forfeit.'

I buttoned up ma jaicket an goes through the door. It was dark, so
the fairmer gien me a lantern tae show me the way doon. It would be
aboot a hundred yairds fae the fairm where the boat was lyin on the
shore. 'Oh there it is', I says. 'This is dead easy.'

I left the lamp doon an went intae the boat and walkit wi ma big
heavy boots tae the end o the boat. I bent doon tae get the bailer an
ma feet slippit an I fell on ma heid an I saw stars! When I came to, I
gropit aboot an got the bailer and pit ma leg owre the bow o the boat
tae get oot on the shore, an I couldnae find the bottom!

This is the opening of a folktale, 'The Man who had no Story to Tell',
tape-recorded during the 1970s from a Scottish 'Traveller' (or tinker, to
use the older and less-favoured term) called Willie McPhee (who was
born in 1910). It is told in a dialect of Central Scotland and has been
transcribed (and lightly edited) by the collector, Dr Sheila Douglas. The
story goes on to describe some miraculous events which befall the hero
(here presented as the storyteller himself); he eventually returns to the
ceilidh (an informal get-together) with 'a story to tell'. The tale itself
can be compared to that in extract *1 above.

Examples of Scots can be found in the forms of verbs: the strong past
tense forms *come* (came) and *gien* (gave), the weak forms *walkit*, *slippit*
and *gropit* (walked, slipped, groped) and the negative forms *canny*, *dinny*
and *couldnae* (can't, don't, couldn't). Scots idioms include *a wee bit* (a
little) and *the morn*. Scots vocabulary includes *ken*, *laddie*, *wee* (know,
lad, little). There are also a number of pronunciations which have been
given a traditional Scots orthography: *o, fairm, sittin, tae dae, hairvest,
wur, ony, aa, sangs, naethin, oot, doon, yairds, fae, ma, heid, pit, ower*.

As we might expect, there are a great many characteristics of
informal speech in the extract. *This*, for instance, is not a demonstrative
but means 'a certain'. There are two examples of the use of present
tense to denote past actions in *says* and *goes*. Traditionally associated
with dramatic immediacy, this use of the present tense, known as the
historic present, is especially common with *say* and *go* in Scottish Traveller folktales. And simple *co-ordinated* constructions with clauses joined
by *and*, as in *an ma feet slippit an I fell on ma heid an I saw stars!* are
common.

It is difficult to know how far back in the history of English and
Scots such features of the oral narrative style can be traced. The so-
called historic present, however, can be found in medieval romance
poetry, and other features can be found in the writing of John Bunyan
in the seventeenth century. Today they can be found in the oral narra-

tive style of the highly educated as well as of those who, like Willie McPhee, are non-literate.

17

YOLLAND:	He knows what's happening.
OWEN:	What is happening?
YOLLAND:	I'm not sure. But I'm concerned about my part in it. It's an eviction of sorts.
OWEN:	We're making a six-inch map of the country. Is there something sinister in that?
YOLLAND:	Not in . . .
OWEN:	And we're taking place-names that are riddled with confusion and. . . .
YOLLAND:	Who's confused? Are the people confused?
OWEN:	. . . . and we're standardising those names as accurately and as sensitively as we can.
YOLLAND:	Something is being eroded.
OWEN:	Back to the romance again. Alright! Fine! Fine! Look where we've got to. (*He drops on his hands and knees and stabs a finger at the map.*) We've come to this crossroads. Come here and look at it, man! Look at it! And we call that crossroads Tobair Vree. And why do we call it Tobair Vree? I'll tell you why. Tobair means a well. But what does Vree mean? It's a corruption of Brian – (*Gaelic pronunciation.*) Brian – an erosion of Tobair Bhriain. Because a hundred-and-fifty years ago there used to be a well there, not at the cross-roads, mind you – that would be too simple – but in a field close to the crossroads. And an old man called Brian, whose face was disfigured by an enormous growth, got it into his head that the water in that well was blessed; and every day for seven months he went there and bathed his face in it. But the growth didn't go away; and one morning Brian was found drowned in that well. And ever since that crossroads is known as Tobair Vree – even though that well has long since dried up. I know the story because my grandfather told it to me. But ask Doalty – or Marie – or Bridget – even my father – even Manus – why it's called Tobair Vree; and do you think they'll know? I know they don't know. So the question I put to you, Lieutenant, is this: What do we do with a name like that? Do we scrap Tobair Vree altogether and call it – what? – The Cross? Crossroads? Or do we keep piety with a man

> long dead, long forgotten, his name 'eroded' beyond recognition, whose trivial little story nobody in the parish remembers?
>
> YOLLAND: Except you.
>
> OWEN: I've left here.
>
> YOLLAND: You remember it.
>
> OWEN: I'm asking you: what do we write in the Name-Book?
>
> YOLLAND: Tobair Vree.
>
> OWEN: Even though the well is a hundred yards from the actual crossroads – and there's no well anyway – and what the hell does Vree mean?
>
> YOLLAND: Tobair Vree.

This extract is from Act 2, Scene 1, of Brian Friel's play *Translations* (1981). The action is set in County Donegal, in the poor north-west of Ireland, in 1833. The British army is making an official map of the area. Owen is a local man now working as an interpreter for the army; Lieutenant George Yolland an English soldier who has come to love Ireland and its language (which he wants to learn). Together they have been going through the local Irish names for the new map and either changing them into their nearest sounds in English, or translating them outright. (Bun na hAbhann, for instance, they have turned into Burnfoot: *bun* is Irish for bottom, *abha* means river, so the name means literally the mouth of the river. The *sounds*, on the other hand, have been anglicised in the past to both Banowen and Binhone.) Yolland, however, no longer has his heart in the enterprise; he is concerned that it is 'an eviction of sorts', and this provokes the argument with Owen.

The extract helps show how the play dramatises the issue of naming. In one respect names, being arbitrary in the linguistic sense, do not matter at all; in social, political and cultural terms, on the other hand, they are crucial. Re-naming the Irish landscape effectively takes the names away from the local Irish-speaking inhabitants. This process of anglicisation, according to Owen, will remove any 'ambiguities'; but as the play proceeds, it becomes clear that anglicisation seems to generate ambiguities rather than remove them, and Owen comes to find that his own feelings about his local place-names are ambivalent.

Translations also deals with the experience of colonisation, and how this experience often strains the loyalties of individuals and makes the issue of personal identity problematic. Above all, it helps us to see how and why a subject people might persist in speaking what the bilingual Owen calls a 'quaint archaic tongue' (but one which his father, the local schoolmaster, argues is more spiritual than the 'commercial' English). The play is an excellent *imaginative* resource for anyone interested in the social history of language.

Histories of English have often used dialogue in literary texts such as plays and novels as evidence for how people of different classes, occupations and localities actually spoke in the past. The problem with this is that literary texts are not *transcripts* of speech (as in the previous extract), but imaginative re-creations of it. Local speech is often used selectively by imaginative writers as a way of distinguishing among *characters*. So in *Translations* Hiberno-English is associated with males, principally those of low social status. One of these is an elderly unmarried peasant, Jimmy, who as the most earnest and erudite pupil at the local Hedge School has learned to read Homer in the original Greek. In one scene (p. 13) he speaks of the Greek goddess Athene, the object of his fantasy. 'If you had a woman like that about the house', he says, '*(I)t's not stripping a turf-bank you'd be thinking about*' (you wouldn't be thinking about stripping a turf-bank, i.e., digging peat for fuel) is the kind of *cleft* construction widespread in Hiberno-English and possibly influenced by a similar construction in Irish. Other examples of Hiberno-English in his speech are the use of *sure* as an adverb in initial position *Sure she can't get her fill of me* and the definite article in *If you had the picking between them, which would you take?*

18

> well sir I was walkin going 'long up Government Hill and just as I get in front of Mr Tudor place he dog rush out and he bite me 'pon me foot. No sir he did bite me 'pon me foot sir. . . . well de ting really put me outa commotion for a couple of weeks very . . . well I can't work at all at all . . . I does sell sweeties at . . . at de school . . . yes sir . . . I does make about tree or four dollars a day. . . . anyway sir and I had to staying home I did been to the doctor too . . . and the doctor say my foot was terribly inflamed . . . no he didn't give me nothing sir . . . he does tell me to bring it to de court . . . do what I like wid he
>
> (Le Page and Tabouret-Keller 1985: 93)

This is an edited extract from the transcription of a story told by a native of the Caribbean island of Barbados. The original transcriber, R.B. Le Page, actually made three transcriptions: one phonetic, one phonemic and one in standard orthography, publishing the last two. Since standard orthography does not convey many of the distinctive characteristics of 'Bajan' speech, I have tried to adapt it to suggest some of the qualities of the phonemic transcription. In this respect it can be compared with Extract 16.

Perhaps one of the most noticeable aspects of the language is the form of verbs. Both present and past tense forms of *do* are used periphrastically in *did bite/been, does sell/make*. This use of *do* may have originated in the English West Country, the source of much indentured labour during the seventeenth century when Barbados was first colonised. Other 'non-standard' verb forms (use of the inflected *does* form with first person *I*, *tell* as a past participle as in *he's tell*) may similarly have a source in dialects of Britain. On the other hand, the uninflected past-tense forms *rush* and *get*, the simplified pronoun forms (*he* = he, him and it) and the lack of a distinctive possessive marker for *Tudor* are more suggestive of creole.

The transcription is also able, through the use of deviant spellings, to show certain features of pronunciation. *Ting* (thing) and *tree* (three) indicate a plosive rather than fricative in initial position. Historically, this may derive from Hiberno-English: Ireland was another important source of seventeenth-century indentured labour. But other pronunciations are not so easily represented in this way. For example, *-ng* in *going* and *staying* represents a nasalised preceding vowel rather than a distinct consonant; in *did* and *what* there is no final consonant sounded. And *me* for 'my' is likely to be misinterpreted as incorrect *grammar* (confusing the possessive form of *my* for the 'accusative' or 'dative') rather than an attempt to represent a *pronunciation* of *my* which happens to sound identical to *me*.

Theoretical postscript

Deeply rooted in European culture are certain stories about language. The Old Testament of the Bible tells of a single original language, spoken by Adam in naming the objects around him. The subsequent splitting of this one language into several mutually unintelligible ones was God's punishment. During the period of their ancient empire, the Greeks too looked back to a linguistic past they felt was better, the 'Golden Age' of Homer's epics. In both traditions, then, there is a sense of linguistic decline.

Such stories of linguistic decline are still very powerful today when, like the Greeks, we apply them to a particular language. This is partly because they overlap with a more general sense that manners and behaviour are not what they were. But it is also possible to see the opposite tendency when particular languages are discussed: the story is not one of decline but progress, overlapping with an opposing tendency to see the past as characterised by ignorance, cruelty and want, conditions from which we are lucky to have been delivered.

Also widespread is a third kind of story which combines elements of both: a language will degenerate if it is not cared for, but can be maintained and even improved by dint of great effort. So Dr Johnson on p. xv of the Preface to his *Dictionary*, looking back over a thousand years of linguistic history, thought the Anglo-Saxons might have been

> a people without learning, and very probably without an alphabet; their speech therefore, having been always cursory and extemporaneous, must have been artless and unconnected, without any modes of transition or involution of clauses; which abruptness and inconnection may be observed even in their later writings. This barbarity may be supposed to have continued during their wars with the Britains, which for a time left them no leisure for softer studies; nor is there any reason for supposing it abated, till the year 570, when

Augustine came from Rome to convert them to Christianity. The Christian religion always implies or produces a certain degree of civility and learning; they then became by degrees acquainted with the Roman language, and so gained, from time to time, some knowledge and elegance, till in three centuries they had formed a language capable of expressing all the sentiments of a civilized people.

In our own time, the Cambridge medievalist John Marenbon tells a story of linguistic progress from the time of the Anglo-Saxons:

It was almost impossible to present clearly a complicated, abstract argument in the English of King Alfred's day, and Chaucer's English was still inadequate for this use; but as, in the sixteenth and seventeenth centuries more and more writers tried to use English for such purposes, the language was gradually shaped to fulfil this function, so that Hume had in his native tongue an instrument perfectly adapted for the subtlest speculations. These differences in adequacy did not lie only in vocabulary, but in the possibilities of grammar and syntax. Chaucer's English allowed him to frame a narrative or a description with ease; but it could not accommodate complicated logical relationships between concepts and arguments.

(Marenbon 1987: 22)

Between Johnson and Marenbon lies the nineteenth-century perspective on language in respect to time, known as philology. Philology is characterised by the patient accumulation of linguistic data and its interpretation as *evidence* for reconstructing the linguistic past. As such it laid the indispensable groundwork for the historical study of language, and it is very difficult for anyone interested in this project to detach themselves from its methods and findings. We shall pursue below the matter of interpretation; meanwhile, we have already seen how problematic is the issue of evidence. Not only are we over-dependent on *written* evidence, we do not know how much writing has been lost and how representative is what remains. We must also remember that in the past only certain types of discourse were written down in the first place, and among these, it is imaginative literature that has been privileged by historians of English. In addition, we have noted the bias towards West Saxon when dealing with the Anglo-Saxon period and standardisation when dealing with the more recent past.

With its emphasis on evidence it might seem that philology eschewed the 'grand narratives' of decline, progress and cyclical change. Indeed, the philologists insisted on the 'scientific' nature of their enterprise, seeing language as an *organism* – a part of nature that is constantly evolving. Like biologists, chemists and physicists the philologists formulated 'laws' to explain the relationships between past and present forms in a language. The aspect of language most amenable to such an approach, however, was pronunciation. The fact that the nature of the available evidence prevented philologists from actually being able to prove any connections between sounds past and present did not appear to undermine their faith in the scientific basis of their project.

One law formulated by the philologists was that, generally speaking, sound-changes admitted no exceptions. Thus, if the sound represented by *a* in Old English *rad* ('long *a*') changed to one represented by *o* or *oa* in Middle English, as in *road*, then *all* instances of Old English 'long *a*' (as in *halig, ac, swa* etc.) would follow the same 'rounding' law. Wherever exceptions did exist, it was incumbent on philologists to find another law or principle to explain them. Thus, the existence of the place-name *Stanton* beside *Stoneton*, from Old English *stan* (stone) can be explained as a result of *shortening* of the long vowel in either Old English or early Middle English, so that like other instances of short *a* it was not subject to the rounding law of 'long *a*'. But, in the case of some forms, such as the famous exceptions to the Great Vowel Shift *great*, *break* and *steak*, philologists could find no satisfactory explanation in terms of general laws or countervailing principles. In fact, so complicated were the processes and pressures involved in linguistic change that philologists also suggested as a general principle that 'every word has its own history'. Even if they were to doubt the applicability of this dictum to the *sounds* of words, most people today would probably agree that in terms of *semantic* development it is almost certainly true.

If language is seen as an organism subject to evolutionary laws, linguistic change can be seen as entirely an *internal* matter. An extreme version of this view holds that a language changes in the way it does quite irrespective of any social, technological, economic or political developments affecting the lives of its users. Most historians of English, however, despite their grounding in philology, have adopted a more moderate view and conceded that invasions, colonisation, religious upheaval, political conflict, printing, computerisation, and so on, have all had an influence on linguistic change. These kinds of phenomena have traditionally been held to constitute the *external* history of a language.

The distinction between internal and external history has many problems. First, it is based on an assumption about the nature of language, that in an important way it is distinguishable from 'non-language'. In practice, it has often proved very difficult indeed to draw the line between what 'language' includes and what it excludes. And since it is impossible to know where to stop when listing all the possible 'external' factors, the temptation has been to treat these in as summary a way as possible, on the view that they are outside language and are therefore not part of the philologist's domain. They are therefore likely to be tacked on to what is primarily an *internal* account in a rather perfunctory way. As we shall see, this has often had undesirable consequences.

With one vital exception, modern linguistics has tended to follow in philology's footsteps when dealing with linguistic change. Although modern linguists have tried to distance themselves from philology by focusing on language's present state and declaring the past as irrelevant to our understanding of the present, they have perpetuated the notion that language is autonomous, and that the 'core' of linguistics is the internal *system* (compare the philologists' notion of organism) of language. Change in language is portrayed as a succession of separate systems. So the system of Old English gives way to Middle English when the grammar has changed, internally, from a synthetic one to an analytical one.

Neither philology nor mainstream linguistics has addressed the details of linguistic change *in progress*. It is this that has been one of the important contributions of the sub-discipline of sociolinguistics. By tracing, with the aid of tape-recorders, the distribution of linguistic innovations among different age-groups, sexes and social classes, and how different phonetic contexts either favour or inhibit their adoption, sociolinguists have at least been able to give us a glimpse of how linguistic change might have occurred in the past. By carefully observing actual language-behaviour they have immeasurably enriched our understanding of issues such as bilingualism, how additional tongues are acquired and even how languages are abandoned.

But sociolinguistics can take us only so far. It is noteworthy, for instance, that once again it is sounds that have proved most amenable to sociolinguistic analysis. And its application to the process of linguistic change in the past depends on an act of faith: that the past is explicable in terms of the present. Does this mean, then, that nothing really changes, because the human condition is always much the same? As we have seen in the case of standardisation, one of the dangers of applying sociolinguistic models to the past is that of anachronism.

To talk about the past as though it were in simple opposition to the present is one of the characteristics of stories of progress or decline. It depends in any case on the assumption that we all agree on what our present is like. And to speak of 'our' and 'we' in this connection is already to assume that that there is something people share in common. One of the most fundamental problems with sociolinguistics is that it assumes the existence of something known as 'society' without clarifying what is meant by the term. So it becomes a category like the 'external' mentioned above, something necessary to include, but beyond the disciplinary boundaries of language study.

Part of the problem is that sociolinguists, like the philologists before them, continue to insist on the 'scientific' nature of their project. 'Society' then is seen as also something to be scientific about, and the required models are taken from sociology. The danger here is that definitions of 'society' are simply taken from sociologists – or, more particularly, *some* sociologists, since they have often argued amongst themselves. This argument is not surprising, given that 'society' is something that everyone has a deep interest in. The models sociolinguists fall back on, those which have the densest aura of science, tend to be those which see society as consensual. If we can assume a consensus then there are no sides to take, and we can carry on in a spirit of disinterested enquiry rather than partisan engagement.

We find the same situation in regard to history. Those phenomena classified as 'external' mentioned above belong to the subject-matter of history, and that is best left to the historians. Except that for most people history, unlike sociology, is something learned in school at an early age. A reason for this is that from one point of view history is made up of stories, which have come to be seen as part of our inheritance. Like sociology, history is often regarded by non-specialists as a largely consensual matter: certain incontrovertible events occurred, and these had discernible effects. Many stories from history are learned so early in our lives that, like our attitudes to dialect and correctness in language, they form part of our identity, and are very difficult to renounce.

The impression given in many histories of language is that history, in the sense of past events which are external to language, is a settled affair. It simply remains to work out how to relate it to change in language. But like sociology, and science in general, history as a subject tends to look settled only from the perspective of those outside it. Historians themselves, on the other hand, have often argued passionately about not only what is supposed to have happened in the past, but about what counts as history in the first place. Who, or what, for instance, should be its subjects?

Christopher Haig, the editor of a recent encyclopaedic history of the British Isles writes:

> to reduce the past to manageable form, historians sub-divide and simplify: we impose our own selective patterns upon time. We break the continuous flow of events into artificial periods for our own

convenience, and we isolate themes which make sense out of the confusion of simultaneous happenings. But the kinds of divisions, simplifications and selections we employ will predetermine the sort of history we produce. A history of the British Isles which divides chapters at the 'great events' of English tradition, in 1066, 1485, 1688, 1815 and 1914, will be a history which stresses drama and disruption; it will centre upon a version of the *English* past which registers the political milestones in an inexorable progress towards the present. The history of Ireland, Scotland and Wales will be subordinated to English political developments, and the social experiences of the British and Irish are likely to be forgotten in the story of wars and revolutions.

(Haig 1985: 7)

It is precisely what Haig calls this 'version of the *English* past' that was traditionally taught in schools throughout the British Empire and which constitutes the stories on which many of us were brought up. Most of the dates cited will be familiar; others could be added, such as 1588 when the Spanish Armada was defeated. It is, in short, a *national* history, which seeks to confirm us in a particular form of belonging, that of the 'nation', and which, like 'society', is largely conceived as consensual.

According to another contemporary historian, history is still largely the history of nations. If this seems like common sense, it shows how pervasive the concept of the nation is. Nationalist historiography, as the quotation shows, often makes use of the story of progress. It seeks individuals – King Alfred, Good Queen Bess – as embodiments of the nation. 'Drama and disruption' are useful to keep the story interesting but also show how nationalism needs the spectre of outside enemies. On the other hand, the sense of progression to the present day is often portrayed as involving a smooth continuity *within* the nation, as though the only conflicts to take place were with those outside it.

Writing history as the history of nations, though it builds on older stories, assumptions and affiliations, belongs to the nationalism of the nineteenth century. Against this background, the claim of philology to be disinterested science cannot be sustained. There is no need to see anything sinister in this: all scholarship takes place in a particular social and political context, and the appeal to science can be seen as a desire for one's work to be seen as above these concerns, and therefore as authoritative. As we have seen, the historical study of the English language was anchored in the attempt to demonstrate a literary continuity from the earliest times to the present. Literature was made to speak for the 'nation' and the language itself was the expression of 'Englishness'. One reason why it is now possible to see this clearly is that so much of this ideology has been revived, in a highly explicit way, by recent British governments. In 1986, for instance, Kenneth Baker, Conservative Minister for Education argued that: 'The English language is our greatest asset as a nation, it is the essential ingredient of the Englishness of England. . . . The thing that has held [the English people] together over the centuries'.

Sentiments such as these have often been aired over the last century at moments of crisis or radical change. They were made, for instance, during the First World War, at a time when English was also supposed to be the language of the British *Empire*. It is hardly surprising if people in Wales, Scotland and Ireland, to say nothing of territories beyond the British Isles, have felt excluded by them. And they help to explain the development, beyond England, of nationalist historiographies that see the issue of language from a very different perspective. Faced with the brute fact that by the 1960s Irish continued to be spoken by only a tiny minority within Eire, the historian An t'Athair Tomás Ó Fiaich writes:

> It is remarkable how clearly the apologists for the Tudor Conquest of Ireland, writing at the end of Elizabeth's reign, saw the extermination of the Irish language as the *sine qua non* for giving permanence to what had been achieved politically.
>
> (Ó Fiaich 1969: 104)

He goes on to quote from the celebrated English poet Edmund Spenser, who was also a government official in Ireland: 'It hath ever been the use of the conquerors to despise the language of the conquered . . . the speech being Irish, the heart must needs be Irish' (p. 104). Similar, rather modern-sounding sentiments were uttered by other state functionaries in Ireland. But how far are these symptoms of a coherent Tudor language-policy, as Ó Fiaich suggests, or how far are they the outbursts of men frustrated by an enemy who fought unconventionally and whose language, like their long hair, was a source of difference and therefore irritation?

Ó Fiaich's interpretation of events sees them, to adapt Haig's phrase in the quotation above, as part of the 'inexorable' march towards 'the present'. Because we know what the situation is today, we look for signs of its origin in the past and link the two in a simple causal relationship. But whereas nationalist histories of a dominant power such as England (often disguised as 'Britain') tend to be progressive, even triumphalist, the story for former colonies such as Ireland tends to involve decline, associated with the period of dominance by England, and then resurgence, associated with independence. Any shortcomings, weaknesses or problems can then be blamed on the former dominant power.

Now that its empire is gone, nationalism in England can no longer be expressed in the form of British imperialism. In England today a widespread nostalgia for the alleged certainties of the past, the pantheon of English heroes and heroines and the drama of 'great' events, is being officially cultivated and promoted, moreover, in the National Curriculum. The danger is that history may acquire the look of a settled affair, in which the voices and perspectives of the victors or the powerful are presented as though they belonged to everyone in the 'nation'. History is then no longer what everyone participates in, and actually makes, but is something 'out there', part of our 'heritage', and helps to form our 'national' identity.

A similar development has occurred in relation to the teaching of English language in the National Curriculum. The contribution of linguistics, especially sociolinguistics, has officially been marginalised, along with the so-called progressive educational ideas associated with the 1960s. The emphasis, officially at least, is now on 'Standard English', even to the extent of admonishing children for not speaking it in the playground. If education is to be about the cultivation of a national identity, then the concept of standard English has a central role to play in this project. Here it is worth quoting once again from John Marenbon, who follows the paragraph cited above with:

> The differences in capacity between modern standard English and the modern dialects of English are even more striking than those between Chaucerian and modern English. When a man speaks a language, he draws on the resources of the culture that has produced that language. He enjoys the achievements of the culture and is restricted by its limitations. Standard English is the language of English culture at its highest levels as it has developed over the last centuries: the language, not just of literature, philosophy and scholarship, but of government, science, commerce and industry. Dialects of English reflect the much more limited range of functions for which they have traditionally been used: the exchanges of everyday life, mainly among those unrefined by education.
>
> (Marenbon 1987: 22)

If 'Standard English' is the language of 'English culture at its highest levels' then it is clearly something to possess, as part of being 'English'.

In a now famous definition, nations have recently been called 'imagined communities'. Since standardisation has played such a central role in the formation of nation-states it seems appropriate, as I have tried to do in this book, to think of standard varieties as imagined rather than actual. But this is not to say that imagination is a misguided or undesirable faculty. Without it, we can hardly do any history at all. And it seems urgently necessary, in the present political climate, for any linguists interested in the history of English to think of themselves as historians rather than scientists. Otherwise, as the sociolinguist Dell Hymes has remarked, the most important work on language in history will be done not by linguists but by historians.

In this book I have only been able to suggest some alternative possibilities for linking the study of language with that of history. Other, far more radical treatments have now been written, and will continue to be written. I trust it is now more difficult to write a history of English without making some use of sociolinguistics, but there are at least four further desiderata. The first is awareness of the pressures which story-patterns involving decline or progress exert on our interpretation of events. The second is a questioning attitude towards alleged ruptures and continuities which shore up traditional nationalist interpretations. It used to be thought, for instance, that the Anglo-Saxon invasion occasioned the virtual extermination of the Romano-Celtic population; nowadays, however, historians and archaeologists are more likely to assert a continuity of settlement-sites and land-usage dating from well before the Roman conquest. The third is sensitivity to point of view, prompting the following question at every turn in the story of English: whose point of view is being adopted here? The serf's or the master's, the men's or the women's, that of the colonialists or of the 'natives'? The use of scare quotes around *native* brings us to the fourth desideratum, a critical attitude to terminology, which I shall finish this postscript by discussing.

For this new edition I made two changes involving the word *native*. First, *American Indians* becomes *Native Americans*, and *native language* becomes *first language*. Neither change is entirely satisfactory, and it is worth discussing why this is so.

To persist in using the term *Indian* in the context of America (it had replaced, in turn, the earlier form *Red Indian*) is to continue to use a colonialists' word, one based, moreover, on mistaken identity. *Native American*, the term preferred by the actual peoples concerned, does however imply a relationship of *belonging*, involving a particular piece of land and a particular group of peoples. Unfortunately, although there is a strong desire among different peoples in many parts of the world to identify with the land they inhabit, it is impossible to claim that anyone is truly 'native' to anywhere. The experience of humanity is migration rather than rootedness (this partly explains, perhaps, the desire for the latter). The term *pre-colonial inhabitants of America* might therefore have been a better choice.

Another problem with the term *native* is its history of use. Colonialist discourse typically refers to the inhabitants of 'exotic' territories as 'natives'. In this context the term often connotes primitiveness, even savagery. Used of others, the term tends to be negative; used of oneself, or one's own, on the other hand, it is positive. One's *native land* connotes something to be proud of if, for instance, one is white and born and brought up in England. The term has a particularly interesting history in Australian English in the nineteenth century when colonial identities were in the process of being re-made. A *native* could be both an Aboriginal and a non-Aboriginal born in Australia. (The latter were also sometimes known as the *Currency*, to be distinguished from the *Sterling*, British-born residents of Australia.)

These connotations have spilt over onto the term *native language*. It tends to associate a particular language with one's own claim to a piece of the Earth. To a white, monoglot speaker of English, born and resident in England, the term seems unproblematic. It is the language of one's ancestral 'nation', and embodies a sense of national identity. But in many areas of the world, such as parts of the Caribbean for example, the issue of identity is not so automatically associated with nationality. The problem with the term, in sum, it that like all terminology it has evolved in a particular social and political context which cannot be applied to very different contexts without difficulties.

Replacing *native language* by *first language* obscures several different issues, that of *when* a language is acquired, *how* it is acquired, and how it is *used*. The language one learns earliest in life may not necessarily be the one used on most occasions. The latter may turn out to be one learned in school, whereas more than one language may be acquired so early in life that the issue of primacy may be irrelevant. The problem is similar to that encountered at many different places in this book: the terminology customarily used is not fine enough to capture all the important distinctions.

One response to this problem might be to dismiss it as a sterile manifestation of 'political correctness'. Another would be that of the scientist: coin new technical terms, or treat existing ones purely as technical terms by sticking strictly to their *denotative* meanings. The first of these 'scientific' courses runs the risk of making a book about language quite unintelligible to the general reader. The second seems to ignore a fundamental quality of words, which is to gather associations over time. One result of this is that eventually they have to be abandoned, or only used in the awareness that they may cause problems. Ultimately, there is no transparent language by means of which we can tell the story of a language. As the study of linguistic history tells us, words too have their own stories.

Exercises and topics for further study

For reasons of space the following exercises have been kept as brief and indicative as possible, with no particular order of difficulty. They are based on the extracts discussed in chapter eight; for the sources of these, see pp. 276–7. Other relevant material will be found in the Index and the Notes and suggested reading as well as the main text above.

1 Try to write out a translation of texts 1–11 into modern English using the glosses. Note any problems you encounter. How much continuity can you find from the earliest texts to the most recent? Do you feel that the 'intelligibility' of the Old and Middle English texts is a single issue, or does it have several dimensions? How 'intelligible', for instance, do you find the Authorised Version discussed alongside Extract 2? Are any problems you find comparable to those you might encounter in respect of the 'legalese' of Extract 9? Are there disadvantages in up-dating the language of these kinds of texts?

2 The *OED* extract talks of an 'accepted uniform spelling and an approximately uniform pronunciation'. Do you find this a reasonable description of English today? Do you think it appropriate for the mid-nineteenth century?

Identify (a) some of the variations in English spelling today and (b) the deviations from a uniform spelling system as evidenced from Extracts 10 onwards. (Examples include u/v, ou/ow, etc.)

Notice the deviations from conventional English spelling in Extract 16. Are they systematic? Are some more 'phonetic' than conventional spelling, and would they also be appropriate for English pronunciation? How far is the argument about American spelling on pages 240–1 relevant for Scots?

Identify spellings in the extracts that may represent variability in pronunciation, for example *er/ar*, *cowde*.

3 The senses of *hag* given in the *OED* (Extract 15) can be summarised by means of a diagram:

13th century   14th century   16th century   19th century

3b *personification*
  of vice

                    3a *ugly old*
                       woman

                              1b *ghost*

                                1a *female*
                                   demon

                                          2 *witch*
                              4a *light*

                                                  5 *fish*

Notice that the last two senses are only tentatively related to this word by the dictionary's editors, and that they consider the general order of senses to be uncertain. Also, the order of senses given does not accord with the date of the earliest.

Using *OED* and, where appropriate, Williams's *Keywords* and *Webster's Dictionary*, draw a diagram for the following words:
(Extract 8) *womb, paunche, meet* (cf. Extract 10 *mete*); (Extract 11) *naturall*, (Extract 15(a)) *genius, declension, policy, dialect, rudeness, speech*, (15(b)) *congress, senate, assembly, court, engine*. Do you find any problems with the dictionary entries?

4 Look up dialectal *hag* (haw) in Upton *et al.* (1993) and compare its modern forms and geographical distribution with those given in Wright. What conclusions can be drawn from the comparison?

Look up the following words in the *English Dialect Dictionary* and the *Oxford English Dictionary*: (Extract 10) *ax(e)* (ask), (Extract 5) *ay(e)* (always), (Extract 3) *withy* (willow). Compare forms and geographical distribution with those given in Upton *et al.* Locate early forms of these words in the textual extracts. Look up the Scots forms listed for Extract 16 in the *Concise Scots Dictionary*. How many are shared with dialects of English?

5 Villages in the vicinity of the Witney estate (Extract 3) are Leafield, Finstock, North Leigh, Cogges, Lew, Crawley and Hailey. Look these forms up in Ekwall (1960), then the individual place-name elements in Gelling (1984). Does the final element in North Leigh, Crawley and Hailey suggest anything about the local landscape at the time of Anglo-Saxon settlement?

The charter names three locations no longer marked on modern maps: Hawkesley, Notley and Henley. Despite appearances, only one of these three contains the same final element as Hailey and Crawley. So are English place-names, like their Irish counterparts (see Extract 17), also, to quote from *Translations*, 'riddled with confusion'?

6 Consider how you wrote up scientific experiments at school. Does Newton's example (Extract 13) conform with what you were taught about pronouns and voice? Compare his style with that of the following extract from *Optics* Book III, Part 1:

> If two equal bodies meet directly *in vacuo*, they will by the laws of motion stop where they meet, and lose all their motion, and remain in rest, unless they be elastick, and receive new motion from their spring. . . . And this may be try'd, by letting two equal pendulums fall against one another from equal heights. If the pendulums be of lead or soft clay, they will lose all or almost all their motions: if of elastick bodies they will lose all but what they recover from their elasticity.

Does this extract have other qualities which are generally associated with scientific style?

7 Today the subjunctive mood can often be recognised by the absence of *-s* in the third person singular of the verb, hence *if she work hard* in Extract 14a. In West Saxon the forms of the subjunctive of *wyrcan* (work) in the present tense were:

	Singular	**Plural**
1st person	*iċ wyrce*	*we wyrcen*
2nd person	*þu wyrce*	*ġe wyrcen*
3rd person	*he* *heo wyrce* *hit*	*hie wyrcen*

The *indicative* (non-subjunctive) forms, on the other hand, were: *iċ wyrce, þu wyrcest, he/heo/hit wyrcþ, we wyrcaþ, ġe wyrcaþ, hie wyrcaþ*.

Using a modern grammar such as Quirk and Greenbaum (1973), find out how, where, and in what styles the subjunctive is used in contemporary English. How many uses are familiar to you? Try to find examples in the extracts. Do you agree with a modern prediction that the subjunctive will one day be obsolete?

8 Identify the different patterns in word-order, negation, the form of questions and the use of *do* in the textual extracts, as discussed in chapter four above.

9 Compare the uses of co-ordination and subordination in the sentence-structures of the textual extracts. How far do they correspond with the differences between speech and writing?

10 A major dimension of variability in Old and Middle English texts is geographical. Locate roughly on a map the areas in which the textual extracts were produced, and see how far you can classify certain features (e.g., *s* rather than *þ* as the verbal ending of the third person singular) as belonging to one region rather than another. Compare what you find with accounts of Old and Middle English dialects in Strang (1970), Mossé (1952), Burnley (1992a) and Milroy (1992b).

Do you feel that geographical variation is more important than the variations associated with different textual functions and levels of formality?

11 Middle English texts have sometimes been discussed in terms of 'internal variation' (see Extract 5). How much internal variation can you find in the different textual extracts? (Look for instance at pronoun and infinitive forms, the form of the past participle, grammatical inflections, final *e*.)

12 How far is the concept of 'Middle English' based on 'internal' evidence, how far on 'external'? Which of the textual extracts would you choose to mark the beginnings of 'Modern' English? What criteria would you use?

13 Collect as many examples as you can of the second person pronoun in the textual extracts. Compare the forms and see how usage varies in relation to social and communicative factors.

14 Compare the adapted Bajan text (Extract 18) with the original in Le Page and Tabouret-Keller (1985: 93). How adequately does it display the crucial linguistic features? What changes would you make in order to 'standardise' the transcription? Do the same with the extract from Scots (16). How similar are the problems and issues?

Appendix: International phonetic alphabet consonant symbols

The chart gives a selection of symbols representing consonants as used in different varieties of English worldwide.

Manner of articulation	Bilabial		Labio-dental		Dental or interdental		Alveolar		Retroflex		Palato-alveolar		Palatal		Velar		Uvular		Labio-velar		Glottal	
Place of articulation	voiceless	voiced	voiceless	voiced	voiceless	voiced	voiceless	voiced	voiceless	voiced	voiceless	voiced	voiceless	voiced	voiceless	voiced	voiceless	voiced	voiceless	voiced	voiceless	voiced
Nasal		m				n̪		n		ɳ				ɲ		ŋ						
Plosive	p	b			t̪	d̪	t	d	ʈ	ɖ					k	g					ʔ	
Fricative	ɸ	β	f	v	θ	ð	s	z	ʂ	ʐ	ʃ	ʒ		j	x	ɣ	χ	ʁ	ʍ		h	
Approximant								ɹ		ɻ				j						w		
Lateral fricative							ɬ															
Lateral approximant								l		ɭ												
Trill								r										ʀ				
Tap or flap								ɾ		ɽ												

Notes and suggested reading

(I have tried to draw attention to the most accessible books and articles. For full details of all works cited, see the Bibliography.)

Most general histories of English have been consulted. Baugh and Cable (1993, 4th edn) is a standard work by an American scholar; it has been valuably up-dated on contemporary varieties. A very readable introduction is Barber (1972, 5th edn); Bolton (1967) is short and very clear. McCrum *et al.* (1986) is lively and accessible but with a highly literary perspective; Burnley (1992a) is a detailed textual history of the traditional kind. More difficult, but infinitely rewarding are Strang (1970) and Samuels (1972). *The Cambridge History of the English Language* (General Editor R. Hogg) is authoritative and highly detailed (1992–). Partridge (1969), Barber (1976), Blake (1977) and Görlach (1991) are invaluable studies of particular periods, as from a more critical and political perspective are Smith (1984) and Crowley (1989). A very useful collection of essays is edited by Lass (1969). Histories of English that have been more clearly influenced by sociolinguistics are Bailey (1991) and Milroy (1992a); Machan and Scott (1992) is a useful collection of chapters on the history of English world-wide; Graddol *et al.* (1996) deals with variation and change from a largely sociolinguistic perspective.

I have used the standard sociolinguistics introductions. A recent and clear one is by Hudson (1980), but the beginner might best start with Trudgill (1974b). A more recent one in Romaine (1994). Bell (1976) is a handy reference book. Two collections of essays are now regarded as classics: Giglioli, and Pride and Holmes (both 1972).

INTRODUCTION

The notion of 're-tribalisation' is taken from Khlief (1979). For multilingualism in contemporary England, see Edwards (1979), Rosen and Burgess (1980) and the Linguistic Minorities Project (1985); for the study of linguistic history, see Bynon (1977); Romaine (1982).

1 LANGUAGES IN CONTACT

A stimulating starting-point is Haugen (1966). See also Stewart (1968). For diglossia, see Ferguson (1959); for bilingualism, Hornby (1977); Romaine (1989); pidgins and creoles, Todd (1974, 1984); Romaine (1988).

On Latin see Elcock (1975); for its imposition, see Brosnahan (1963). For the multilingual heritage of the British Isles, see Jackson (1953), Lockwood (1975), Trudgill, ed. (1984). The Anglo-Saxons are the subject of Whitelock (1965), Loyn (1962), and to some extent Finberg (1976). See also Myres (1986).

Place-names are a subject of inexhaustible fascination, but the student requires knowledge of their early forms. See Ekwall (1960) and for recent research, Cameron and Gelling (1976). Gelling (1984) is invaluable.

On the Vikings, see Loyn (1977). Norman-French relations with English are discussed by Berndt (1965). An interesting study of English in the fourteenth century is by Cottle (1969).

For up-to-date surveys on all these topics see the relevant chapters in *The Cambridge History of the English Language* (vol. 1 ed. R. Hogg; vol. 2 ed. N. Blake). A fascinating study of literacy after the Norman Conquest is by Clanchy (1993). See also chapter 3 in Graddol *et al.* (1996).

2 STANDARDISATION AND WRITING

The four stages of standardisation are proposed by Haugen (1966). A great deal of the data in this chapter is from Dobson (1955). Williams (1961) offers a clear social and political perspective. See Milroy and Milroy (1985) and Joseph (1987). Crowley (1989) is essential reading. See also Leith and Graddol (1996).

Discussions of 'standard English' in Britain critical of the role of linguists are Honey (1983) and Marenbon (1987). Responses by linguists are Stubbs (1986), Cameron and Bourne (1988), Hudson (1992) and Perera (1994).

On spellings, see Scragg (1975) alphabets and literacy in general, Goody and Watt (1962), and Oxenham (1980). Street (1985) offers a different perspective. Medieval English is discussed by Blake (1977) who elsewhere (1976) provided the basis for the discussion of Kentish. A very useful study of literary representations of non-standard speech is by Page (1973). On Cockney see Matthews (1938) and Sivertsen (1960).

For sixteenth-century attitudes to English see Jones (1953) and J. Williams in Machan and Scott (1992). A very good introduction to Shakespeare's language is by Quirk (1974). On prose, see Gordon (1966). For contemporary attitudes to usage, Mittins *et al.* (1970) is excellent; it discusses the history of certain shibboleths. On the middle-class 'market' for correctness, see Wyld (1936) and Labov (1972a).

Invaluable contributions to this topic from historians include Brennan (1989), Smith (1984) and Joyce (1991). For an educationalist's view of the history of English as a taught language see Michael (1987).

3 WORDS AND MEANINGS

A good general history of English vocabulary is by Sheard (1954). The discussion of Anglo-Saxon topographical terms is based on Strang (1970); that of euphemism, and of emphatic variants, on Samuels (1972). Burnley's chapter in Blake, ed. (1992) is a very useful study of vocabulary in the medieval period. Williams (1988) has proved indispensable in writing this chapter.

An excellent chapter, 'Lexis', in Strang (1968) provided the basis for the discussion of dictionaries. The categories of meaning are those of Leech (1974), who has a good chapter called 'Semantics and Society'. For other examples and insights see Waldron (1967); for detailed studies of individual words, see Lewis (1968) and Tucker (1967, 1972). An invaluable and accessible recent study of semantic change is by Adamson in Ricks and Michael (eds) (1990).

Letters of complaint to the press about usage are reproduced in Strang (1970, pp. 3–5). Status terms are discussed in Barber (1976), and the section on Elizabethan terms of address is based on Salmon (1967). See also J. Williams in Machan and Scott (1992). An invaluable contribution from an historian is Wrightson (1991). Schulz (1975) provided the basis for the discussion on words denoting women. See also Cameron (1995).

4 GRAMMAR

The list of misconceptions about grammar is taken from Palmer (1971), an excellent introduction to the subject of grammar. On the grammar of speech and contemporary varieties of English, see Quirk (1968) and Crystal and Davy (1969). On 'standard' grammar, see Quirk and Greenbaum (1973); on 'non-standard', see Trudgill and Hughes (1979), Edwards, Trudgill and Weltens (1984), Milroy and Milroy (eds) (1993), Trudgill and Chambers (eds) (1991). For a useful introduction to a number of issues see Thomas's chapter in Graddol *et al.* (1996).

On the loss of inflexions, and sixteenth-century hypercorrection, see Samuels (1972). For sociolinguistic study of forms of address, see Brown and Gilman (1960) and Ervin-Tripp (1969); on the history of *thou* and *you*, see Byrne (1936), Leith (1984), and J. Williams in Machan and Scott (1992). For Bernstein's early ideas, see his 1970 article; those of Whorf can be found in Carroll (ed.) (1956).

5 PRONUNCIATION

Indispensable for the study of English sounds, present and past, is Gimson (1980, 3rd edn). See also Wells (1982). The sociolinguistic framework derives from Labov (1972a). On dialect pronunciations, see Sanderson *et al.*, *The Linguistic Atlas of England* (1978); on regional sounds, both rural and urban, see the works and editions of Trudgill (1974, 1975, 1978) and Trudgill and Hughes (1979). A recent and accessible introduction is by Wright in Graddol *et al.* (1996). More advanced is Labov (1994). On the conditioning effect of consonants on vowels, see C.-J. Bailey (1973). The section on the Great Vowel Shift is based on Labov (1974). A more recent and different perspective is Jones (1989).

On the rise of new accents, see Kerswill in Graddol *et al.* (1996). The controversial role of gender in pronunciation change is discussed in Coates (1986) and Cameron and Coates (1988).

6 THE IMPOSITION OF ENGLISH IN THE BRITISH ISLES

Most standard histories of English do not deal in any detail with the linguistic minorities of the British Isles. An accessible place to start is Lockwood (1975). Perhaps the most useful sociohistorical account to supplement the present work is Trudgill (ed.) (1984). Stephens (1976) is a classic nationalist account. A useful corrective by an historian is T. Williams (1989). On internal colonisation in the Celtic periphery see Bartlett (1993). See also Trudgill (1974b) and Trudgill and Hughes (1979). On Scots, the collection of essays edited by Aitken and McArthur (1979) is indispensable, as are the chapters by Aitken in Trudgill (ed.) (1984). The discussion of border usage is based on Glauser (1974), Mather and Speitel (1975/7), and Speitel (1978). On recent research in Edinburgh, see essays by Reid and Romaine in Trudgill (1978). More recent polemical accounts inspired by nationalist ideology are Kay (1986) and McClure (1988). The New Testament in Scots is translated by Lorimer (1983). See also Donaldson (1986) and Devitt (1989).

A helpful introduction to languages of Ireland is edited by Ó'Muirithe (1977). See also Bliss (1979) and O'Cuiv (1969). Recent studies of Irish (or Hiberno-) English are: Harris (1991a and b, 1993). The section on Gaelic in contemporary Ireland is based on Turvey (1978) and Ó'Riagáin and Ó'Gliasáin (1979). On usage in Ulster, see Gregg (1972) and McCafferty (1996), and in Belfast, J. and L. Milroy in Trudgill (1978).

Recent sociolinguistic studies of Gaelic in Scotland are by Mackinnon (1977, 1991, 1996). See also Thomson (1976). On Welsh, see Lewis (1978), R.M. Jones (1979), and Khlief (1979); on Cornish, Berresford Ellis (n.d.). The phenomenon of the semi-speaker is discussed by Dorian (1980).

7 ENGLISH AS AN INTERNATIONAL LANGUAGE

A number of general introductions to English as a world language have appeared since the early 1980s: Pride (1982), Platt, Weber and Ho (1984), Trudgill and Hannah (3rd edn 1994). There is also useful material in later editions of Baugh and Cable (1993), and in Bailey and Robinson (1973), Bailey (1991), Graddol *et al.* (1996), McCrum *et al.* (1986) and Kachru (2nd edn 1992; 1986); more oppositional is Tripathi (1992). The journals *English World-Wide* and *English Today* are invaluable.

The status of 'Standard British English' in the Anglophone world is debated by Quirk (1990) and Kachru (1991). A valuable critique of the global English language teaching 'industry' is by Phillipson (1992).

Cheshire (ed.) (1991) is an invaluable collection of more advanced sociolinguistic essays dealing with most of the Anglophone world, many with a historical dimension. On the formation of colonial varieties see Trudgill (1986).

On Caribbean varieties, see Cassidy (1961), Ramchand (1970), Craig (1976), and Edwards (1979). Le Page and Tabouret-Keller (1985) is not only informative but is important in its treatment of language as the expression of multiple identities. See also Winer (1993). On Black slavery see Walvin (1993). On British Black English see Edwards (1986) and Sebba (1993).

Not surprisingly, there is no dearth of books on American English. A good, short introduction is by Strevens (1972). On varieties of American English, see Reed (1967), Kurath (1972), McDavid (1973, 1980). On contemporary sociolinguistic variation, see Labov (1972a and 1972b). There are two fascinating chapters on relations between American and British English by Quirk (1972). On standardisation in American English, see Smith and Lance (1979), Heath (1976), and Švejcer (1978). For American Indian languages, see Spolsky and Kari (1974) and Stoller (1976); for Chicano English, Metcalf (1974), Thompson (1974), Sawyer (1964). See also Bailey (1973, 1991), Ferguson and Heath (eds) (1991). For a fascinating literary treatment of American linguistic nationalism see Simpson (1986).

On Canadian English, see Orkin (1971); further material can be found in Trudgill (1986) and Cheshire (ed.) (1991); for relations with Canadian French, Inglehart and Woodward (1967) and Vallée and de Vries (1978); see also Wardhaugh (1987) and Heller (1992). For South African English, see Lanham and McDonald (1980) and for the recent linguistic situation see McLean and McCormick (1996). For Australian English see Turner (1972), Ramson (1988), Horvath (1985), Romaine (1991) and Bradley (1991). On New Zealand English see Gordon and Deverson (1989) and Bell and Holmes (1990).

There is a fairly extensive literature on English in Africa, much of it concerned with language planning. See Spencer (1963 and 1971a), Whiteley (1971), Ladefoged *et al.* (1972). The article by Angogo and Hancock (1980) is excellent. See also Mazrui (1967) and Adeniran (1979). See also Bamgbose (1992) and Myers-Scotton (1993).

On English in India, see Kachru (1986, 1992), Verma (1982) and Tripathi (1992) and in Singapore and Malaysia, Platt (1980). Singapore English is discussed by Foley (1988) and Gupta (1993).

On colonial language policies in general, see Spencer (1963, 1971b). A good introduction to problems of language planning is by Le Page (1964).

8 A CRITICAL LINGUISTIC HISTORY OF ENGLISH TEXTS

Extracts 1, 2, 4, 7, 11, 12 and parts of 15 are contextualised more fully and discussed from a philological perspective in Burnley (1992a). The West Saxon version of 2 can be found in D. Whitelock, ed. *Sweet's Anglo-Saxon Reader*, Oxford, Clarendon, 1967. Extract 3 is taken from an article by M. Gelling, 'English place-names derived from the compound *wicham*' in *Medieval Archaeology XI*, (1967) pp. 87–104; her map can be interpreted with the aid of the Ordnance Survey 'Landranger' Sheet 164 (better still, the larger scale 1091 and 1115 'Pathfinder' sheets). Extract 5 is taken from, and discussed by, Milroy (1992b); 6 from K. Sisam (ed.), *Fourteenth Century Verse and Prose*, Oxford, Clarendon, 1921, 8 from A. Barratt (ed.), *Women's Writing in Middle English*, London, Longman, 1992, 9 from Blake (ed.) (1992). Extract 10, from the Preface to Caxton's *Eneydos*, is discussed in detail by Harris and Taylor (1989) and, in part, by Hamer (1993). Puttenham's *The Arte of English Poesie* (Extract 11) is edited by G.D. Willcock and A. Walker, Cambridge, Cambridge University Press, 1936. *The Letters of Lady Brilliana Harley* is edited by L.T. Lewis, London, Camden Society 58, 1854. Extract 13 is from p. 1 of *Opticks*. The quotation from *Arcadia*, published in 1590, is taken from A.C. Partridge, *Tudor to Augustan English*, London, Deutsch, 1969, p. 213. Extract 14(a) is from page 89 of Helen Wood's *A Grammatical Reading Class Book*, 1828; the quotation is from p. 87. R. Lowth's definition of the subjunctive is on pages 140–1 of his *A Short Introduction to English Grammar*, London, 1762. Extract 14(b) is on p. 46 of W. Cobbett's *A grammar of the English Language in a Series of Letters*, London, 1819 (2nd edn). Extract 15(a) is from p. ix of the Preface to Samuel Johnson's *A Dictionary of the English Language*, London, 1773 (4th edn); his *Plan of A Dictionary of the English Language* was published in London in 1747. Extract 15(b) is from N. Webster's *American Dictionary*, Boston, 1828; the other quotations are from his *Dissertations on the English Language*, Boston, 1789. Extract 15(c) is from p. xxv of the General Explanations to the *Oxford English Dictionary*, Oxford, 1989 (2nd edn). The *Proposal* for the *OED* is in the

Appendix to the *Transactions of the Philological Society*, London, 1858. Further points about Extracts 15(a), (b) and (c) are made by Crowley (1991). Extract 15(d) is on p. i of the Preface to Joseph Wright's *English Dialect Dictionary*, Oxford, Oxford University Press, 1898–1905. Nowell's citation of *haȝan* can be found in A.H. Marckwardt (ed.), *Lawrence Nowell's Vocabularium Saxonicum*, Ann Arbor, Michigan, 1952. Extract 16 is taken from Sheila Douglas, ed. *The King o the Black Art and Other Folktales*, Aberdeen, Aberdeen University Press, 1987, p. 67. Extract 17 is from pp. 43–4 of Brian Friel's *Translations*, London, Faber, 1991. Extract 18 is adapted from R. Le Page and A. Tabouret-Keller, *Acts of Identity*, Cambridge, Cambridge University Press, 1985, p. 93.

THEORETICAL POSTSCRIPT

The quotation from Johnson is taken from his 'A History of the English Language', which follows the Preface to his *Dictionary*. Both quotations from John Marenbon are on p. 22 of his *English Our English* (1987). The quotation from Haig is in the Editor's Preface to Haig (1985); the extract from Kenneth Baker's speech is from his Alan Palmer Lecture of 7 November 1986, and is quoted by J. Donald on p. 14 of his 'Beyond our Ken: English, Englishness and the National Curriculum', in P. Brooker and P. Humm (eds), *Dialogue and Difference: English into the 90s*, London, Routledge, 1989, pp. 13–30. The quotations from Ó Fiaich are on p. 104 of Ó Fiaich (1969).

See also Harris and Taylor (1989), R. Williams (1977), Labov (1994), Anderson (1983), Fairclough (1991), Leith (1996), Crowley (1989, 1990), Milroy (1992a), G. Williams (1992), Haig, ed. (1985), Ó'Fiaich (1969), Hymes (1991) and Cameron (1995).

Bibliography

Below is a list of books and articles consulted in the writing of this book. Fuller bibliographies can be found in the standard histories of English.

Adamson, A. (1990), 'The what of the language' in C. Ricks and L. Michaels (eds) *The State of the Language*, pp. 503–14.

Adeniran, A. (1979), 'Personalities and policies in the establishment of English in northern Nigeria (1900–1943)', *International Journal of the Sociology of Language*, vol. 22, pp. 55–77.

Aitken, A.J. and McArthur, T. (1979), *Languages of Scotland*, Edinburgh, Chambers.

Anderson, B. (1983), *Imagined Communities: Reflections on the Origin and Spread of Nationalism*, London, Verso.

Andrew, S.O. (1940), *Syntax and Style in Old English*, Cambridge, Cambridge University Press.

Angogo, R. and Hancock, I. (1980), 'English in Africa', *English World-Wide*, vol. 1, no. 1, pp. 67–96.

Bailey, C.-J.N. (1973), 'The patterning of language variation', in Bailey and Robinson (eds), pp. 156–87.

Bailey, R.W. (1973), 'Write off versus write on: dialects and the teaching of composition' in R.W. Bailey and J.L. Robinson (eds), *Varieties of Present-Day English*, New York, Macmillan, pp. 384–408.

Bailey, R.W. (1991), *Images of English*, Cambridge, Cambridge University Press.

Bailey, R.W. and Robinson, J.L. (eds) (1973), *Varieties of Present-Day English*, New York, Macmillan.

Baldi, P. and Werth, R.N. (eds) (1978), *Readings in Historical Phonology*, Pennsylvania State University Press.

Bamgbose, A. (1982), 'Standard Nigerian English: issues of identification' in B.B. Kachru (ed.), *The Other Tongue*, pp. 99–111.

Barber, C.L. (1964), *Linguistic Change in Present-Day English*, Edinburgh, Oliver and Boyd.

Barber, C.L. (1972), *The Story of Language*, 5th edn, London, Pan.

Barber, C.L. (1976), *Early Modern English*, London, Deutsch.

Barry, M. (1967), 'Yorkshire sheep-scoring numerals', *Transactions of the Yorkshire Dialect Society*, part LXVII, pp. 21–32.

Bartlett, R. (1993), *The Making of Europe*, Harmondsworth, Penguin.

Baugh, A.C. and Cable, T. (1993), *A History of the English Language*, 4th edn, London, Routledge & Kegan Paul.

Bell, D. and Holmes, J. (1990), *New Zealand Ways of Speaking English*, Clevedon, Multilingual Matters.

Bell, R.T. (1976), *Sociolinguistics: Goals, Approaches and Problems*, London, Batsford.

Bellin, W. (1984), 'Welsh and English in Wales' in P. Trudgill (ed.), *Language in the British Isles*, pp. 449–79.

Berndt, R. (1965), 'The linguistic situation in England from the Norman Conquest to the loss of Normandy (1066–1204)', *Philologica Pragensica*, 8, pp. 145–63, reprinted in Lass (1969).

Bernstein, B. (1970), 'Social class, language, and socialisation', in Bernstein, B. (1971), *Class, Codes and Control*, pp. 170–89.

Bernstein, B. (1971), *Class, Codes and Control*, vol. 1: *Theoretical Studies Towards a Sociology of Language*, London, Routledge & Kegan Paul.

Bernstein, B. (ed.) (1973), *Class, Codes and Control*, vol. 2: *Empirical Studies*, London, Routledge & Kegan Paul.

Berresford Ellis, P. (n.d.), *The Story of the Cornish Language*, Truro, Tor Mer Press.

Blake, N. (1976), 'Born in Kent', *Lore and Language*, vol. 2, no. 5, pp. 5–9.

Blake, N. (1977), *The English Language in Medieval Literature*, London, Dent.

Blake, N. (ed.) (1992), *The Cambridge History of the English Language*, vol. II, *1066–1476*, Cambridge, Cambridge University Press.

Bliss, A.J. (1979), *Spoken English In Ireland 1600–1740*, Dublin, Dolmen; Humanities Press.

Bolton, W.F. (1967), *A Short History of Literary English*, London, Arnold.

Bradley, D. (1991), '/ae/ and /aː/ in Australian English' in J. Cheshire (ed.), *English Around the World: Sociolinguistic Perspectives*, pp. 227–34.

Brennan, G. (1989), 'Patriotism, language and power: English translations of the Bible 1520–80', *History Workshop Journal* 27, Ruskin College, Oxford, pp. 18–36.

Brosnahan, L.F. (1963), 'Some historical cases of language imposition', in J. Spencer (ed.), *Language in Africa. Papers of the Leverhulme Conference on Universities and the Language Problems of Tropical Africa Held at University College Ibadan*, Cambridge, Cambridge University Press, pp. 7–24, reprinted in Bailey and Robinson (1973).

Brown, R. and Gilman, A. (1960), 'The pronouns of power and solidarity', in T.A. Sebeok (ed.), *Style in Language*, MIT Press, pp. 253–76; reprinted in Giglioli (1972).

Burke, P. and Porter, R. (eds) (1987), *The Social History of Language*, Cambridge, Cambridge University Press.

Burke, P. and Porter, R. (eds) (1991), *Language, Self, and Society: a Social History of Language*, Oxford, Polity.

Burnley, D. (1992a), *The History of the English Language*, London, Longman.

Burnley, D. (1992b), 'Lexis and semantics' in N. Blake (ed.), *The Cambridge History of the English Language*, pp. 409–98.

Bynon, T. (1977), *Historical Linguistics*, Cambridge University Press.

Byrne, Sister St G. (1936), *Shakespeare's Use of the Pronouns of Address, its Significance in Characterisation and Motivation*, New York, Haskell House.

Cameron, D. (1995), *Linguistic Hygiene*, London, Routledge.

Cameron, D. and Bourne, J., (1988), 'No common ground: Kingman, grammar and the nation', *Language and Education*, vol. 2, no. 3, pp. 147–60.

Cameron, D. and Coates, J., (1988), *Women in their Speech Communities*, London, Longman.

Cameron, K. and Gelling, M. (eds) (1976), *Place-name Evidence for the Anglo-Saxon Invasion and Scandinavian Settlements*, Cambridge, English Place Name Society.

Carroll, J.B. (ed.) (1956), *Language, Thought and Reality: Selected Writings of Benjamin Lee Whorf*, MIT Press.

Cassidy, F.G. (1961), *Jamaica Talk: Three Hundred Years of the English Language in Jamaica*, London, Macmillan.

Cheshire, J. (ed.) (1991), *English Around the World: Sociolinguistic Perspectives*, Cambridge, Cambridge University Press.

Clanchy, M.T. (1993), *From Memory to Written Record*, 2nd edn, Oxford, Blackwell.

Clark, J.W. (1957), *Early English*, London, Deutsch.

Coates, J. (1986), *Women, Men and Language*, 2nd edn, London, Longman.

Corfield, P.J. (ed.) (1991), *Language, History and Class*, Oxford, Blackwell.

Cottle, B. (1969), *The Triumph of English 1350–1400*, London, Blandford.

Craig, D.R. (1976), 'Bi-dialectal education: creole and standard in the West Indies', *International Journal of the Sociology of Language*, vol. 8, pp. 94–105.

Crowley, T. (1989), *The Politics of Discourse: the Standard Language Question in British Cultural Politics*, London, Macmillan.

Crowley, T. (1990), 'That obscure object of desire: a science of language' in J.E. Joseph and T.J. Taylor (eds), *Ideologies of Language*, London, Routledge, pp. 27–50.

Crowley, T. (1991), *Proper English? Readings in Language, History and Cultural Identity*, London, Routledge.

Crystal, D. and Davy, D. (1969), *Investigating English Style*, London, Longman.

Davidson, B. (1978), *Africa in Modern History: The Search for a New Society*, London, Allen Lane.

Devitt, A. (1989), *Standardising Written English: Diffusion in the Case of Scotland 1520–1659*, Cambridge, Cambridge University Press.

Dittmar, N. (1976), *Sociolinguistics*, London, Arnold.

Dobson, E.J. (1955), 'Early modern standard English', *Transactions of the Philological Society*, pp. 25–54, reprinted in Lass (1969).

Dobson, E.J. (1968), *English Pronunciation 1500–1700*, Oxford, Oxford University Press.

Donaldson, W. (1986), *Popular Literature in Victorian Scotland: Language, Fiction and the Press*, Aberdeen, Aberdeen University Press.

Dorian, N.C. (1980), 'Language shift in community and individual: the phenomenon of the laggard semi-speaker', *International Journal of the Sociology of Language*, vol. 25, pp. 85–94.

Edwards, J. (1984), 'Irish and English in Ireland' in P. Trudgill (ed.), *Language in the British Isles*, pp. 480–98.

Edwards, V. (1979), *The West Indian Language Issue in British Schools*, London, Routledge & Kegan Paul.

Edwards, V. (1986), *Language in a Black Community*, Clevedon, Multilingual Matters.

Edwards, V.K., Trudgill, P. and Weltens, B. (1984), *The Grammar of English Dialect*, London, ESRC.

Ekwall, E. (1956), *Studies in the Population of Medieval London*, Lund, Lund Studies in English.

Ekwall, E. (ed.) (1960), *The Concise Oxford Dictionary of English Place Names*, 4th edn, Oxford, Oxford University Press.

Elcock, W.D. (1975), *The Romance Languages*, London, Faber.

Ervin-Tripp, S. (1969), 'Sociolinguistic rules of address', from 'Sociolinguistics' in L. Berkowitz (ed.), *Advances in Experimental Social Psychology*, vol. 4, pp. 93–107, reprinted in Pride and Holmes (1972).

Fairclough, N. (1991), *Discourse and Social Change*, Cambridge, Polity.

Ferguson, C. and Heath, S.B. (eds) (1981), *Language in the United States of America*, Cambridge, Cambridge University Press.

Ferguson, C.A. (1959), 'Diglossia', *Word*, 15, pp. 325–40, reprinted in Giglioli (1972).

Finberg, H.P.R. (1976), *The Formation of England*, St Albans, Paladin.

Fisher, J.H. and Bornstein, D. (1974), *In Forme of Speche is Chaunge*, Englewood Cliffs, Prentice-Hall.

Fishman, J.A. (1965), 'Who speaks what language to whom and when?', *La Linguistique*, 2, pp. 67–88, reprinted in Pride and Holmes (1972).

Fishman, J. A. (1971), *Sociolinguistics: A Brief Introduction*, Rowley, Newbury House.

Fishman, J.A. (1972), 'The sociology of language', in Giglioli (1972).

Fishman, J.A. (ed.) (1978), *Advances in the Study of Societal Multilingualism*, The Hague, Mouton.

Fishman, J.A., Ferguson, C.A. and Das Gupta, J. (eds) (1968), *Language Problems of Developing Nations*, New York, Wiley.

Fishman, J.A., Cooper, R.L. and Conrad, W. (eds) (1977), *The Spread of English: The Sociology of English as a Second Language*, Rowley, Mass., Newbury House.

Foley, J. (1988), *New Englishes: the Case of Singapore*, Singapore, Singapore University Press.

Freeborn, D. (1993), *From Old English to Standard English*, London, Macmillan.

Gelling, M. (1984), *Place-Names in the Landscape*, London, Dent.

Giglioli, P.P. (ed.) (1972), *Language and Social Context*, Harmondsworth, Penguin.

Gimson, A.C. (1980), *An Introduction to the Pronunciation of English*, 3rd edn, London, Arnold.

Glauser, B. (1974), *The Scottish-English Linguistic Border: Lexical Aspects*, The Cooper Monographs, Berne, Francke Verlag.

Goody, J. and Watt, I. (1962), 'The consequences of literacy', *Comparative Studies in Society and History*, 5, pp. 304–26, 332–95, reprinted in Giglioli (1972).

Gordon, E. and Deverson, T. (1989), *Finding a New Zealand Voice: Attitudes Towards English Use in New Zealand*, Auckland, New House.

Gordon, I.A. (1966), *The Movement of English Prose*, London, Longman.

Görlach, M. (1991), *Introduction to Early Modern English*, Cambridge, Cambridge University Press.

Graddol, D., Leith, D. and Swann, J. (eds) (1996), *English: History, Diversity and Change*, London, Open University/Routledge.

Green, A.E. (1972), 'Folksong and dialect', *Transactions of the Yorkshire Dialect Society*, part LXXII, vol. 13, pp. 20–47.

Gregg, R.J. (1972), 'The Scottish–Irish dialect boundaries in Ulster', in M. Wakelin (ed.), *Patterns in the Folk Speech of the British Isles*, London, Athlone, pp. 109–39.

Gupta, A.F. (1993), 'The debate over a standard in Singapore English', *Style on the Move: Proceedings of Style Council*, 92, Dictionary Research Centre, NSW, Macquarie University, pp. 12–19.

Haig, C. (ed.) (1985), *The Cambridge Historical Encyclopedia of Great Britain and Ireland*, Cambridge, Cambridge University Press.

Hall, R.A. Jr (1980), 'Language, dialect and regional Italian', *International Journal of the Sociology of Language*, vol. 25, pp. 95–106.

Hamer, A. (1993), 'Early standard English: linguistic confidence and insecurity' in *Proceedings of the English Association*, vol. VII, pp. 31–42.

Harris, J. (1991a), 'Conservatism versus substratal transfer in Irish English', in P. Trudgill and J.K. Chambers (eds), *Dialects of English: Studies in Grammatical Variation*.

Harris, J. (1991b), 'Ireland' in J. Cheshire (ed.), *English Around the World: Sociolinguistic Perspectives*, pp. 37–46.

Harris, J. (1993), 'The grammar of Irish English' in J. Milroy and L. Milroy (eds), *Real English: The Grammar of English Dialects in the British Isles*, pp. 139–86.

Harris, R. (1980), *The Language Makers*, London, Duckworth.

Harris, R. and Taylor, T.J. (1989), *Landmarks in Linguistic Thought: the Western Tradition From Socrates to Saussure*, London, Routledge.

Haugen, E. (1966), 'Dialect, language, nation', *American Anthropologist*, 68, pp. 922–35, reprinted in Pride and Holmes (1972).

Heath, S.B. (1976), 'A National language Academy? Debate in the new nation', *International Journal of the Sociology of Language*, vol. 11, pp. 9–43.

Heller, M. (1992), 'The politics of code-switching and language choice', *Journal of Multilingual and Multicultural Development*, vol.13, nos. 1 and 2, pp. 123–42.

Hobsbawm, E. (1990), *Nations and Nationalism since 1780*, Cambridge, Cambridge University Press.

Hogg, R. (ed.) (1992), *The Cambirdge History of the English Language*, vol. I, *The Beginnings to 1066*, Cambridge, Cambridge University Press.

Holm, J. (1980), 'African features in white Bahama English', *English World-Wide*, vol. 1, no. 1, pp. 45–65.

Honey, J. (1983), *The Language Trap: Race, Class and the 'Standard Language' Issue in British Schools*, London, National Council for Educational Standards.

Hornby, P. (ed.) (1977), *Bilingualism: Psychological, Social and Educational Implications*, London, Academic Press.

Horvath, B. (1985), *Variation in Australian English*, Cambridge, Cambridge University Press.

Hudson, R. (1980), *Sociolinguistics*, Cambridge, Cambridge University Press.

Hudson, R. (1992), 'What is Standard English?' in R. Hudson (ed.), *Teaching*

Grammar: A Guide for the National Curriculum, Oxford, Blackwell, pp. 39–57.

Huffines, M.L. (1980), 'Pennsylvania German: maintenance and shift', *International Journal of the Sociology of Language*, vol. 25, pp. 43–57.

Hymes, D. (1991), 'Afterword' in P. Burke and R. Porter (eds), *Language, Self and Society: A Social History of Language*, pp. 331–48.

Inglehart, R.F. and Woodward, M. (1967), 'Language conflicts and the political community', *Comparative Studies in Society and History*, 10, pp. 27–45, reprinted in Giglioli (1972).

Jackson, K. (1953), *Language and History in Early Britain*, Edinburgh University Press.

Jesperson, O. (1968), *Growth and Structure of the English Language*, 9th edn, Oxford, Blackwell.

Jones, C. (1989), *A History of English Phonology*, London, Longman.

Jones, R.F. (1953), *The Triumph of the English Language*, Oxford University Press.

Jones, R.M. (1979), 'Welsh bilingualism: four documents', in W.F. Mackey and J. Ornstein (eds), *Sociolinguistic Studies in Language Contact*, The Hague, Mouton, pp. 231–43.

Joseph, J.E. (1987), *Eloquence and Power. The Rise of Language Standards and Standard Languages*, London, Pinter.

Joyce, P. (1991), *Visions of the People*, Cambridge, Cambridge University Press.

Kachru, B. (1969), 'English in South Asia', in T.A. Sebeok (ed.), *Current Trends in Linguistics*, vol. 5, The Hague, Mouton, pp. 627–78, reprinted in Fishman (1978).

Kachru, B.B. (1986), *The Alchemy of English: The Spread, Models and Functions of Non-native Englishes*, Oxford, Pergamon.

Kachru, B.B. (1991), 'Liberation linguistics and the Quirk concern', *English Today*, vol. 25, no. 7, 1 January, pp. 3–13.

Kachru, B.B. (1992), *The Other Tongue: English Across Cultures*, 2nd edn, Urbana/Chicago, University of Illinois Press.

Katzner, K. (1977), *The Languages of the World*, London, Routledge & Kegan Paul.

Kay, B (1986), *Scots: the Mither Tongue*, Edinburgh, Mainstream.

Kerswill, P. (1996), 'Milton Keynes and dialect levelling in southeast British English' in Graddol *et al.* (eds) *English: History, Diversity and Change*, pp. 292–300.

Khlief, B. (1979), 'Language as an ethnic boundary in Welsh–English relations', *International Journal of the Sociology of Language*, vol. 20, pp. 59–74.

Kurath, H. (1972), *Studies in Area Linguistics*, Indiana University Press.

Labov, W. (1969), 'The logic of non-standard English', *Georgetown Monographs in Language and Linguistics*, vol. 22, pp. 1–22, 26–31, reprinted in Giglioli (1972).

Labov, W. (1970), 'The study of language in its social context', *Studium Generale*, vol. 23, pp. 66–84, reprinted in Giglioli (1972).

Labov, W. (1972a), *Sociolinguistic Patterns*, University of Pennsylvania Press; Oxford, Blackwell.

Labov, W. (1972b), *Language in the Inner City*, University of Pennsylvania Press; Oxford, Blackwell.

Labov, W. (1974), 'On the use of the present to explain the past', *Proceedings of the Eleventh International Congress of Linguists*, vol. 2, Bologna, pp. 825–51, reprinted in P. Baldi and R.N. Werth (1978).

Labov, W. (1994), *Principles of Linguistic Change: Internal Factors*, Oxford, Blackwell.

Ladefoged, P., Glick, R. and Criper, C. (1972), *Language in Uganda*, Oxford University Press.

Lanham, L. and McDonald, C.A. (1980), *The Standard in South African English and its Social History*, Heidelberg, Julius Groos Verlag.

Lass, R. (1969), *Approaches to English Historical Linguistics*, New York, Holt, Rinehart and Winston.

Leech, G.N. (1974), *Semantics*, Harmondsworth, Penguin.

Leith, D. (1984), 'Tudor London: sociolinguistic stratification and linguistic change', *Anglo-American Studies*, vol. IV, no. 1, pp. 59–72.

Leith, D. (1987), 'The social contexts of English' in W.F. Bolton and D. Crystal (eds), *Penguin History of English Literature*, vol. 10, *The English Language*, London, Sphere, pp. 295–321.

Leith, D. (1996), 'The origins of English' and 'English colonial to postcolonial' in Graddol *et al.* (eds), *English: History, Diversity and Change*, pp. 95–135 and pp. 136–76.

Leith, D. and Graddol, D. (1996), 'Modernity and English as a national language' in Graddol *et al.* (eds), *English: History, Diversity and Change*, pp. 180–221.

Leith, R. (1973), The Traditional Phonology of North London Speech, unpublished MPhil thesis, University of Leeds.

Le Page, R.B. (1964), *The National Language Question*, Oxford University Press.

Le Page, R. and Tabouret-Keller, A. (1985), *Acts of Identity: Creole-based Approaches to Language and Ethnicity*, Cambridge, Cambridge University Press.

Lewis, C.S. (1968), *Studies in Words*, Cambridge, Cambridge University Press.

Lewis, G. (1978), 'Migration and the decline of the Welsh language', in Fishman (ed.) (1978), pp. 263–351.

Linguistic Minorities Project (1985), *The Other Languages of England*, London, Routledge.

Lockwood, W.B. (1975), *Languages of the British Isles Past and Present*, London, Deutsch.

Lorimer, W.L. (1983), *The New Testament in Scots*, Harmondsworth, Penguin.

Loyn, H.R. (1962), *Anglo-Saxon England and the Norman Conquest*, London, Longman.

Loyn, H.R. (1977), *The Vikings in Britain*, London, Batsford.

Macafee, C. (1980), review of A.J. Aitken and T. McArthur, *Languages of Scotland*, in *English World-Wide*, vol. I, no. 1, pp. 137–8.

McCafferty, K. (1996), 'Frae "wile norn aksints" tae oor ain national leid?' *Causeway* 3: 1, pp. 39–44.

McClure, J.D. (1988), *Why Scots Matters: the Scots Language is a Priceless National Possession*, Edinburgh, Saltire Society.

McCrum, R., Cran, W. and MacNeil, R. (1986), *The Story of English*, London, Faber.

McDavid, R. (1973), 'Go slow in ethnic attributions: geographical mobility and dialect prejudice', in Bailey and Robinson (1973), pp. 258–73.

McDavid, R. (1980), *Varieties of American English*, Stanford University Press.

Machan, T.W. and Scott, C.T., (eds) (1992), *English in its Social Contexts: Essays in historical sociolinguistics*, Oxford, Oxford University Press.

Mackey, W.F. and Ornstein, J. (1979), *Sociolinguistic Studies in Language Contact*, The Hague, Mouton.

Mackinnon, K. (1977), *Language, Education and Social Processes in a Gaelic Community*, London, Routledge & Kegan Paul.

Mackinnon, K. (1991), *Gaelic: A Past and Future Prospect*, Saltire Society, Edinburgh.

Mackinnon, K. (1995/6), 'Gaelic and "The other languages of Scotland" in the 1991 census', *Scottish Language* 14/15, Association of Scottish Literary Studies, Aberdeen, pp. 104–17.

McLean, D. and McCormick, K. (1996), 'English in South Africa 1940–1993' in J. Fishman, A. Conrad and A. Rubal-Lopez (eds), *Post-Imperial English*, Amsterdam, Mouton de Gruyter.

Marenbon, J. (1987), *English Our English: the 'New Orthodoxy' Examined*, London, Centre for Policy Studies.

Mather, J.Y. and Speitel, H. (1975/7), *The Linguistic Atlas of Scotland: Scots Sections*, vols 1 and 2, London, Croom Helm.

Matthews, W. (1938), *Cockney Past and Present*, London, Routledge & Kegan Paul.

Mazrui, A.A. (1967), 'The English language and the origins of African nationalism', *Mawazo*, vol. I, no. 1, reprinted in Bailey and Robinson (1973), pp. 56–70.

Mazrui, A.A. (1975), *The Political Sociology of the English Language*, The Hague, Mouton.

Metcalf, A.A. (1974), 'The study of Californian Chicano English', *International Journal of the Sociology of Language*, vol. 2, pp. 53–8.

Michael, I. (1987), *The Teaching of English*, Cambridge, Cambridge University Press.

Milroy, J. (1992a), *Linguistic Variation and Change*, Oxford, Blackwell.

Milroy, J. (1992b), 'Middle English Dialectology' in N. Blake (ed.), *The Cambridge History of the English Language*, pp. 156–206.

Milroy, J. and Milroy, L. (1978), 'Belfast: change and variation in an urban vernacular', in P. Trudgill (ed.) (1978), pp. 19–36.

Milroy, J. and Milroy, L. (1985), *Authority in Language: Investigating Language Prescription and Standardisation*, London, Routledge.

Milroy, J. and Milroy, L. (eds) (1993), *Real English: the Grammar of English Dialects in the British Isles*, London, Longman.

Mioni, A.M. and Arnuzzo-Lanszweert, A.M. (1979), 'Sociolinguistics in Italy', *International Journal of the Sociology of Language*, vol. 21, pp. 81–107.

Mittins, W. *et al.* (1970), *Attitudes to English Usage*, Oxford University Press.

Mossé, F. (1952), *A Handbook of Middle English*, Johns Hopkins University Press; Oxford University Press.

Mossé, F. (1952) *A Handbook of Middle English*, Baltimore, Johns Hopkins University Press.

Myres, J. (1986), *The English Settlements*, Oxford, Clarendon.

Myers-Scotton, C. (1993), *Social Motivations for Code-Switching: Evidence from Africa*, Oxford, Clarendon.

O'Cuiv, B. (ed.) (1969), *A View of the Irish Language*, Dublin, Stationery Office.

O'Donnell, W.R. and Todd, L. (1980), *Variety in Contemporary English*, London, Allen and Unwin.

Ó'Fiaich, An t'Athair Tomás (1969), 'The language and political history' in B. O'Cuiv (ed.), *A View of the Irish Language*, Dublin, Stationery Office, pp. 101–11.

O'Muirithe, D. (1977), *The English Language in Ireland*, Dublin, Mercier Press.

O'Riagáin, P. and Ó'Gliasáin, M. (1979), *All-Irish Primary Schools in the Dublin Area*, publication 16(b), Dublin, Institiúid Teangeolaíochta Éireann.

Orkin, M. (1971), *Speaking Canadian English*, London, Routledge & Kegan Paul.

Orton, H. and Wright, N. (1974), *A Word Geography of England*, London, Seminar Press.

Oxenham, J. (1980), *Literacy: Writing, Reading and Social Organisation*, London, Routledge & Kegan Paul.

Pace, S. (1975), 'A sociolinguistic consideration of the English spoken in Grenada, British West Indies', in Mackey and Ornstein (1979), pp. 265–76.

Page, N. (1973), *Speech in the English Novel*, London, Longman.

Palmer, F. (1971), *Grammar*, Harmondsworth, Penguin.

Partridge, A.C. (1969), *Tudor to Augustan English*, London, Deutsch.

Perera, K. (1994), 'Standard English: the debate' in S. Brindley (ed.) *Teaching English*, London, Routledge, pp. 79–88.

Phillipson, R. (1992), *Linguistic Imperialism*, Oxford, Oxford University Press.

Platt, J., Weber, H. and Ho, M.L. (1984), *The New Englishes*, London, Routledge.

Platt, J. (1980), 'Varieties and functions of English in Singapore and Malaysia', *English World-Wide*, vol. 1, no. 1, pp. 97–121.

Pride, J. (ed.) (1982), *New Englishes*, Rowley, Mass., Newbury House.

Pride, J. and Holmes, J. (1972), *Sociolinguistics: Selected Readings*, Harmondsworth, Penguin.

Quirk, R. (1968), *The Use of English*, London, Longman.

Quirk, R. (1972), 'Philology, politics and American English', and 'Linguistic bonds across the Atlantic', *The English Language and Images of Matter*, Oxford University Press, pp. 1–13, 14–31.

Quirk, R. (1974), 'Shakespeare and the English language', *The Linguist and the English Language*, London, Arnold, pp. 46–64.

Quirk, R. (1985), 'The English language in a global context' in R. Quirk and H. Widdowson (eds), *English in the World: Teaching and Learning the Language and Literatures*, Cambridge, Cambridge University Press, pp. 1–6.

Quirk, R. (1990), 'Language varieties and standard language' *Language Today*, vol. 6, no. 1, January, pp. 3–10.

Quirk, R. and Greenbaum, S. (1973), *A University Grammar of English*, London, Longman.

Ramchand, K. (1970), 'The language of the master', from *The West Indian Novel and its Background*, London, Faber, reprinted in Bailey and Robinson (1973), pp. 115–46.

Rampton, B. (1990), 'Displacing the "native speaker": expertise, affiliation and inheritance', *ELT Journal*, 44/2, pp. 97–101.

Rampton, B. (1995), *Crossing: Language and Ethnicity among Adolescents*, London, Longman.

Ramson, W.S. (ed.) (1988), *The Australian National Dictionary*, Melbourne, Oxford University Press.

Rayfield, J.R. (1970), *The Languages of a Bilingual Community*, The Hague, Mouton.

Reed, C. (1967), *Dialects of American English*, New York, World Publishing Co.

Reid, E. (1978), 'Social and stylistic variation in the speech of children: some evidence from Edinburgh', in Trudgill (1978), pp. 158–71.

Ricks, C. and Michaels, L. (eds) (1990), *The State of the Language*, London, Faber.

Romaine, S. (1978), 'Post-vocalic /r/ in Scottish English: a sound-change in progress?' in Trudgill (1978), pp. 144–57.

Romaine, S. (1982), *Sociohistorical Linguistics*, Cambridge, Cambridge University Press.

Romaine, S. (1989), *Bilingualism*, Oxford, Blackwell.

Romaine, S. (1991), *Language in Australia*, Cambridge, Cambridge University Press.

Romaine, S. (1994), *Language in Society: an Introduction to Sociolinguistics*, Oxford, Oxford University Press.

Rosen, H. and Burgess, T. (1980), *Languages and Dialects of London School-children*, London, Ward Lock.

Salmon, V. (1967), 'English colloquial language in the Falstaff plays', *Leeds Studies in English*, New Series, vol. 1, pp. 37–70.

Samuel, R. (ed.) (1989), *Patriotism: the Making and Unmaking of British National Identities*, vols 1–3, London, Routledge.

Samuels, M.L. (1972), *Linguistic Evolution*, Cambridge, Cambridge University Press.

Sanderson, S. *et al.* (1978), *The Linguistic Atlas of England*, London, Croom Helm.

Sawyer, J.B. (1964), 'Social aspects of bilingualism in San Antonio, Texas', *Publications of the American Dialect Society*, 41, pp. 7–15, reprinted in Bailey and Robinson (1973).

Schulz, M.R. (1975), 'The semantic derogation of women', in B. Thorne and N. Henley (eds), *Language and Sex: Difference and Dominance*, Rowley, Mass., Newbury House, pp. 64–75.

Scragg, D.G. (1975), *History of English Spelling*, Manchester University Press.

Sebba, M. (1993), *London Jamaican: Language Systems in Interaction*, London, Longman.

Sheard, J.A. (1954), *The Words we Use*, London, Deutsch.

Simpson, D. (1986), *The Politics of American English 1776–1850*, Oxford, Oxford University Press.

Sivertsen, E. (1960), *Cockney Phonology*, Oslo, Oslo Studies in English, no. 8.

Smith, O. (1984), *The Politics of Language 1791–1819*, Oxford, Oxford University Press.

Smith, R.B. and Lance, D.M. (1979), 'Standard and disparate varieties of English in the United States: educational and sociopolitical implications', *International Journal of the Sociology of Language*, vol. 21, pp. 127–40.

Speitel, H.H. (1978), 'The word geography of the Borders', in H. Speitel (ed.), *The Scottish Literary Journal*, Supplement no. 6, Spring 1978.

Spencer, J. (1963), *Language in Africa*, Cambridge University Press.

Spencer, J. (1971a), *The English Language in West Africa*, London, Longman.

Spencer, J. (1971b), 'Colonial language policies and their legacies', in T. Sebeok (ed.), *Current Trends in Linguistics*, vol. 7, The Hague, Mouton, pp. 537–47.

Spolsky, B. and Kari, J. (1974), 'Apachean language maintenance', *International Journal of the Sociology of Language*, vol. 2, pp. 92–100.

Stallybrass, P. (1988), 'An inclosure of the best people in the world: nationalism and imperialism in late sixteenth-century England' in R. Samuel (ed.), *Patriotism*, vol. 1, pp. 199–214.

Stephens, M. (1976), *Linguistic Minorities of Western Europe*, Llandysul, Gomer Press.

Stewart, W.A. (1968), 'A sociolinguistic typology for describing national multilingualism', in J. Fishman (ed.) (1968), *Readings in the Sociology of Language*, The Hague, Mouton, pp. 531–45.

Stoller, P. (1976), 'The language planning activities of the US office of bilingual education', *International Journal of the Sociology of Language*, vol. 11, pp. 45–60.

Strang, B. (1968), *Modern English Structure*, 2nd edn, London, Arnold.

Strang, B. (1970), *A History of English*, London, Methuen.

Street, B. (1985), *Literacy in Theory and Practice*, Cambridge, Cambridge University Press.

Strevens, P. (1972), *British and American English*, London, Collier-Macmillan.

Stubbs, M. (1986), 'What is Standard English?' in M. Stubbs, *Educational Linguistics*, Oxford, Blackwell, pp. 83–97.

Švejcer, A.D. (1978), *Standard English in the United States and England*, The Hague, Mouton.

Thomas, L. (1996), 'Variation in English grammar' in Graddol *et al.* (eds), *English: History, Diversity and Change*, pp. 222–58.

Thompson, R.M. (1974), 'Mexican American language loyalty and the validity of the 1970 census', *International Journal of the Sociology of Language*, vol. 2, pp. 7–17.

Thomson, D. (ed.) (1976), *Gaelic in Scotland: A Blueprint for Official and Private Initiatives*, Glasgow, Gairm.

Todd, L. (1974), *Pidgins and Creoles*, London, Routledge & Kegan Paul.

Todd, L. (1984), *Modern Englishes: Pidgins and Creoles*, Oxford and London, Blackwell and Deutsch.

Traugott, E.C. (1972), *A History of English Syntax*, New York, Holt, Rinehart & Winston.

Tripathi, P.D. (1992), 'The chosen tongue', *English Today*, vol. 32, no. 8, 4 October, pp. 3–11.

Trudgill, P. (1974a), *The Social Differentiation of English in Norwich*, Cambridge, Cambridge University Press.

Trudgill, P. (1974b), *Sociolinguistics: An Introduction*, Harmondsworth, Penguin.

Trudgill, P. (1975), *Accent, Dialect and the School*, London, Arnold.

Trudgill, P. (ed.) (1978), *Sociolinguistic Patterns in British English*, London, Arnold.

Trudgill, P. (ed.) (1984), *Language in the British Isles*, Cambridge, Cambridge University Press.

Trudgill, P. (1986), 'Koineization in colonial English' in P. Trudgill, *Dialects in Contact*, Oxford, Blackwell, pp. 127–68.

Trudgill, P. and Hughes, A. (1979), *English Accents and Dialects: An Introduction to Social and Regional Varieties of British English*, London, Arnold.

Trudgill, P. and Hannah, J. (1994), *International English*, 3rd edn, London, Edward Arnold.

Trudgill, P. and Chambers, J.K. (eds.) (1991), *Dialects of English: Studies in Grammatical Variation*, London, Longman.

Tucker, S. (1967), *Protean Shape: A Study in Eighteenth Century Vocabulary and Usage*, London, Athlone.

Tucker, S. (1972), *Enthusiasm: A Study in Semantic Change*, Cambridge, Cambridge University Press.

Turner, G.W. (1972), *The English Language in Australia and New Zealand*, London, Longman.

Turner, G.W. (1973), *Stylistics*, Harmondsworth, Penguin.

Turvey, H. (1978), *Language Policy and Socioeconomic Development in Ireland*, occasional paper 4, Dublin, Institiúid Teangeolaíochta Éireann.

Underwood, G. (1974), 'American English dialectology: alternatives for the south west', *International Journal of the Sociology of Language*, vol. 2, pp. 19–40.

Upton, C., Widdowson, J. & Parry, D. (1993), *Survey of English Dialects: The Dictionary and Grammar*, London, Routledge.

Vallée, F. and de Vries, J. (1978), 'Trends in bilingualism in Canada', in Fishman, (ed.) (1978).

Verma, S.K. (1982), 'Swadeshi English: form and function' in J. Pride (ed.), *New Englishes*, pp. 174–87.

Wakelin, M.F. (1972), *English Dialects: An Introduction*, London, Athlone.

Wakelin, M.F. (ed.) (1972), *Patterns in the Folk Speech of the British Isles*, London, Athlone.

Waldron, R.A. (1967), *Sense and Sense Development*, London, Deutsch.

Walker, J. (1836), *A Critical Pronouncing Dictionary*, Preston, Banks.

Wallwork, J.F. (1978), *Language and People*, London, Heinemann.

Walvin, J. (1993), *Black Ivory: a History of British Slavery*, London, Fontana.

Wardhaugh, R. (1987), *Languages in Competition: Dominance, Diversity and Decline*, Oxford, Blackwell.

Wells, J. (1982), *Accents of English*, Cambridge, Cambridge University Press.

Whiteley, W.H. (1971), *Language Use and Social Change: Problems of Multilingualism with Special Reference to Eastern Africa*, Oxford University Press.

Whitelock, D. (1965), *The Beginnings of English Society*, revised edn, Harmondsworth, Pelican.

Williams, G. (1992), *Sociolinguistics: a Sociological Critique*, London, Routledge.

Williams, J.M. (1992), ' "O! when degree is shak'd": sixteenth-century anticipations of some modern attitudes towards usage' in T.W. Machan and C.T. Scott (eds), *English in its Social Contexts*, pp. 69–101.

Williams, R. (1961), 'Standard English', *The Long Revolution*, Harmondsworth, Penguin.

Williams, R. (1977), 'Language' in R. Williams, *Marxism and Literature*, Oxford, Oxford University Press, pp. 21–44.

Williams, R. (1988), *Keywords*, rev. edn, London, Fontana.

Williams, T. (1989), 'The anglicisation of South Wales' in R. Samuel (ed.) *Patriotism*, vol. 2, pp. 193–203.

Williamson, R.C. and Van Eerde, J.A. (1980), 'Sub-cultural factors in the survival of secondary languages: a cross-national sample', *International Journal of the Sociology of Language*, vol. 25, pp. 59–83.

Winer, L. (1993), *Varieties of English Around the World: Trinidad and Tobago*, Amsterdam, John Benjamins.

Wright, S. (1996), 'Accents of English' in Graddol *et al.* (eds), *English: History, Diversity and Change*, pp. 259–300.

Wrightson, K. (1991), 'Estates, degrees and sorts: changing perceptions of class in Tudor and Stuart England,' in P.J. Corfield (ed.), *Language, History and Class*, pp. 30–52.

Wyld, H.C. (1936), *A History of Modern Colloquial English*, Oxford University Press.

General index

Index of words and forms

(In matters of pronunciation or morphology the relevant segment is italicised.)